250

Essential Chinese Characters

Volume 2
Revised Edition

Philip Yungkin Lee
Revised by **Darell Tibbles**

TUTTLE PUBLISHING
Tokyo • Rutland, Vermont • Singapore

Published by Tuttle Publishing, an imprint of Periplus Editions (HK) Ltd., with editorial offices at 364 Innovation Drive, North Clarendon, Vermont 05759 U.S.A. and at 61 Tai Seng Avenue #02-12, Singapore 534167.

Copyright © 2010 Periplus Editions (HK) Ltd
Illustrator: Jon Ng

Library of Congress Cataloging-in-Publication Data
Lee, Philip Yungkin. 250 essential Chinese characters / Philip Yungkin Lee;
revised by Darell Tibbles.—Rev. ed.
    p. cm.
  ISBN 978-0-8048-4035-4 (v. 1 : pbk.)
  ISBN 978-0-8048-4036-1 (v. 2 : pbk.)
1. Chinese language—Textbooks for foreign speakers—English. 2. Chinese characters. I.
Title: Two hundred fifty essential Chinese characters.
  PL1129.E5 L45 2009
  495.1'82421—dc22
                           2009075104

ISBN 978-0-8048-4036-1

Distributed by

North America, Latin America & Europe
Tuttle Publishing
364 Innovation Drive
North Clarendon, VT 05759-9436 U.S.A.
Tel: 1 (802) 773-8930
Fax: 1 (802) 773-6993
info@tuttlepublishing.com
www.tuttlepublishing.com

Asia Pacific
Berkeley Books Pte. Ltd.
61 Tai Seng Avenue #02-12
Singapore 534167
Tel: (65) 6280-1330
Fax: (65) 6280-6290
inquiries@periplus.com.sg
www.periplus.com

First edition
14 13 12 11 10 09   10 9 8 7 6 5 4 3 2 1

Printed in Singapore

Contents

Introduction

Beginning Chinese language learners frequently wonder as to the number of Chinese characters necessary for basic written fluency. Effectively answering that question is neither simple nor straightforward. Simple conversations and interactions can be covered with a few hundred known characters. Advanced and specialized conversations would, on the other hand, require specialized vocabulary.

This second volume of *250 Essential Chinese Characters for Everyday Use* offers the essential characters present in expressions of concepts, ideas, and opinions in increasingly advanced language situations. This volume will often prompt greater understanding between each section to effectively utilize new characters. Complete information is given for each character including the meaning, pronunciation, and written components.

The 250 characters have been selected and arranged based on a range of criteria. First, many characters should be instantly familiar in meaning for any language learner. These characters are important in language to convey critical aspects and understandings of events, items, people, and thought. Across most language contexts, characters selected for this volume communicate, with increasing clarity, often complicated aspects of understanding. Second, characters have been chosen for usefulness in a variety of word and language settings. A frequent indicator of usefulness and variety was the range of two character compound vocabulary words that utilize the character. Knowing these characters can increase vocabulary acquisition as the patterns of use and meaning are built. Finally, characters have been selected that show great frequency and meaning in spoken language.

Each **character** is presented in an independent entry that provides both the simplified (*jiantizi*) and traditional (*fantizi*) form for the character. Each character's stroke order, the recognized order for character composition, is given for the simplified character form. *Pinyin* romanization is also provided. The meaning and radical for each character is given, along with the radical index number found in standard dictionary indexes. A variety of examples are given that demonstrate effective use of the character. These examples feature use of the two character compound vocabulary and multiple character phrases that often appear in modern written and spoken Chinese.

The character entries are arranged into 23 lessons of 10 to 12 characters per lesson. A longer review appears every fourth or fifth lesson, after each new 50 characters as appropriate. A short selection of exercises at the end of each lesson provides different opportunities to practice the vocabulary of the lesson.

The **Review Activities** for each lesson provide 3 related components for character mastery. Generally, the first section of the exercises focuses on *pinyin* or character recall. The second section asks for effective grammatical utilization of the previous vocabulary. The final section is a broader exercise to develop communicative proficiency. Exercises in this section require short paragraphs or responses that depend on understanding the lesson. These offer each learner the opportunity to grow and strengthen individual proficiency.

Each **Section Review** is composed of 4 sections, with each section growing in linguistic complexity. The first exercise is a larger vocabulary and character recognition for the combined lesson vocabulary. Next, the second exercise will challenge for grammatical understanding and accuracy. The bulk of the section review is a longer open format exercise to allow individual proficiency growth. The topic of discussion for the section will depend on the characters from the previous lessons. Taken together, these first 3 exercises in the section review can provide effective opportunity to review and practice for advanced proficiency examination such as the College Board AP examination or an American Council on the Teaching of Foreign Languages Oral Proficiency Interview (OPI). The final exercise in each section review is a series of questions offered to prompt greater depth in the previous section. If possible, these questions can be asked and answered orally, preparing the learner for oral interview interactions and assessments.

An answer key is provided for those exercises formatted for single answers. However, many exercises prompt for independent responses. For those, a sample answer is sometimes provided with the understanding that there are many additional effective possibilities.

The activities and exercises provided are intended to allow each learner to grow at their level and individual pace. For a new language student the character entries will provide much to consider and many new examples of language use. Lesson exercises will often challenge and exceed the domain of one particular lesson. For a language student reviewing previously known characters, many entries will confirm examples and constructions well practiced. Lesson exercises will review and strengthen existing skills.

For each learner the process of mastering Chinese character writing is also a development of individual learning and recall strategies. With the stroke order given for each character and many different examples of vocabulary use, each learner is invited to utilize the most effective learning strategy for him or her. Best practices in character memory include mindfulness and repetition. When practicing character formation, be aware of each stroke, stroke order, and composition. Character recall is further strengthened by much repetition including the physical act of character writing, especially writing individual characters and words multiple times.

The new edition's contents have been revised to match the development of Chinese language instruction. The character order has been restructured to help learners connect characters based on function. This has necessitated slight variations in lesson length, with some lessons of 10 characters, and some lessons of up to 12 characters. As a result, the expressive possibilities of the vocabulary have been increased for each lesson. Additionally, the exercises have been completely revised to reflect the growing focus on proficiency assessment throughout the field. Each lesson and section review features exercises designed to challenge and grow expressive proficiency. Finally, greater attention is paid to incorporating spoken language throughout the exercises. While the volume focuses on character vocabulary growth, examples throughout the exercises invite learners to engage in spoken review and development.

The 250 characters contained in Volume 2, when taken together, compose a significant opportunity to expand language proficiency. Whether you are new to the subject or coming back for review, each of these characters provides a wealth of expressive opportunity.

Learners' Guide

Chinese Characters

For many learners of Chinese language, one of the most engaging and fulfilling challenges is mastering the Chinese character writing system. From the first character learned, understanding and utilizing a refined system with a long history is very compelling. In this book you'll be introduced to 250 characters, with a demonstration of the writing system for each.

Every character has a basic form recognized for reading and visual accuracy. The basic form is the result of a precise stroke order that allows for clear and accurate character formation. Through accurate stroke order, the composition of each character is achieved. Every character is the formation of several components. As important as the shape of the overall character is the relationship between these different components. These relationships are seen in the composition of the character. Finally, characters contain many repeated components, and across the 250 characters in this volume many components will repeat. These commonly used character components help create predictable patterns for composition, stroke order, and pronunciation.

Most characters contain a significant component: the character radical. In the Chinese character writing system, the vast majority of characters are considered to be "radical-phonetic" characters. By identifying the radical component you often reveal a key insight into the character meaning and use. Additionally, the remaining character component, the "phonetic," is a clue to pronunciation. The identification of character radicals is critical to utilizing a character index by radical, which is common in Chinese dictionaries.

These 250 characters establish the foundation for identifying patterns in the Chinese character writing system. There are patterns in character stroke order, composition, and overall form. There are also patterns in meaning, pronunciation, and use identified in part by character components. Yet there are also those characters that defy easy compartmentalization. Often these are fundamental characters and constructions for expressive language.

The Basic Strokes

Chinese characters are written in various strokes. Although we can identify over 30 different strokes, only 8 are basic ones and all the others are their variants. Certain arrangements of strokes form components, or the building blocks for characters.

The strokes that make up a component of a character and by extension the whole character are given names. Here are the 8 basic strokes:

[—] The **héng** or "horizontal" stroke is written from left to right.

[|] The **shù** or "vertical" stroke is written from top to bottom.

[丿] The **piě** or "downward-left" stroke is written from top-right to bottom-left.

[乀] The **nà** or "downward-right" stroke is written from top-left to bottom-right.

[丶] The **diǎn** or "dot" stroke is written from top to bottom-right, finishing firmly. It can also be finished to bottom-left, depending on how the dot is written.

[乛] The **zhé** or "turning" stroke can begin with a horizontal stroke with a downward turn, or it can be a vertical stroke with a horizontal turn to the right.

[亅] The **gōu** or "hook" stroke is written by a quick flick of the pen or Chinese brush. There are five types of **gōu** "hook" strokes. They are:

    [⼀] the **hénggōu** or "horizontal hook,"

    [亅] the **shùgōu** or "vertical hook,"

    [乚] the **wān'gōu** or "bending hook,"

    [乀] the **xiégōu** or "slanting hook,"

    [⺄] the **pínggōu** or "level hook."

[丿] The **tí** or "upward stroke to the right" is written from bottom-left to top-right.

Stroke Order

The long history of Chinese character writing has developed a strong aid to character memory and recognition: stroke order. Each character has a recognized stroke order that is the preferred method of character formation. Learning and repeating this stroke order for every written character is recommended as an aid for memory, recognition, and writing clarity.

Stroke orders are the product of a long continuous history of the writing system. Each stroke order offers benefits to character production. First, the recognized stroke order is the most accurate method for character composition. With each stroke in proper order, a character is clear, readable, and accurate. Second, the recognized stroke order is the most efficient method for character construction. The progression of strokes between character components have developed to move effectively through each component and to the next character to be written. Third, the recognized stroke order, when practiced, is the most repeatable method to write the character. Mastering a stroke order allows, much like a singer mastering a song, the character to be produced without having to cognitively recall each component. Instead of having to learn all of the constituent components, a character is learned as a process.

The recognized stroke orders have developed for right-handed character writing. This is shown in the stroke progression and stroke formation. For left-handed writers the stroke orders may appear inefficient or counter-intuitive. There is no easy remedy for this aspect of character writing; the benefits for consistent stroke orders are still valid for left-handed writers and should be considered.

The following examples illustrate patterns in character stroke orders. These general rules can help you understand specific stroke orders.

1. From top to bottom:

三		一	二	三	
学		⺌	⺍	兴	学
是		日	旦	early	是

2. From left to right:

你		亻	伬	你	
好		女	奵	好	
她		女	奵	奵	她

3. The horizontal before the vertical:

十		一	十	
七		一	七	
天		二	天	天

4. The horizontal before the down stroke to the left:

大		一	ナ	大	
有		一	ナ	有	有
在		一	ナ	才	在

5. The down stroke to the left before that to the right:

人		丿	人		
八		丿	八		
文		亠	𠂇	文	

6. The enclosing strokes first, then the enclosed and finally the sealing stroke:

四		丨	冂	㸚	四
国		冂	国	国	国
回		冂	回	回	回

7. The middle stroke before those on both sides:

小		亅	小	小	
你		仁	竹	你	你
水		亅	水	水	水

8. Inside stroke before side stroke:

这		亠	亠	文	这
过		寸	寸	讨	过
道		丷	丷	首	道

Simplified Characters versus Traditional Characters

Many of the 250 characters in this volume have both simplified and traditional character forms. If only one character form is given for a character then the simplified and traditional forms are identical. Becoming acquainted with both forms is useful for many reasons. First, the simplified form is related to the traditional form of the character. The techniques for simplification are outlined below, with many of the simplifications being a confirmation of the evolution of character writing through the history of Chinese characters. Second, both forms are used in current Chinese language communities. Different communities generally prefer the use of one character form or the other; however both forms can be seen and used within one community. Advanced Chinese language use necessitates at least basic familiarity with both character forms.

Simplified characters have existed long before the government of the People's Republic of China sanctioned their use in 1986. For example, the characters **cóng** 从 (from), **wàn** 万 (ten thousand), and **bǐ** 笔 (writing brush) existed side by side with the traditional forms 從, 萬, and 筆 in classical Chinese. The official sanction only means the elevation of the simplified forms.

Several techniques were employed to create simplified characters. One was to replace the original component of a character with a component of fewer strokes but having the same sound as the given character. For example, the simplified character for "recognize" is **rèn** 认. The component 人 is pronounced **rén** which is also the pronunciation for **rěn** 忍 in the traditional form 認 (despite different tones).

Another technique was to take one section of a traditional character and use it as the simplified character. Compare the traditional form for "family" **qīn** 親 and the simplified form 亲 that uses only the left component. Other examples of such simplification include **ér** 兒 (son), **yī** 醫 (doctor), and **xí** 習 (practice) with respective simplified forms of 儿, 医, and 习.

Some characters are simplified on the basis of having adopted cursive forms and in the process eliminating some strokes. For example the radical **yán** 言 (speech) is simplified to 讠 by the adoption of its cursive form. Other radicals simplified on the same basis include 门 (door) and 车 (vehicle). Simplification involving radicals is responsible for many simplified forms being created as it is often the case that only the radical is simplified; **shuō** 说, **yǔ** 语, and **wèn** 问 are examples. Other cursive forms are adopted as the simplified form such as **ài** 爱 for 愛 and **lè/yuè** 乐 for 樂.

Some cursive forms use an arbitrary stroke order created for the sake of writing a character quickly. These are used to replace some complicated phonetic components. One common example is **yòu** 又 written in only two strokes. It is used in the characters **huān** 欢, **hàn** 汉, and **duì** 对 replacing 歡, 漢, and 對 respectively.

The Pinyin System of Romanization

The system used in this book to write Chinese with Roman letters is the *Hanyu Pinyin* system which is the standard in the People's Republic of China and is now used almost everywhere else in the world. The imitated pronunciation should be read as if it were English, bearing in mind the following main points:

Consonants

b, d, f, g, h, k, l, m, n, p, s, t, w, y as in English

c	like English **ts** in i**ts**
j	like English **j** in **j**eer
q	like English **ch** in **ch**eer, with a strong puff of air
r	like English **ur** in leis**ur**e, with the tongue rolled back
x	like English **see** (whole word)
z	like English **ds** in ki**ds**
ch	like English **ch** in **ch**urch, with the tongue rolled back and a strong puff of air
sh	like English **sh** in **sh**e, with the tongue rolled back
zh	like English **j**, with the tongue rolled back

Vowels

a	like English **ar** in f**ar**
e	like English **ur** in f**ur**
i	like English **ee** in f**ee**
o	like English **or** in f**or**
u	like English **ue** in s**ue**
ü	like French **u**

Tones

A tone is a variation in pitch by which a syllable can be pronounced. In Chinese, a variation of pitch or tone changes the meaning of the word. There are four tones each marked by a diacritic. In addition there is a neutral tone which does not carry any tone marks. Below is a tone chart which describes tones using the 5-degree notation. It divides the range of pitches from lowest (1) to highest (5). Note that the neutral tone is not shown on the chart as it is affected by the tone that precedes it.

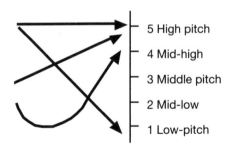

The first tone is a high-level tone represented by a level tone mark (–).

The second tone is a high-rising tone represented by a rising tone mark (´).

The third tone is a low-dipping tone represented by a dish-like tone mark (ˇ).

The fourth tone is a high-falling tone represented by a falling tone mark (`).

In addition to the above tones, there is a neutral tone which is pronounced light and soft in comparison to other tones. A neutral tone is not marked by any tone mark. A syllable is said to take on a neutral tone when it forms part of a word or is placed in various parts of a sentence.

How to Use the Alphabetical Index

The words and phrases collected in the Chinese-English Glossary (approximately 1,200 items) are arranged alphabetically according to the *Hanyu Pinyin* system of romanization. In this system each syllable (represented by a character) is a unit. The first character in a word or phrase is the head character. Each word or phrase is ordered in the first instance according to the phonetic value of this character. In a succession of entries having the same head character, alphabetical order is then determined by the phonetic value of the second character. This arrangement has the advantage of enhancing meaning by grouping together words which share a common character root, even though it is done at the expense of a straight alphabetical ordering.

The ordering of characters is affected by two other considerations. Firstly, in the case of characters represented by the same Roman letters, alphabetization is determined by the tone of each character (represented in *Hanyu Pinyin* by diacritics), in the order first, second, third, fourth and neutral tone. Secondly, in the case of characters represented by the same Roman letters which also have the same tone, alphabetization follows the principle that simpler characters (those composed of fewer strokes) are listed before more complex characters (those composed of more strokes).

For example, the first 8 entries under J have as their head character variations of the syllable **ji** (pronounced like *jee* in English). These entries are **jī** — first tone (2 instances); **jí** — second tone (2 instances); **jǐ** — third tone (1 instance); **jì** — fourth tone (3 instances).

In the case of a character taking more than one tone, e.g. **bu** 不 which can take on **bú**, **bù** or **bu**, the words or phrases sharing the head character are also arranged in the descending order of the tones.

How to Use the Radical Index

The radical index is based on the 189 radicals used by *The Chinese-English Dictionary 1995,* published by the Foreign Language Teaching and Research Press in Beijing. When you look up a character, first determine which part of the character constitutes the radical and then count the remaining number of strokes to locate the character under that radical. Where a character is made up of two components which can function as radicals, it is sometimes classified under both radicals. For example, the character **měi** 美 "beautiful" is classified under both components which are treated as radicals: **yáng** 羊 "sheep" and **dà** 大 "big" in the same way as found in the *Chinese-English Dictionary 1995*.

Explanatory Notes for Character Pages

Below is an annotated character page, showing the range of information offered:

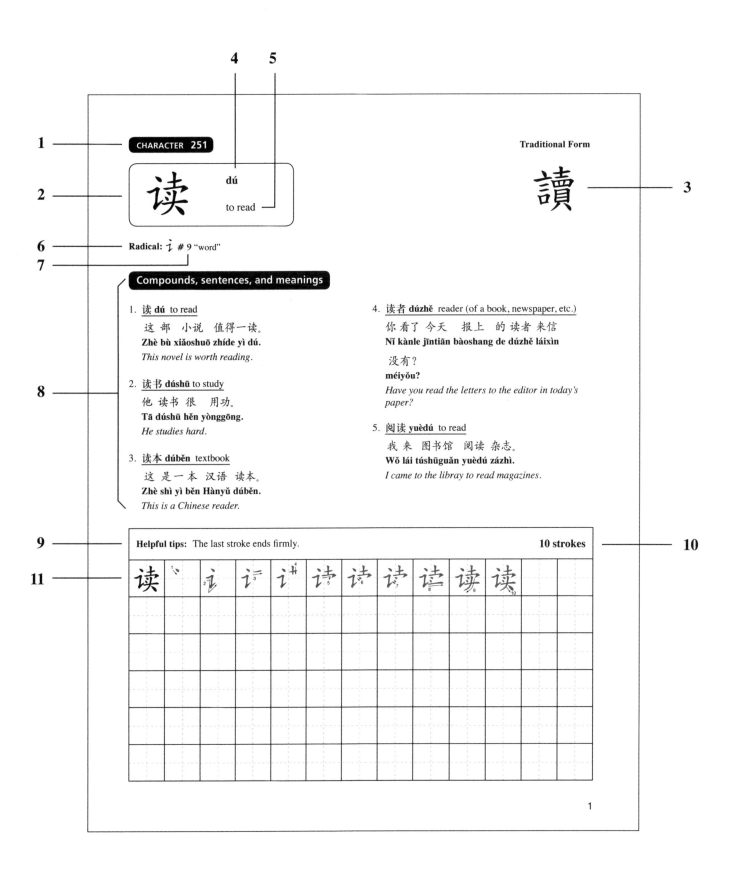

4 **5**

1 — CHARACTER 251

Traditional Form

2 — 读   **dú**

to read

讀 — **3**

6 — **Radical:** 讠 # 9 "word"

7 — **Compounds, sentences, and meanings**

1. 读 **dú** to read
这 部 小说 值得一读。
Zhè bù xiǎoshuō zhíde yì dú.
This novel is worth reading.

2. 读书 **dúshū** to study
他 读书 很 用功。
Tā dúshū hěn yònggōng.
He studies hard.

3. 读本 **dúběn** textbook
这 是一本 汉语 读本。
Zhè shì yì běn Hànyǔ dúběn.
This is a Chinese reader.

4. 读者 **dúzhě** reader (of a book, newspaper, etc.)
你 看了 今天 报上 的 读者 来信
Nǐ kànle jīntiān bàoshang de dúzhě láixìn
没有？
méiyǒu?
Have you read the letters to the editor in today's paper?

5. 阅读 **yuèdú** to read
我 来 图书馆 阅读 杂志。
Wǒ lái túshūguǎn yuèdú zázhì.
I came to the library to read magazines.

8

9 — **Helpful tips:** The last stroke ends firmly.   **10 strokes** — **10**

11 — 读 ﹀ 讠 讠 讠 读 读 读 读 读

1

KEY:

1. character number as sequenced in volume
2. character
3. traditional form of character (when appropriate)
4. *pinyin* romanization and tone
5. character definition
6. character radical
7. radical index number (based on *The Chinese-English Dictionary 1995*)
8. character vocabulary examples with sentences, pronunciation, and meaning
9. points to note when writing character
10. number of strokes of the character
11. character stroke order

读 **dú**

to read

讀

Radical: 讠 # 9 "word"

Compounds, sentences, and meanings

1. 读 **dú** to read

   这 部 小说 值得一读。

   Zhè bù xiǎoshuō zhíde yì dú.

   This novel is worth reading.

2. 读书 **dúshū** to study

   他 读书 很 用功。

   Tā dúshū hěn yònggōng.

   He studies hard.

3. 读本 **dúběn** textbook

   这 是 一 本 汉语 读本。

   Zhè shì yì běn Hànyǔ dúběn.

   This is a Chinese reader.

4. 读者 **dúzhě** reader (of a book, newspaper, etc.)

   你 看了 今天 报上 的 读者 来信

   Nǐ kànle jīntiān bàoshang de dúzhě láixìn

   没有?

   méiyǒu?

   Have you read the letters to the editor in today's paper?

5. 阅读 **yuèdú** to read

   我 来 图书馆 阅读 杂志。

   Wǒ lái túshūguǎn yuèdú zázhì.

   I came to the library to read magazines.

Helpful tips: The last stroke ends firmly.　　　　　　　　　　**10 strokes**

读	丶	讠	讠	计	读	读	读	读	读	读		

běn

[measure word]; root, base

Radical: 木 # 81 "tree"

Compounds, sentences, and meanings

1. 本 **běn** [measure word]

   我 去 图书馆 借了 两 本 书。

   Wǒ qù túshūguǎn jièle liǎng běn shū.

   I went to the library and borrowed two books.

2. 本地 **běndì** local

   我 是 本地人。

   Wǒ shì běndìrén.

   I was born here.

3. 本行 **běnháng** one's own profession

   搞 电脑 是 我的 本行。

   Gǎo diànnǎo shì wǒde běnháng.

   Computers are my line of work.

4. 本来 **běnlái** original

   他 本来 身体 很 瘦弱。

   Tā běnlái shēntǐ hěn shòuruò.

   He used to be thin and weak.

5. 本领 **běnlǐng** ability

   他的 本领 很 大。

   Tāde běnlǐng hěn dà.

   He's very capable.

Helpful tips: Make sure the bottom horizontal stroke is not too low.												**5 strokes**
本	一	十	才	木	本								

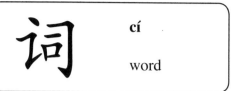

cí

word

词

Radical: 讠 # 9 "word"

Compounds, sentences, and meanings

1. 词 **cí** words

   调子 我记得, 可是词儿我 忘 了。

   Diàozi wǒ jìde, kěshì cír wǒ wàng le.

   I remember the tune all right, but I've forgotten the words.

2. 词典 **cídiǎn** dictionary

   这 本 词典 很 有用。

   Zhè běn cídiǎn hěn yǒuyòng.

   This dictionary is very useful.

3. 生词 **shēngcí** new words

   这 篇 短文 生词 太 多。

   Zhè piān duǎnwén shēngcí tài duō.

   This narrative has too many new words.

4. 单词 **dāncí** single word

   我 学 的 单词 不够 用。

   Wǒ xué de dāncí búgòu yòng.

   I haven't learned enough words.

5. 词汇表 **cíhuìbiǎo** glossary

   书 后面 有 词汇表。

   Shū hòumiàn yǒu cíhuìbiǎo.

   There's a glossary at the back of the book.

Helpful tips: The second stroke is a horizontal-bend-lift.										**7 strokes**
词	讠	讠	诃	诃	词	词	词			

典　diǎn

standard

Radical: 八 # 17 "eight"

Compounds, sentences, and meanings

1. 典 **diǎn** ceremony

校长　邀请 我 参加 五十 年
Xiàozhǎng yāoqǐng wǒ cānjiā wǔshí nián

校庆　盛典。
xiàoqìng shèngdiǎn.

The headmaster invited me to take part in the school's 50th anniversary ceremony.

2. 典礼 **diǎnlǐ** ceremony

校长　邀请 我 参加 五十 年
Xiàozhǎng yāoqǐng wǒ cānjiā wǔshí nián

校庆　典礼。
xiàoqìng diǎnlǐ.

The headmaster invited me to take part in the school's 50th anniversary ceremony.

3. 典型 **diǎnxíng** typical

这是 典型 的 中国　村庄。
Zhè shì diǎnxíng de Zhōngguó cūnzhuāng.

This is a typical Chinese village.

4. 词典 **cídiǎn** dictionary

这 本 词典 很 有用。
Zhè běn cídiǎn hěn yǒuyòng.

This dictionary is very useful.

5. 古典 **gǔdiǎn** classical

我 喜欢 古典 音乐。
Wǒ xǐhuan gǔdiǎn yīnyuè.

I like classical music.

| Helpful tips: The bottom horizontal stroke is longer. | | | | | | | | | **8 strokes** |

4

杂 zá

mixed, assorted

雜

Radical: 木 # 81 "tree"

Compounds, sentences, and meanings

1. 杂货 **záhuò** groceries, sundries

   很 大 的 超市 有 各种 的 杂货。

   Hěn dà de chāoshì yǒu gèzhǒng de záhuò.

   Very large supermarkets have every sort of product.

2. 杂乱 **záluàn** messy, disorderly

   你的 房间 太 杂乱 啊!

   Nǐ de fángjiān tài záluàn ā!

   Your room is too messy!

3. 杂志 **zázhì** magazine

   大人 跟 小孩 的 杂志 不 一样。

   Dàrén gēn xiǎohái de zázhì bù yíyàng.

   Adult's and children's magazines are not the same.

4. 复杂 **fùzá** complicated

   现代 社会 的 问题 一定 非常 复杂。

   Xiàndài shèhuì de wèntí yídìng fēicháng fùzá.

   The problems of modern societies are necessarily complicated.

Helpful tips: The top two strokes should be the same length when combined as the horizontal stroke.												**6 strokes**
杂	丿	九	九	杂	杂	杂						

志 **zhì**

ideal, aspiration

誌

Radical: 心 # 76 "heart"

Compounds, sentences, and meanings

1. 志愿 **zhìyuàn** aspiration, hope

   你 有 什么 志愿?

   Nǐ yǒu shénme zhìyuàn?

   What are your dreams?

2. 志气 **zhìqi** ambition, goal

   世界 年轻 人有 丰富 的 志气。

   Shìjiè niánqīng rén yǒu fēngfù de zhìqi.

   The young people of the world have varied goals.

3. 同志 **tóngzhì** comrade

   以前 中国 大陆人 常常 说:

   Yǐqián Zhōngguó Dàlù rén chángcháng shuō:

   "同志们!"

   "tóngzhì men!"

   Previously, Mainland Chinese people often said: "Comrades!"

Helpful tips: The top horizontal stroke is longer than the bottom horizontal stroke.											**7 strokes**	
志	一	十	士	士	志	志	志					

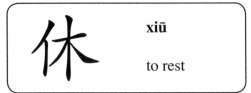

CHARACTER 257

休 xiū

to rest

Radical: 亻 # 19 "upright person"

Compounds, sentences, and meanings

1. **休 xiū** to stop

   他们 两个 争论 不休。

   Tāmen liǎng ge zhēnglùn bùxiū.

   The two of them cannot stop arguing.

2. **休假 xiūjià** to take a holiday

   今年 国庆节 休假一 周。

   Jīnián Guóqìngjié xiūjià yì zhōu.

   This year we have a week off for National Day.

3. **休养 xiūyǎng** to recuperate

   他 到 北戴河 休养 去了。

   Tā dào Bědàihé xiūyǎng qù le.

   He has gone to Beidaihe to convalesce.

4. **休息 xiūxi** rest

   百货 公司 元旦 不休息。

   Bǎihuò gōngsī Yuándàn bù xiūxi.

   Department stores are open as usual on New Year's Day.

5. **休业 xiūyè** suspend business

   今天 休业一 天。

   Jīntiān xiūyè yì tiān.

   Closed today.

Helpful tips: The last stroke tapers off.											**6 strokes**
休	丿	亻	仁	什	休	休					

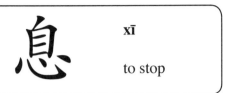

息   xī

to stop

Radical: 自 # 147 "self" or 心 # 76 "heart"

Compounds, sentences, and meanings

1. 息 **xī** to stop

   生命 不息, 战斗 不止。

   Shēngmìng bù xī, zhàndòu bù zhǐ.

   Life does not stop as struggles continue.

2. 信息 **xìnxī** news

   我 很 久 没 收到 她的信息。

   Wǒ hěn jiǔ méi shōudào tāde xìnxī.

   I haven't received news from her for a long time.

3. 利息 **lìxī** interest (on an investment)

   这家 银行 给的利息很 高。

   Zhè jiā yínháng gěi de lìxī hěn gāo.

   This bank gives high interest.

4. 作息 **zuòxī** to work and rest

   我们 应该 按时 作息。

   Wǒmen yīnggāi ànshí zuòxī.

   We should work and rest according to schedule.

5. 歇息 **xiēxi** to put up for the night

   今晚 就 在 我 这里歇息吧。

   Jīnwǎn jiù zài wǒ zhèlǐ xiēxi ba.

   Stay here tonight.

Helpful tips: The second stroke of 心 is a level curve ending in a hook.　　**10 strokes**

息	⺊¹	自²	白³	自⁴	自⁵	自⁶	自⁷	息⁸	息⁹	息¹⁰		

念 niàn

to think

Radical: 心 # 76 "heart"

Compounds, sentences, and meanings

1. 念 **niàn** to think of, miss (loved ones)

   我们 老 念着 你。

   Wǒmen lǎo niànzhe nǐ.

   We miss you very much.

2. 念书 **niànshū** to study

   我弟弟在 美国 念书。

   Wǒ dìdi zài Měiguó niànshū.

   My younger brother is studying in the United States.

3. 念头 **niàntóu** thought, idea

   你最好 放弃 这 个 念头。

   Nǐ zuìhǎo fàngqì zhè ge niàntóu.

   You'd better give up the idea.

4. 念课文 **niàn kèwén** to read aloud a text

   要 养成 大声 念 课文的 习惯。

   Yào yǎngchéng dàshēng niàn kèwén de xíguàn.

   We should get into the habit of reading the text aloud.

5. 纪念 **jìniàn** to commemorate

   人们 集会纪念这 位 伟大 的 音乐家。

   Rénmen jíhuì jìniàn zhè wèi wěidà de yīnyuèjiā.

   They held a commemorative function for the great musician.

Helpful tips: The last stroke of 今 does not touch the middle stroke of 心.									**8 strokes**		
念	丿	人	仒	今	今	念	念	念			

脑 **nǎo** brain

腦

Radical: 月 # 103 "flesh/moon"

Compounds, sentences, and meanings

1. 脑 **nǎo** brain
   我 今天 用 脑 过度。
   Wǒ jīntiān yòng nǎo guòdù.
   I overtaxed my brain today.

2. 脑筋 **nǎojīn** brain
   多 动 脑筋 才 能 解决 问题。
   Duō dòng nǎojīn cái néng jiějué wèntí.
   By exercising one's brain more often, one can resolve problems.

3. 脑汁 **nǎozhī** brain
   我 绞尽 脑汁 也 想不出 解决 方法。
   Wǒ jiǎojìn nǎozhī yě xiǎngbuchū jiějué fāngfǎ.
   I racked my brain but I still couldn't work it out.

4. 电脑 **diànnǎo** computer
   她 刚 买了一台 电脑。
   Tā gāng mǎile yì tái diànnǎo.
   She had just bought a computer.

5. 豆腐脑儿 **dòufu'nǎor** jellied beancurd
   我 喜欢 吃 豆腐脑儿。
   Wǒ xǐhuan chī dòufu'nǎor.
   I'm fond of jellied beancurd.

Helpful tips: The ninth stroke is a vertical bend.									**10 strokes**
脑	丿	几	月	月	月"	肷	肷	肷	脑	脑

A. *Pinyin* and Character Practice

Please complete the verbs in Part 1 with an appropriate object. Then supply the *pinyin* for those characters as appropriate. In Part 2, add a character to each blank to create a two-character noun. Then supply *pinyin* for the word as appropriate.

Part 1

看 _____   读 _____   休 _____   念 _____   打 _____

kàn _____   dú _____   xiū _____   niàn _____   dǎ _____

Part 2

杂 _____   词 _____   课 _____   电 _____   老 _____

zá _____   cí _____   kè _____   diàn _____   lǎo _____

B. Day Description

Please use each of the following nouns to create a sentence describing a day in which an activity associated with the noun occurs. Remember that a key construction to utilize in such sentences is 有一天.

1.（日报）_____

2.（杂志）_____

3.（词典）_____

4.（电脑）_____

5.（休息）_____

C. Short Description

The diagram here shows a small library and some of its contents. Add to the diagram as you see fit. Then, write a paragraph that describes the items in the library and the activities that would happen at each location.

书架

服务员台

电脑

书架　书架　书架

桌子

_____

_____

_____

_____

_____

_____

_____

_____

_____

活　**huó**

to live

Radical: 氵 # 32 "3 drops of water"

Compounds, sentences, and meanings

1. 活 **huó** to live

   我 爸爸 活到 八十五 岁。

   Wǒ bàba huódào bāshíwǔ suì.

   My father lived to be eighty-five.

2. 活力 **huólì** energy

   这 个 小伙子 充满 活力。

   Zhè ge xiǎohuǒzi chōngmǎn huólì.

   This young man is full of energy.

3. 活泼 **huópò** lively

   这 个 孩子 真 活泼。

   Zhè ge háizi zhēn huópò.

   This child is really lively.

4. 活动 **huódòng** activity

   这 个 周末 你 有 什么 活动？

   Zhè ge zhōumò nǐ yǒu shénme huódòng?

   What activities have you planned for this weekend?

5. 生活 **shēnghuó** life

   在 中国 生活 要 用 汉语。

   Zài Zhōngguó shēnghuó yào yòng Hànyǔ.

   You have to use Chinese if you live in China.

Helpful tips: The fourth stroke sweeps down from right to left.　　　　　　**9 strokes**

活	氵	氵	氵	氵	汗	汗	活	活			

动 **dòng**

to move

動

Radical: 力 # 31 "strength"

Compounds, sentences, and meanings

1. 动 **dòng** to move

   这 东西 一个人 拿不动。

   Zhè dōngxi yí ge rén nábudòng.

   This thing can't be moved by one person.

2. 动身 **dòngshēn** to set out on a journey

   我们 明天 一早 就 动身。

   Wǒmen míngtiān yì zǎo jiù dòngshēn.

   We'll leave early tomorrow.

3. 动人 **dòngrén** moving, touching

   这 个 电影 故事 很 动人。

   Zhè ge diànyǐng gùshi hěn dòngrén.

   The plot of this movie is very touching.

4. 动听 **dòngtīng** pleasant to listen to

   她 唱歌 很 动听。

   Tā chànggē hěn dòngtīng.

   She sings beautifully.

5. 动物园 **dòngwùyuán** zoo

   北京 动物园 有 大熊猫。

   Běijīng Dòngwùyuán yǒu dàxióngmāo.

   There are pandas in Beijing Zoo.

Helpful tips: The last stroke tapers off.						6 strokes
动	二	三	云	云	习	动

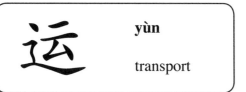

Traditional Form

运　yùn

transport

運

Radical: 辶 # 38 "movement"

Compounds, sentences, and meanings

1. 运 **yùn** luck

   祝 你 好 运!

   Zhù nǐ hǎo yùn!

   Good luck!

2. 运气 **yùnqi** luck

   我 最近 运气 不 太 好。

   Wǒ zuìjìn yùnqi bú tài hǎo.

   I've had some bad luck recently.

3. 幸运 **xìngyùn** fortunate

   我 觉得 我 很 幸运。

   Wǒ juéde wǒ hěn xìngyùn.

   I think that I'm very fortunate.

4. 运动 **yùndòng** sport

   游泳 是 我 喜爱 的 运动。

   Yóuyǒng shì wǒ xǐ'ài de yùndòng.

   Swimming is my favorite sport.

5. 运用 **yùnyòng** to utilize

   她 把 学过 的 东西 运用 在

   Tā bǎ xuéguo de dōngxi yùnyòng zài

   生活 里。

   shēnghuó li.

   She applies what she learned to everyday situations.

Helpful tips: End the last stroke of 云 firmly.　　　　**7 strokes**

运	一	二	云	云	运	运					

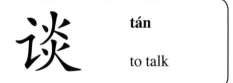

tán

to talk

談

Radical: 讠 # 9 "word"

Compounds, sentences, and meanings

1. 谈 **tán** to talk

   我 跟 他 很 谈得来。
   Wǒ gēn tā hěn tándelái.
   I get along with him very well.

2. 谈话 **tánhuà** talk

   我们 进行了 友好 的 谈话。
   Wǒmen jìnxíngle yǒuhǎo de tánhuà.
   We had a friendly talk.

3. 谈判 **tánpàn** to negotiate

   两 国 进行了 贸易 谈判。
   Liǎng guó jìnxíngle màoyì tánpàn.
   The two countries held trade negotiations.

4. 谈天 **tántiān** chat

   有空儿 到 我 这里 谈天。
   Yǒukòngr dào wǒ zhèlǐ tántiān.
   Come for a chat when you're free.

5. 谈吐 **tántù** style of conversation

   从 她的 谈吐 看得出 她 是 有 教养
   Cóng tāde tántù kàndechū tā shì yǒu jiàoyǎng

   的 人。
   de rén.
   From her style of speech, I can see that she's well educated.

| Helpful tips: The second stroke lifts at the end. | | | | | | | | | | 10 strokes |

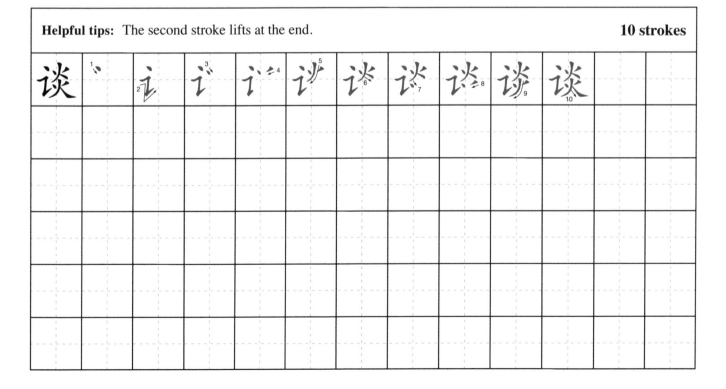

話

话　**huà**

speech

話

Radical: 讠 # 9 "word"

Compounds, sentences, and meanings

1. 话 **huà** word, talk

话 不能 这么 说。

Huà bùnéng zhème shuō.

I wouldn't say that.

2. 大话 **dàhuà** to brag, talk big

他 常常 说 大话。

Tā chángcháng shuō dàhuà.

He often brags.

3. 电话 **diànhuà** telephone

今晚 请 给我 回个 电话。

Jīnwǎn qǐng gěi wǒ huí ge diànhuà.

Please give me a call tonight.

4. 好话 **hǎohuà** word of praise

请 给我 说 句 好话。

Qǐng gěi wǒ shuō jù hǎohuà.

Please put in a good word for me.

5. 听话 **tīnghuà** obedient

这个孩子 很 听话。

Zhè ge háizi hěn tīnghuà.

This child is very obedient.

Helpful tips: The top stroke of 舌 sweeps from right to left.										**8 strokes**
话	丶	讠	订	讦	讦	话	话	话		

帮 | **bāng**

to help

幫

Radical: 巾 # 52 "napkin"

Compounds, sentences, and meanings

1. 帮 **bāng** to help

   我 帮 她 搬了 行李。

   Wǒ bāng tā bānle xíngli.

   I helped her with her luggage.

2. 帮助 **bāngzhù** to help

   他 帮助 我学 汉语。

   Tā bāngzhù wǒ xué Hànyǔ.

   He helps me to learn Chinese.

3. 帮手 **bāngshǒu** helper

   你 真 是 个 好 帮手。

   Nǐ zhēn shì ge hǎo bāngshǒu.

   You really are a good helper.

4. 帮忙 **bāngmáng** to help

   我 要 请 她 帮忙。

   Wǒ yào qǐng tā bāngmáng.

   I'll ask her to help.

5. 帮倒忙 **bāngdàománg** to make the matter worse with one's help

   请 小心 点儿, 别 给 我 帮倒忙 了。

   Qǐng xiǎoxīn diǎnr, bié gěi wǒ bāngdàománg le.

   Please be careful, don't make things worse.

Helpful tips: The fourth stroke sweeps down and tapers off.   **9 strokes**

帮	一	三	三	扌	邦	邦	邦	帮	帮			

助 **zhù**

assistance

Radical: 力 # 31 "strength"

Compounds, sentences, and meanings

1. 助 **zhù** to help

   感谢 你 助 我 一臂之力。

   Gǎnxiè nǐ zhù wǒ yí bì zhī lì.

   Thanks for lending me a helping hand.

2. 帮助 **bāngzhù** to help

   他 帮助 我学 汉语。

   Tā bāngzhù wǒ xué Hànyǔ.

   He helps me learn Chinese.

3. 助手 **zhùshǒu** assistant

   他是我的 助手。

   Tā shì wǒde zhùshǒu.

   He is my assistant.

4. 助兴 **zhùxìng** to add to the fun

   给大家 唱 支歌 助助兴。

   Gěi dàjiā chàng zhī gē zhùzhuxìng.

   Sing us a song to liven things up.

5. 助学金 **zhùxuéjīn** grant-in-aid

   他是 领 助学金的 学生。

   Tā shì lǐng zhùxuéjīn de xuésheng.

   He is a grant-in-aid student.

Helpful tips: The fifth stroke lifts slightly. **7 strokes**

助 | 刀 | 刀 | 月 | 且 | 且 | 助 | 助

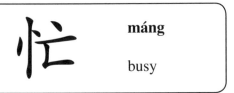

忙

máng

busy

Radical: 忄 # 33 "upright heart"

Compounds, sentences, and meanings

1. 忙 **máng** busy

   我 最近 很 忙。

   Wǒ zuìjìn hěn máng.

   I've been very busy lately.

2. 忙着 **mángzhe** be busy with something

   他 正 忙着 做饭 呢。

   Tā zhèng mángzhe zuòfàn ne.

   He's busying himself preparing the meal.

3. 忙人 **mángrén** busy person

   他 是 个 大 忙人。

   Tā shì ge dà mángrén.

   He's a very busy man.

4. 忙碌 **mánglù** be busy

   她 忙碌了 一个 上午，结果 把 饭菜

   Tā mánglùle yí ge shàngwǔ, jiéguǒ bǎ fàncài

   做好。

   zuòhǎo.

   She was busy all morning, and eventually got the cooking done.

5. 帮忙 **bāngmáng** to help

   他 来 找 人 帮忙。

   Tā lái zhǎo rén bāngmáng.

   He came for help.

Helpful tips: The last stroke is a vertical bend.											**6 strokes**
忙	丶	丷	忄	忄	忙	忙					

懂   dǒng

to understand

Radical: 忄 # 33 "upright heart"

Compounds, sentences, and meanings

1. **懂 dǒng** to understand

   不要 不 懂 装 懂。

   Búyào bù dǒng zhuāng dǒng.

   Don't pretend to understand when you don't.

2. **懂得 dǒngde** to understand

   你 懂得 这 句 话 的 意思 吗?

   Nǐ dǒngde zhè jù huà de yìsi ma?

   Do you understand the meaning of this sentence?

3. **懂事 dǒngshì** sensible, intelligent

   她 是 一个 懂事 的 孩子。

   Tā shì yí ge dǒngshì de háizi.

   She is a sensible child.

4. **看懂 kàndǒng** to understand (by reading)

   我 看不懂 中文 报。

   Wǒ kànbudǒng Zhōngwén bào.

   I can't understand Chinese newspapers.

5. **听懂 tīngdǒng** to understand (by hearing)

   我 能 听懂 上海话。

   Wǒ néng tīngdǒng Shànghǎihuà.

   I can understand Shanghai dialect.

Helpful tips: Write the two dots before the vertical stroke in the upright heart 忄.   **15 strokes**

懂	1	2	3	忄	5	6	7	8	9	10	11	12
懂	懂	懂										

zhǎo

to look for

Radical: 扌 # 48 "hand"

Compounds, sentences, and meanings

1. 找 **zhǎo** to look for

   我 到处 在 找 你。

   Wǒ dàochù zài zhǎo nǐ.

   I've been looking for you all over the place.

2. 找钱 **zhǎoqián** to give change

   这 是 找 给 你 的 钱。

   Zhè shì zhǎo gěi nǐ de qián.

   Here's your change.

3. 找麻烦 **zhǎo máfan** to look for trouble

   对不起, 我 给 你们 找 麻烦 了。

   Duìbuqǐ, wǒ gěi nǐmen zhǎo máfan le.

   I'm sorry to have caused you so much trouble.

4. 找对象 **zhǎo duìxiàng** to look for a partner in marriage

   她 念 大学 为 的 是 找 对象。

   Tā niàn dàxué wèi de shì zhǎo duìxiàng.

   She's only going to university to find a husband.

5. 找不开 **zhǎobukāi** to have no small change

   对不起, 你 这 张 五十 元 票子 我

   Duìbuqǐ, nǐ zhè zhāng wǔshí yuán piàozi wǒ

   找不开。

   zhǎobukāi.

   Sorry, I can't change a fifty.

Helpful tips: The two components do not join in the middle.							**7 strokes**

找　一　扌　才　扌　扌　找　找

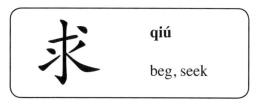

qiú

beg, seek

Radical: 一 # 2 "horizontal stroke"

Compounds, sentences, and meanings

1. 求 **qiú** beg, request

   我 求 你 帮 个 忙, 行 吗?

   Wǒ qiú nǐ bāng ge máng, xíng ma?

   May I ask you a favor?

2. 求教 **qiújiào** come to seek advice

   不懂 的 事 要 向 别人 求教。

   Bùdǒng de shì yào xiàng biéren qiújiào.

   If you don't understand, you should ask someone.

3. 求情 **qiúqíng** plead

   他 父母 来 学校 为 儿子 求情。

   Tā fùmǔ lái xuéxiào wèi érzi qiúqíng.

   His parents came to the school to plead for their son.

4. 求之不得 **qiú zhī bù dé** all one could wish for

   这 是 个 求 之 不 得 的 好 机会。

   Zhè shì ge qiú zhī bù dé de hǎo jīhuì.

   This is a most welcome opportunity.

5. 要求 **yāoqiú** requirement

   父母 不要 对 孩子 要求 过 高。

   Fùmǔ búyào duì háizi yāoqiú guò gāo.

   Parents should not ask too much of their children.

Helpful tips: The vertical stroke ends with a hook.

7 strokes

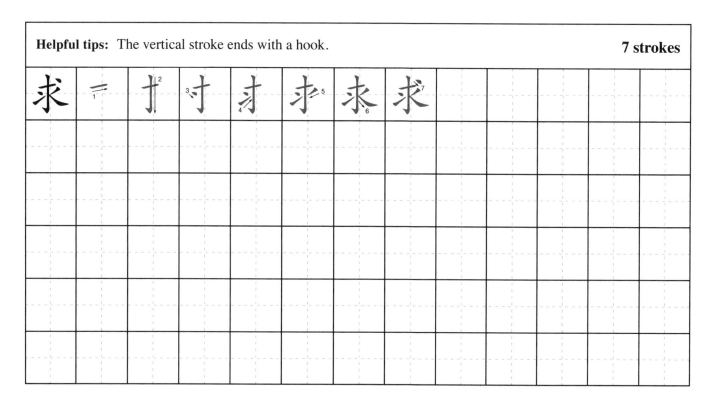

教

jiāo/jiào

teach

Radical: 攵 # 99 "tap"

Compounds, sentences, and meanings

1. 教 **jiāo** teach

我 教 汉语 已经 三十 年 了。

Wǒ jiāo Hànyǔ yǐjīng sānshí nián le.

I've taught Chinese for thirty years.

2. 教书 **jiāoshū** teach

我 哥哥 在 小学 教书。

Wǒ gēge zài xiǎoxué jiāoshū.

My older brother teaches in a primary school.

3. 教师 **jiàoshī** teacher

当 教师 要 有 耐心。

Dāng jiàoshī yào yǒu nàixīn.

You need patience to be a teacher.

4. 教堂 **jiàotáng** church

我 每个 星期天 都 去 教堂。

Wǒ měi ge xīngqītiān dōu qù jiàotáng.

I go to church every Sunday.

5. 教育 **jiàoyù** education

我 母亲 受过 高等 教育。

Wo mǔqin shòuguo gāoděng jiàoyù.

My mother had tertiary education.

Helpful tips: Note the difference between 攵 and 又.									**11 strokes**	
教	二	并	土	夬	耂	孝	孝	孝	教	教

Lesson 25: Review Activities

A. *Pinyin* and Pronunciation Practice

Please transcribe the following questions into *pinyin*. Then, for additional practice, ask and answer the questions.

1. 她汉语说得很清楚, 你们都听得懂吗?

   _____

2. 这张画很有意思, 你怎么看得懂?

   _____

3. 介绍完了, 你懂了吗?

   _____

B. Sentence Completion

Please complete each of the following sentences using one of the following words. Then translate the resulting sentence into English.

应该　　　　需要　　　　喜欢　　　　别做　　　　得

1. 我的朋友_____踢足球。

   _____

2. 我的母亲常常告诉我_____危险的运动。

   _____

3. 医生说每天人都_____锻炼锻炼。

   _____

4. 离开家以前你_____查有家的钥匙。

   _____

5. 去别的国家你_____有护照。

   _____

C. Conversation Practice

Please create 7 questions that you would ask during a phone conversation with a friend. A clear phone conversation would move between different activities and timeframes clearly and with purpose; write your questions to reflect that.

1. _____

2. _____

3. _____

4. _____

5. _____

6. _____

7. _____

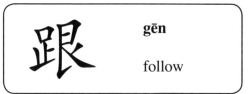

跟 gēn

follow

Radical: 足 # 164 "foot"

Compounds, sentences, and meanings

1. 跟 **gēn** with

   她 跟 父母 住 在 一起。

   Tā gēn fùmǔ zhù zài yìqǐ.

   She lives with her parents.

2. 跟⋯⋯一样 **gēn ... yíyàng** the same as

   弟弟 长得 跟 我 一样 高。

   Dìdi zhǎngde gēn wǒ yíyàng gāo.

   My younger brother is as tall as me.

3. 跟上 **gēnshàng** to keep pace with

   你 走得 太 快, 我 跟不上。

   Nǐ zǒude tài kuài, wǒ gēnbúshàng.

   You walk too fast, I can't keep up with you.

4. 跟着 **gēnzhe** follow

   请 跟着 我 念。

   Qǐng gēnzhe wǒ niàn

   Please read after me.

5. 高跟鞋 **gāogēnxié** high-heeled shoes

   她 喜欢 穿 高跟鞋。

   Tā xǐhuan chuān gāogēnxié.

   She likes to wear high-heeled shoes.

Helpful tips: The last two strokes of 足 are vertical and lift, respectively.												**13 strokes**
跟	丶 1	口 2	口 3	口 4	卟 5	卟 6	足 7	足 8	足 9	足 10	跟 11	跟 12
跟 13												

dé/de/děi

to obtain; [particle]; must

Radical: 彳 # 54 "double person"

Compounds, sentences, and meanings

1. 得 **dé** obtain

   他 考试 得了第一 名。

   Tā kǎoshì déle dìyī míng.

   He came in first in the exam.

2. verb + 得 **verb + de** [verbal particle]

   她 乒乓球 打得不错。

   Tā pīngpāngqiú dǎde búcuò.

   She plays table tennis quite well.

3. 得意 **déyì** proud of oneself

   我 对自己的 成绩 感到 得意。

   Wǒ duì zìjǐ de chéngjì gǎndào déyì.

   I was proud of my results.

4. 得罪 **dézuì** offend

   我的 话 把他给 得罪了。

   Wǒde huà bǎ tā gěi dézuìle.

   My words offended him.

5. 得 **děi** certainly will

   要不 快 走，我们 就 得 迟到 了。

   Yàobú kuài zǒu, wǒmen jiù děi chídào le.

   We'll be late if we don't hurry.

Helpful tips: The second horizontal stroke is longer.										**11 strokes**
得	丿	彡	彳	彳	彳日	得	得	得	得	得

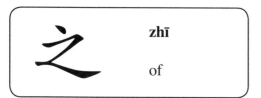

之   **zhī**

of

Radical: 丶 # 1 "dot"

Compounds, sentences, and meanings

1. 之 **zhī** of

   人民 是 国家 之 材。

   Rénmín shì guójiā zhī cái.

   The people are a country's raw materials.

2. 之后 **zhīhòu** afterwards

   毕业 之后 你 不 能 再 上 高中

   Bìyè zhīhòu nǐ bù néng zài shàng gāozhōng

   学校 的课。

   xuéxiào de kè.

   After graduating you can't go back to high school classes.

3. 之前 **zhīqián** beforehand

   节日 之前 你 不可以 打开 礼物。

   Jiérì zhīqián nǐ bù kěyǐ dǎkāi lǐwù.

   Before a holiday you can't open presents.

4. 五分之一 **wǔ fēnzhī yī** one-fifth

   世界 人口里, 五 分 之一 是 中国 人。

   Shìjiè rénkǒulǐ, wǔ fēnzhī yī shì Zhōngguó rén.

   Of the world's population, one-fifth is Chinese.

Helpful tips: The second stroke should be even in length with both sections.   **3 strokes**

之	之	之	之							

因 **yīn**

reason

Radical: # 51 "4-sided frame"

Compounds, sentences, and meanings

1. 因 **yīn** because of

   这次他是因病请假。

   Zhè cì tā shì yīn bìng qǐngjià.

   On this occasion he asked for sick leave.

2. 因此 **yīncǐ** so, therefore

   她没有小孩子,因此养了一只猫。

   Tā méiyǒu xiǎoháizi, yīncǐ yàngle yì zhī māo.

   She has no children, so she keeps a cat.

3. 因循 **yīnxún** be in a rut

   老人经常是因循守旧。

   Lǎorén jīngcháng shì yīnxún shǒujiù.

   Old folks often stick to old ways.

4. 因为 **yīnwèi** because

   因为喝了酒,所以不能开车。

   Yīnwèi hēle jiǔ, suǒyǐ bù néng kāichē.

   I can't drive because I've been drinking.

5. 原因 **yuányīn** reason

   你知道是什么原因吗?

   Nǐ zhīdào shì shénme yuányīn ma?

   Do you know the reason?

Helpful tips: The fifth stroke ends firmly.											**6 strokes**
因	丨	冂	冋	因	因	因					

为 wéi/wèi

do / on behalf of

為

Radical: 丶 # 1 "dot"

Compounds, sentences, and meanings

1. 为 **wéi** do, act
   事 在 人 为。
   Shì zài rén wéi.
   Human effort is the decisive factor.

2. 为难 **wéinán** make things difficult for
   请 别 故意 为难 我。
   Qǐng bié gùyì wéinán wǒ.
   Please don't deliberately make things difficult for me.

3. 为期 **wéiqī** last for a period (of time)
   会议 为期 三 天。
   Huìyì wéiqī sān tiān.
   The meeting is scheduled to last for three days.

4. 为了 **wèile** in order to, for
   我 学 英语 是 为了 以后 出国。
   Wǒ xué Yīngyǔ shì wèile yǐhòu chūguó.
   I'm studying English so that I can study abroad later.

5. 为什么 **wèishénme** why
   你 为什么 不去 美国 看看?
   Nǐ wèishénme bú qù Měiguó kànkan?
   Why don't you go to the US for a visit?

Helpful tips: The first dot is placed on the top left, the second dot goes inside.　　　　**4 strokes**

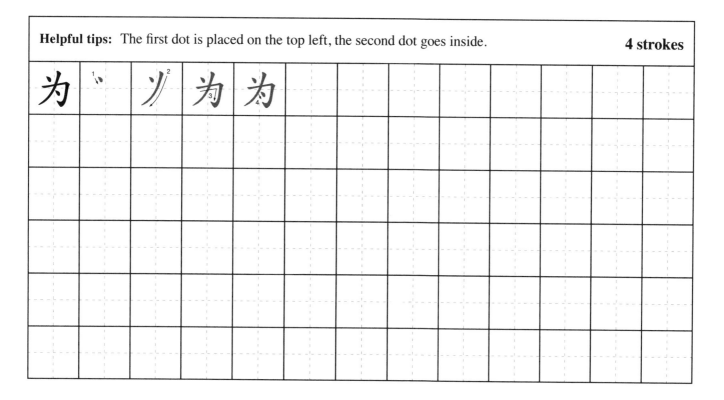

CHARACTER 278

或   huò

or; perhaps

Radical: 戈 # 85 "spear"

Compounds, sentences, and meanings

1. 或 **huò** or

   无论 唱歌 或 跳舞, 她 都 行。

   Wúlùn chànggē huò tiàowǔ, tā dōu xíng.

   She is good at both singing and dancing.

2. 或是 **huòshì** or

   无论 唱歌 或是 跳舞, 她 都 行。

   Wúlùn chànggē huòshì tiàowǔ, tā dōu xíng.

   She is good at both singing and dancing.

3. 或许 **huòxǔ** perhaps, maybe

   他 或许 没有 赶上 火车。

   Tā huòxǔ méiyǒu gǎnshàng huōchē.

   Perhaps he has missed the train.

4. 或者 **huòzhě** either ... or

   你 早上 或者 下午 来 都 可以。

   Nǐ zǎoshang huòzhě xiàwǔ lái dōu kěyǐ.

   You may come either in the morning or in the afternoon.

Helpful tips: The bottom horizontal stroke goes up slightly.   **8 strokes**

或	二	一	一	豆	戈	或	或				

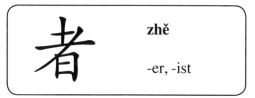

者　zhě

-er, -ist

Radical: 曰 # 91 "speech"

Compounds, sentences, and meanings

1. 者 **zhě** one of those who; the thing or things which

   独身主义者。

   Dúshēnzhǔyìzhě.

   One who prefers to be single.

2. 作者 **zuòzhě** author

   他是这本书的作者。

   Tā shì zhè běn shū de zuòzhě.

   He's the author of this book.

3. 读者 **dúzhě** reader

   这本书的读者很广。

   Zhě běn shū de dúzhě hěn guǎng.

   This book has a wide readership.

4. 记者 **jìzhě** reporter

   他是当记者的。

   Tā shì dāng jìzhě de.

   He is a reporter.

5. 旁观者 **pángguānzhě** onlooker

   旁观者　清。

   Pángguānzhě qīng.

   The spectator sees most clearly.

Helpful tips: The top horizontal stroke is shorter.							**8 strokes**			
者	一	土	土	耂	者	者	者			

33

着

zhe/zháo/zhuó

[verbal particle]

著

Radical: 羊 # 133 "sheep"

Compounds, sentences, and meanings

1. 着 **zhe** [verbal suffix]

她 穿着 一 身 新衣服。
Tā chuānzhe yì shēn xīn yīfu.
She is wearing new clothes.

2. 着急 **zháojí** get worried

冷静 点儿, 别 着急。
Lěngjìng diǎnr, bié zháojí.
Keep calm, don't panic.

3. 着凉 **zháoliáng** catch a chill

外面 有点 冷, 当心 着凉。
Wàimiàn yǒudiǎn lěng, dāngxīn zháoliáng.
It's chilly outside, be careful not to catch cold.

4. 着想 **zhuóxiǎng** consider (the interest of somebody or something)

他是 为你 着想, 才 劝 你不要
Tā shì wèi nǐ zhuóxiǎng, cái quàn nǐ búyào
去 的。
qù de.
It was for your own good that he advised you not to go.

5. 着重 **zhuózhòng** stress, emphasize

这里我 想 着重地 讲 一个问题。
Zhèlǐ wǒ xiǎng zhuózhòngde jiǎng yí ge wèntí.
Here I would like to go into one question in particular.

Helpful tips: The second horizontal stroke is shorter.										**11 strokes**

着

才 cái

only then, just; talent

Radical: 一 # 2 "horizontal stroke"

Compounds, sentences, and meanings

1. 才 **cái** only then (late occurrence)

   下雪 路 滑, 汽车 晚了 半 个 小时
   Xiàxuě lù huá, qìchē wǎnle bàn ge xiǎoshí
   才 到。
   cái dào.
   It was snowing and the road was slippery so the bus was half an hour late.

2. 刚才 **gāngcái** just now

   他 刚才 还 说 要 去 呢。
   Tā gāngcái hái shuō yào qù ne.
   He was saying only a moment ago that he wanted to go.

3. 才华 **cáihuá** literary or artistic talent

   他 是 一 位 很 有 才华 的 作家。
   Tā shì yí wèi hěn yǒu cáihuá de zuòjiā.
   He is a gifted writer.

4. 才识 **cáishí** ability and insight

   我 觉得 你 哥哥 才识 过 人。
   Wǒ juéde nǐ gége cáishí guò rén.
   I think your older brother is extraordinarily talented.

5. 人才 **réncái** talent

   她 是 个 难得 的 人才。
   Tā shì ge nándé de réncái.
   She is a person of extraordinary ability.

Helpful tips: The final sweeping stroke comes down from the intersection of the first two strokes.					**3 strokes**

才 一 才 才

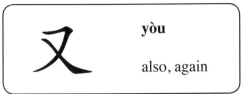

又

yòu

also, again

Radical: 又 # 24 "again"

Compounds, sentences, and meanings

1. 又 **yòu** again

   她把信看了又看。

   Tā bǎ xìn kànle yòu kàn.

   She read the letter over and over again.

2. 又 **yòu** in addition to

   跳舞是一种娱乐，又是一种

   Tiàowǔ shì yì zhǒng yúlè, yòu shì yì zhǒng

   运动。

   yùndòng.

   Dancing is a form of entertainment and a sport.

3. 又⋯又 **yòu ... yòu** both ... and

   这种汽车又便宜又好。

   Zhè zhǒng qìchē yòu piányi yòu hǎo.

   This type of automobile is cheap and good.

4. 又 **yòu** but

   我想去，又怕没时间。

   Wǒ xiǎng qù, yòu pà méi shíjiān.

   I'd like to go, but I'm not sure if I can find the time.

Helpful tips: The last stroke comes down firmly and then tapers off.										**2 strokes**
又	ㄱ	又								

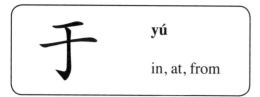

于   yú

in, at, from

於

Radical: 一 # 2 "horizontal stroke"

Compounds, sentences, and meanings

1. 于 **yú** in, at

关心 只 感觉 于心。

Guānxīn zhǐ gǎnjué yú xīn.

Care is only felt in the heart.

2. 于 **yú** from (lit.)

河水 流于 源 到海。

Hé shuǐ liú yú yuán dào hǎi.

A river's water flows from the source to the sea.

3. 于今 **yújīn** up to the present

于今 汽车 都 需要 石油。

Yújīn qìchē dōu xūyào shíyóu.

Up to now all cars need gasoline.

4. 于是 **yúshì** therefore, thereupon

我的 朋友 希望 写书, 于是她

Wǒ de péngyou xīwàng xiěshū, yúshì tā

常常 读现代 小说。

chángcháng dú xiàndài xiǎoshuō.

My friend dreams of writing a book, therefore she often reads modern novels.

Helpful tips: The bottom horizontal stroke is the longest.   **3 strokes**

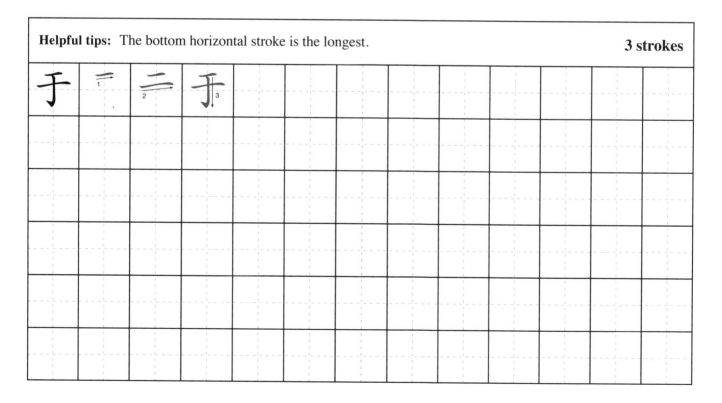

A. Character and Pronunciation Practice

Please provide a conjunction in Chinese that has the same meaning as the English conjunction given. First give the characters for the conjunction and then the *pinyin* for each word.

	If	Must	Thus	But	Or	With
汉字	_____	_____	_____	_____	_____	_____
(pinyin)	_____	_____	_____	_____	_____	_____

B. Sentence Creation

Construct a sentence with each of the topics provided. In each sentence utilize one of the following grammatical structures.

跟　　　因为　　　于是　　　或者　　　才

1. （来朋友的家）

_____

2. （要看新的电影）

_____

3. （两个人去花园）

_____

4. （不能吃饭）

_____

5. （写很长的文章）

_____

C. Connected Discourse

For each of the following situations, create a statement connected by the conjunction or construction provided. Make sure that the statement created is connected logically with the original situation.

1. (得买一辆新汽车)

因为 _____

所以 _____

于是 _____

2. (要去亚洲旅游)

因为 _____

或者 _____

于是 _____

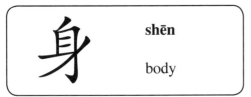

身   **shēn**

body

Radical: 身 # 168 "body"

Compounds, sentences, and meanings

1. 身 **shēn** body, oneself

   身 在 福 中 不 知 福。

   Shēn zài fú zhōng bù zhī fú.

   When you're happy you don't know it.

2. 身体 **shēntǐ** health

   跳舞 可以 锻炼 身体。

   Tiàowǔ kěyǐ duànliàn shēntǐ.

   Dancing can improve your physique.

3. 身上 **shēnshang** (carry something) on one

   你 身上 有 零钱 吗?

   Nǐ shēnshang yǒu língqián ma?

   Have you got any change on you?

4. 身材 **shēncái** body line

   王 菲的 身材 苗条。

   Wáng Fēi de shēncái miáotiáo.

   Faye Wong has a slim figure.

5. 身高 **shēn'gāo** stature

   王 菲 身 高 一点六五 米。

   Wáng Fēi shēn'gāo yìdiǎnliùwǔ mǐ.

   Faye Wong is 1.65 meters tall.

Helpful tips: The third stroke ends with a hook.   **7 strokes**

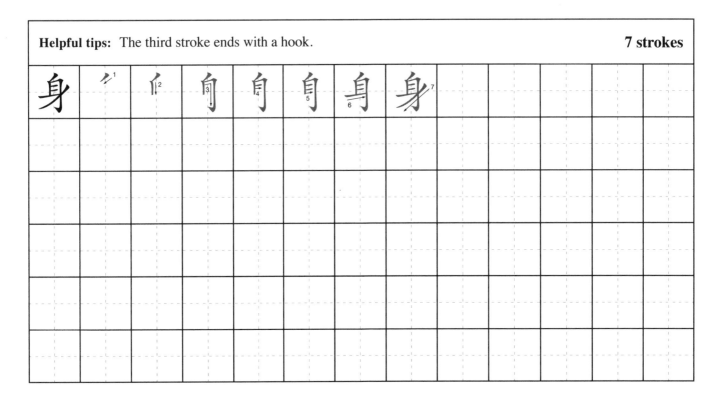

体　　tǐ

body

體

Radical: 亻 # 19 "upright person"

Compounds, sentences, and meanings

1. **体 tǐ** style of writing

你写的是 什么 体?

Nǐ xiě de shì shénme tǐ?

What style of calligraphy are you writing?

2. **身体 shēntǐ** health

跳舞可以 锻炼 身体。

Tiàowǔ kěyǐ duànliàn shēntǐ.

Dancing can improve your physique.

3. **体温 tǐwēn** body temperature

你的体温是 三十九 度, 发烧了。

Nǐde tǐwēn shì sānshíjiǔ dù, fāshāo le.

You have a fever, your temperature is 39 degrees.

4. **体力 tǐlì** bodily strength

运动 能 增强 体力。

Yùndòng néng zēngqiáng tǐlì.

Sports can build up your strength.

5. **体贴 tǐtiē** considerate

他 对妻子很 体贴。

Tā duì qīzi hěn tǐtiē.

He's very considerate to his wife.

Helpful tips: The bottom horizontal stroke is shorter.						7 strokes

体	丿	亻	仁	什	仕	休	体					

病　bìng

sick, ill

Radical: 疒 # 112 "sickness"

Compounds, sentences, and meanings

1. 病 **bìng** sick

   他 有 病。

   Tā yǒu bìng.

   He is ill.

2. 病假 **bìngjià** sick leave

   医生 给 我 三 天 病假。

   Yīshēng gěi wǒ sān tiān bìngjià.

   The doctor gave me three days' sick leave.

3. 病历 **bìnglì** medical history

   请 填上 病历。

   Qǐng tiánshàng bìnglì.

   Please fill in your medical history.

4. 病情 **bìngqíng** patient's condition

   孩子的 病情 有 好转。

   Háizi de bìngqíng yǒu hǎozhuǎn.

   The child's condition took a turn for the better.

5. 病人 **bìngrén** patient

   这 家 医院 医生 不够, 病人 太 多。

   Zhè jiā yīyuàn yīshēng búgòu, bìngrén tài duō.

   This hospital does not have enough doctors; there are too many patients.

Helpful tips: The sixth stroke is shorter than the one above it.									**10 strokes**
病	丶	二	广	疒	疒	疒	病	病	病

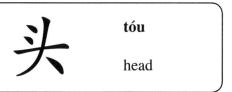

头　tóu

head

頭

Radical: 丶 # 1 "dot"

Compounds, sentences, and meanings

1. 头 **tóu** head

   走路 要 抬高 头。

   Zǒulù yào táigāo tóu.

   One should lift one's head when walking.

2. 头等 **tóuděng** first class

   他 买 的 是 头等舱。

   Tā mǎi de shì tóuděngcāng.

   He bought tickets for a first-class cabin.

3. 头发 **tóufa** hair

   她 把 头发 染成 金色。

   Tā bǎ tóufa rǎnchéng jīnsè.

   She dyed her hair blonde.

4. 头脑 **tóunǎo** brains, mind

   她 很 有 头脑。

   Tā hěn yǒu tóunǎo.

   She has plenty of brains.

5. 头痛 **tóutòng** (have a) headache

   我 头痛得 很 厉害。

   Wǒ tóutòngde hěn lìhai.

   I have a very bad headache.

| Helpful tips: End the last stroke firmly. | | | | | | | | | | | 5 strokes |

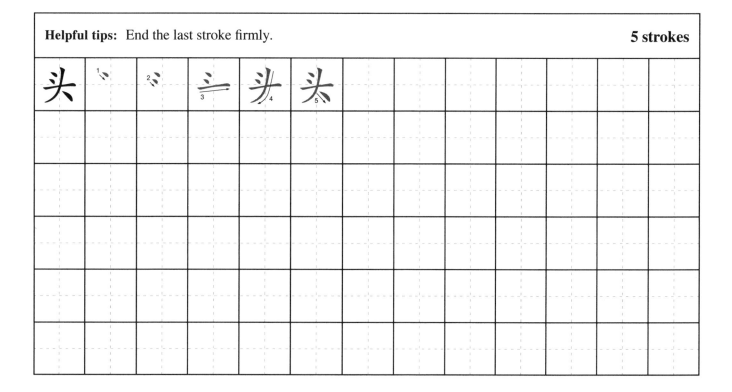

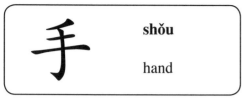

shǒu

hand

Radical: 手 # 96 "whole hand"

Compounds, sentences, and meanings

1. 手 **shǒu** hand

   这 是 手织 的 毛衣。

   Zhè shì shǒuzhí de máoyī.

   This is a hand-knitted sweater.

2. 手纸 **shǒuzhǐ** toilet paper

   厕所 没有 手纸 了。

   Cèsuǒ méiyǒu shǒuzhǐ le.

   There's no toilet paper in the lavatory.

3. 手气 **shǒuqì** luck at gambling

   我 今晚 打牌 的 手气 好得 出奇。

   Wǒ jīnwǎn dǎpái de shǒuqì hǎode chūqí.

   I've had a lot of luck at cards/mahjong tonight.

4. 手艺 **shǒuyì** craftsmanship

   那个 裁缝 的 手艺 很 好。

   Nà ge cáifeng de shǒuyì hěn hǎo.

   That tailor is very skillful.

5. 手续 **shǒuxù** formalities

   请 过来 这边 办 入境 手续。

   Qǐng guòlai zhèbian bàn rùjìng shǒuxù.

   Please come over here to go through the entry formalities.

Helpful tips: The last stroke ends with a hook.											4 strokes

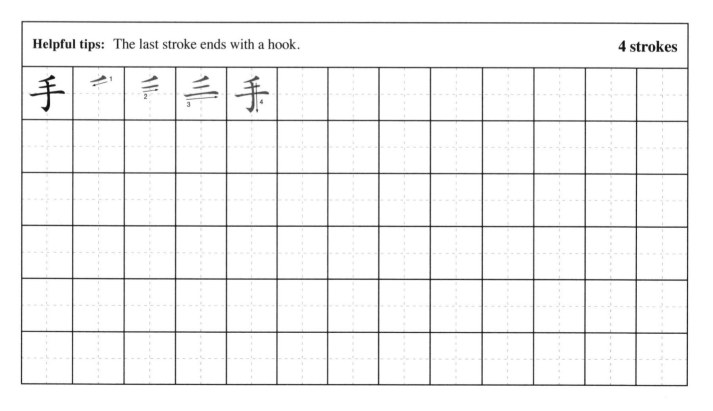

痛

tòng

sore, hurt

Radical: 疒 # 112 "sickness"

Compounds, sentences, and meanings

1. 痛 **tòng** pain

   这里 痛 不 痛?

   Zhèlǐ tòng bu tòng?

   Does it hurt here?

2. 痛哭 **tòngkū** weep bitterly

   她 为 这 件 事 痛哭了 一 场。

   Tā wèi zhè jiàn shì tòngkūle yì cháng.

   She had a good cry about it.

3. 痛苦 **tòngkǔ** suffering

   我 得 离开 老家, 感到 很 痛苦。

   Wǒ děi líkāi lǎojiā, gǎndào hěn tòngkǔ.

   It pains me to have to leave my home.

4. 痛快 **tòngkuài** delighted

   今天 遇到了 一件 不 痛快 的事。

   Jīntiān yùdàole yí jiàn bú tòngkuài de shì.

   I had an unpleasant experience today.

5. 痛心 **tòngxīn** distressed

   这样 浪费 食物 令 人 痛心。

   Zhèyàng làngfèi shíwù lìng rén tòngxīn.

   It is distressing to see food being wasted like this.

Helpful tips: The sixth stroke is a horizontal-bend.　　　　**12 strokes**

痛	丶	亠	广	疒	疒	疒	疒	痡	痛	痛	痛

心 **xīn**

rest

Radical: 心 # 76 "heart"

Compounds, sentences, and meanings

1. 心 **xīn** heart

   他 人 在 这儿, 心 不 在。

   Tā rén zài zhèr, xīn bú zài.

   He is physically present, but his thoughts are elsewhere.

2. 心理 **xīnlǐ** psychology, mentality

   这 是 一般 人 的 心理。

   Zhè shì yìbān rén de xīnlǐ.

   This is how ordinary people feel about it.

3. 心情 **xīnqíng** mood

   她 今天 的 心情 不 好。

   Tā jīntiān de xīnqíng bù hǎo.

   She is in a bad mood today.

4. 心疼 **xīnténg** be distressed

   这么 浪费, 叫 人 看了 心疼。

   Zhème làngfèi, jiào rén kànle xīnténg.

   It makes your heart ache to see such waste.

5. 小心 **xiǎoxīn** be careful

   过 马路 要 小心。

   Guò mǎlù yào xiǎoxīn.

   Be careful when crossing the street.

Helpful tips: The second stroke ends with a hook.											**4 strokes**
心	心	心	心	心							

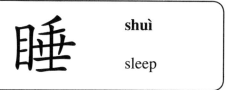

shuì

sleep

Radical: 目 # 118 "eye"

Compounds, sentences, and meanings

1. 睡 **shuì** sleep

   昨晚 我 睡了八 小时。

   Zuówǎn wǒ shuìle bā xiǎoshí.

   I slept for eight hours last night.

2. 睡觉 **shuìjiào** sleep

   该 睡觉 了。

   Gāi shuìjiào le.

   It's time to go to sleep.

3. 午睡 **wǔshuì** afternoon nap

   中国人 有 午睡 的 习惯。

   Zhōngguórén yǒu wǔshuì de xíguàn.

   Chinese have the habit of taking an afternoon nap.

4. 睡眠 **shuìmián** sleep

   医生 说我 睡眠 不足。

   Yīshēng shuō wǒ shuìmián bùzú.

   The doctor said that I don't have enough sleep.

5. 睡衣 **shuìyī** pyjamas

   我 忘了 带 睡衣。

   Wǒ wàngle dài shuìyī.

   I forgot to bring my pyjamas.

Helpful tips: Each horizontal stroke is evenly spaced.

13 strokes

睡	丨	冂	目	目	目	目	眤	眊	睡	睡	睡	睡

觉　**jiào/jué**

sleep; feel

覺

Radical: 见 # 93 "see"

Compounds, sentences, and meanings

1. 觉 **jiào** sleep

一 觉 醒 来 已经 十点半 了。

Yí jiào xǐng lái yǐjīng shídiǎnbàn le.

When I woke up it was already 10:30.

2. 睡懒觉 **shuì lǎnjiào** sleep in

周末 我 喜欢 睡 懒觉。

Zhōumò wǒ xǐhuan shuì lǎnjiào.

At the weekend, I like to sleep in.

3. 睡午觉 **shuì wǔjiào** afternoon nap

中国人 有 睡 午觉 的 习惯。

Zhōngguórén yǒu shuì wǔjiào de xíguàn.

Chinese have the habit of taking an afternoon nap.

4. 觉得 **juéde** feel

我 觉得 我的 中文 进步了。

Wǒ juéde wǒde Zhōngwén jìnbù le.

I feel that my Chinese has improved.

5. 感觉 **gǎnjué** perception

这 只 是 我 个人 的 感觉。

Zhè zhǐ shì wǒ gèrén de gǎnjué.

This is only my personal feeling.

Helpful tips: The last stroke is a vertical-bend-hook.									**9 strokes**		
觉											

足   zú

foot; complete

Radical: 足 # 164 "foot"

Compounds, sentences, and meanings

1. 足球 **zúqiú** soccer, football

   巴西人 都 喜欢 踢足球。

   Bāxī rén dōu xǐhuan tī zúqiú.

   Brazilians all enjoy playing soccer.

2. 足够 **zúgòu** sufficient, enough

   三个人喝六杯咖啡, 足够了!

   Sān ge rén hē liù bēi kāfēi, zúgōu le!

   Three people having six cups of coffee, that's enough!

3. 足以 **zúyǐ** sufficient

   这 个 办法足以解释 我们 的 问题。

   Zhè ge bànfǎ zúyǐ jiěshì wǒmen de wèntí.

   This method is sufficient to resolve our problem.

4. 满足 **mǎnzú** satisfied

   吃 饱了, 喝足了, 我 觉得 很 满足。

   Chī bǎole, hē zú le, wǒ juéde hěn mǎnzú.

   I have eaten enough, drunk enough, and feel satisfied.

Helpful tips: The last two strokes do not cross.   **7 strokes**

足	丨	口	口	尸	무	尸	足				

肥　**féi**

fat/loose-fitting

Radical: 月 # 103 "flesh/moon"

Compounds, sentences, and meanings

1. 肥 **féi** loose-fitting

   这 条 裤子太肥了。

   Zhè tiáo kùzi tài féi le.

   These trousers are too baggy.

2. 肥大 **féidà** loose, large

   现在 流行 肥大 的 衣服。

   Xiànzài liúxíng féidà de yīfu.

   Loose clothing is fashionable at the moment.

3. 肥胖 **féipàng** fat, obese

   如今 中国 的 小孩 偏向 肥胖。

   Rújīn Zhōngguó de xiǎohái piānxiàng féipàng.

   Nowadays Chinese children tend to be overweight.

4. 肥瘦 **féishòu** the girth of a garment

   你 看 这 件 外衣的 肥瘦 怎么样?

   Nǐ kàn zhè jiàn wàiyī de féishòu zěnmeyàng?

   Do you think this coat is a good fit?

5. 肥沃 **féiwò** fertile, rich

   这里土地肥沃。

   Zhèlǐ tǔdì féiwò.

   The land here is fertile.

Helpful tips: The last stroke ends with a hook.							**8 strokes**					
肥	丿	月	月	月	肝	肝	肥	肥				

瘦

shòu

thin

Radical: 疒 # 112 "sickness"

Compounds, sentences, and meanings

1. 瘦 **shòu** thin

我 的 哥哥 很 瘦。

Wǒ de gēgē hěn shòu.

My elder brother is very skinny.

2. 瘦弱 **shòuruò** weak, emaciated

生 病 以后 你 的 身体 很 瘦弱。

Shēng bìng yǐhòu nǐ de shēntǐ hěn shòuruò.

After having an illness your physical body is weak.

3. 瘦小 **shòuxiǎo** small, short

赛马 骑士 需要 比较 瘦小。

Sàimǎ qíshi xūyào bǐjiào shòuxiǎo.

Jockeys need to be comparatively short and small.

4. 瘦肉 **shòuròu** lean meat

人 都 要 吃 瘦 牛肉。

Rén dōu yào chī shòu niúròu.

People all want to eat lean beef.

Helpful tips: The radical should surround the other character components evenly.											**14 strokes**

瘦	丶	二	广	疒	疒	疒	疒	疒	疒	瘦	瘦
瘦	瘦										

A. Vocabulary and Pronunciation

Using characters, label the illustration with each body part. Then write the *pinyin* for each of the terms.

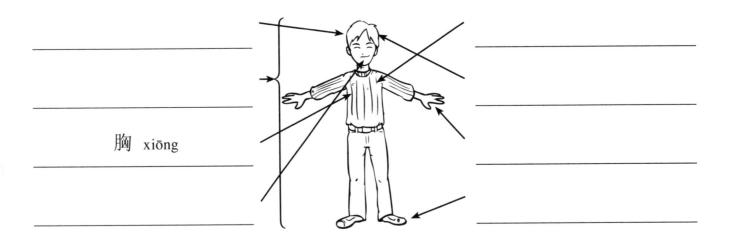

胸 xiōng

B. Answering Questions

Please answer each of the following questions in complete sentences with effective demonstration of context. For additional practice, say and then respond to these questions aloud.

1. 有时候你的身体很瘦，为什么？

_____

2. 为什么也有时候你的身体很肥？

_____

3. 去年你生病，为什么？

_____

4. 你说昨天你不能睡好觉，为什么？

_____

5. 为什么现在你觉得不舒服？

_____

C. Short Description

Please respond to the following situation with advice consistent with the description. A strong response will demonstrate an understanding of cause and effect, along with effective describing.

你的朋友头疼，她头疼很厉害。你要告诉她什么？

_____

_____

_____

_____

_____

_____

_____

A. Vocabulary Review and Identification

Using characters, for each of the following items of clothing write the item's name and then identify the body part that it covers.

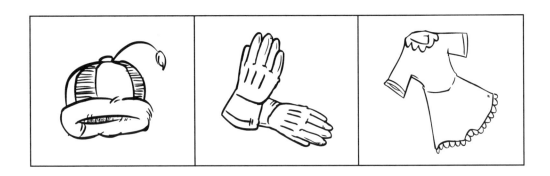

身体： _____   _____   _____

衣服： _____   _____   _____

身体： _____   _____   _____

衣服： _____   _____   _____

B. Sentence Creation

Please create a sentence that responds to the general question given below for each feature provided. First demonstrate understanding of the basic feature by sketching a small illustration of it in the lefthand box.

现代化的课堂需要什么东西？为什么一个好的课堂要有这些东西？

（老师）_____

	（课本）_____ 55
	（黑板）_____
	（电脑）_____
	（学生）_____

C. Lifestyle Description

Consider the following topic. Then create a description that demonstrates an understanding of the various components of one's lifestyle. Your description should express both the physical aspects of one's life and the connections to the more intellectual or emotional aspects. Attempt to show strong use of specific conjunctions and other constructions that allow for effective connected discourse.

想一想你自己的生活, 你天天喜欢做什么? 你天天应该做什么? 有时生活或身体可能出了问题, 在那个时候你需要做什么?

_____

_____

_____

_____

_____

_____

_____

D. Reflective Questions

Use these questions to both check the expressiveness of the previous section and to confirm your understanding of the previous topic. For additional practice, say and then respond to these questions aloud.

你的生活有很多部分, 很多活动。你喜欢哪些活动? 哪些活动你不喜欢?

你天天做喜欢的活动吗?

每天你先做什么? 然后又做什么?

你得天天做什么?

你在几点钟做各种的活动?

星期六和星期天的活动是不是一样? 周末你喜欢做什么?

介绍只能在星期六做的活动, 你先做什么? 然后又做什么?

为什么你不能天天做这种的活动?

你喜欢跟谁做这个活动?

你得天天跟谁做不喜欢的活动?

Traditional Form

応　yīng/yìng

ought to/answer

應

Radical: 广 # 36 "broad"

Compounds, sentences, and meanings

1. 应 **yīng** ought to

    发现 错误 应 马上 纠正。

    Fāxiàn cuòwù yīng mǎshàng jiūzhèng.

    When a mistake is discovered, it should be corrected at once.

2. 应该 **yīnggāi** ought to

    不用 谢, 这 是 我们 应该 做 的。

    Búyòng xiè, zhè shì wǒmen yīnggāi zuò de.

    Don't mention it, it's the least we could do.

3. 应酬 **yìngchóu** social engagement

    今天 晚上 有 个 应酬。

    Jīntiān wǎnshang yǒu ge yìngchóu.

    I've been invited to a social event this evening.

4. 应当 **yīngdāng** ought to

    我们 是 朋友, 应当 互相 帮助。

    Wǒmen shì péngyou, yīngdāng hùxiāng bāngzhù.

    We are friends, we ought to help each other.

5. 应付 **yìngfu** deal with, cope with

    定单 过多, 难 于 应付。

    Dìngdān guòduō, nán yú yìngfu.

    We cannot cope with such a flood of orders.

Helpful tips: The third stroke tapers down to the left.　　　　　**7 strokes**

应	丶	二	广	广	応	応	应					

该　**gāi**

ought to

該

Radical: 讠 # 9 "word"

Compounds, sentences, and meanings

1. 该 **gāi** ought to

   我 该 走 了。
   Wǒ gāi zǒu le.
   I must be off now.

2. 该死 **gāisǐ** exclamation (showing anger)

   该死!我 又 忘了 带 钥匙 了。
   Gāisǐ, wǒ yòu wàngle dài yàoshi le.
   Oh no! I've forgotten my key again.

3. 活该 **huógāi** exclamation (it serves someone right)

   活该, 谁 叫 你 不听 我的 话。
   Huógāi, shéi jiào nǐ bùtīng wǒde huà.
   It serves you right for not listening to me.

4. 该当 **gāidāng** deserve

   你 晚来了 一个 小时, 该当 何罪?
   Nǐ wǎnláile yí ge xiǎoshí, gāidāng hé zuì?
   You are an hour late. What punishment do you think you deserve?

5. 应该 **yīnggāi** ought to

   不用 谢, 这 是 我们 应该 做 的。
   Búyòng xiè, zhè shì wǒmen yīnggāi zuò de.
   Don't mention it, it's the least we could do.

Helpful tips: The last stroke ends firmly.											8 strokes
该	丶	讠	计	诣	该	该	该				

感 **gǎn**

feel

Radical: 心 # 76 "heart"

Compounds, sentences, and meanings

1. 感 **gǎn** feel, sense

他 感到 自己 错了。

Tā gǎndào zìjǐ cuòle.

He sensed that he was wrong.

2. 感觉 **gǎnjué** feel, perceive

你 感觉 怎么样?

Nǐ gǎnjué zěnmeyàng?

How do you feel now?

3. 感冒 **gǎnmào** common cold, flu

医生 说 我得了 感冒。

Yīshēng shuō wǒ déle gǎnmào.

The doctor said that I've got the flu.

4. 感情 **gǎnqíng** feeling, emotion

这 两 年来, 我 对她 产生了 感情。

Zhè liǎng nián lái, wǒ duì tā chǎnshēngle gǎnqíng.

I've grown very close to her these past two years.

5. 感谢 **gǎnxiè** thank

非常 感谢你的 帮助。

Fēicháng gǎnxiè nǐde bāngzhù.

Thanks very much for your help.

Helpful tips: The seventh stroke ends with a hook.											**13 strokes**
感	一	厂	厅	后	后	后	咸	咸	咸	咸	感	感
感											

情　　qíng

emotion

Radical: 忄 # 33 "upright heart"

Compounds, sentences, and meanings

1. 情 **qíng** emotion, affection

   她 情 不自禁地 笑起来。

   Tā qíng bú zì jìn de xiàoqǐlai.

   She can't help laughing.

2. 情节 **qíngjié** plot

   这个 剧本 情节 很复杂。

   Zhè ge jùběn qíngjié hěn fùzá.

   The play has a very complicated plot.

3. 情况 **qíngkuàng** situation

   现在 情况 不同 了。

   Xiànzài qíngkuàng bùtóng le.

   Now things are different.

4. 情趣 **qíngqù** temperament and interest

   他们 两 人 情趣 相投。

   Tāmen liǎng rén qíngqù xiāngtóu.

   The two of them are compatible.

5. 情人 **qíngrén** lover

   情人 眼里 出 西施。

   Qíngrén yǎnlǐ chū Xīshī.

   The beloved is always beautiful. (Literally, Xishi, a famous beauty).

Helpful tips: Each horizontal stroke is evenly spaced.										**11 strokes**

情　丶　忄　忄　忄￝　忄￦　忄＃　情　情　情　情　情

Traditional Form

饿   è

hungry, famished

餓

Radical: 饣 # 59 "food"

Compounds, sentences, and meanings

1. 饿 è hungry

锻炼 以后我 常常 很饿。

Duànliàn yǐhòu wǒ chángcháng hěn è.

After exercising I am often hungry.

2. 饿死了 è sǐ le extremely hungry

你吃了吗? 我饿死了!

Nǐ chī le ma? Wǒ è sǐ le!

Have you eaten? I'm so very hungry!

Helpful tips: The left component of the character should be one-third of the total character size.											**10 strokes**
饿	⺈¹	⺈²	⻊³	⻟⁴	⻟⁵	饣⁶	饩⁷	饿⁸	饿⁹	饿¹⁰	

累 **léi/lěi/lèi**

tired

Radical: 田 # 119 "field" or 糸 # 152 "raw silk"

Compounds, sentences, and meanings

1. 累 **lèi** tired
   我 累 了, 想 去 睡觉。
   Wǒ lèi le, xiǎng qù shuìjiào.
   I'm tired and I want to sleep.

2. 累赘 **léizhui** burden, nuisance
   行李 带得 太 多 了, 是 个 累赘。
   Xíngli dàide tài duō le, shì ge léizhui.
   Too much luggage is a nuisance.

3. 积累 **jīlěi** accumulate
   他 在 工作 上 积累了 很多 经验。
   Tā zài gōngzuò shàng jīlěile hěnduō jīngyàn.
   He has built up a lot of experience in his work.

4. 日积月累 **rìjī-yuèlěi** accumulate (literally, over days and months)
   日积月累地 练习 就 能 学好。
   Rìjī-yuèlěide liànxí jiù néng xuéhǎo.
   Practice makes perfect.

5. 连累 **liánlěi** get someone into trouble
   这 件 事 连累了 你, 真 不 好意思。
   Zhè jiàn shì liánlěile nǐ, zhēn bù hǎo yìsi.
   I'm sorry to have involved you in this matter.

Helpful tips: The last stroke of 幺 is a dot.										**11 strokes**

死 **sǐ**

die; extremely

Radical: 歹 # 83 "evil"

Compounds, sentences, and meanings

1. 死 **sǐ** die

   这 次 车祸 死了三个 人。

   Zhè cì chēhuò sǐle sān ge rén.

   The accident took three lives.

2. 死板 **sǐbǎn** rigid, stiff

   她的 表情 死板。

   Tāde biǎoqíng sǐbǎn.

   She's got an expressionless face.

3. 死心 **sǐxīn** drop the idea forever

   你 还是死了这 条 心 吧。

   Nǐ háishì sǐle zhè tiáo xīn ba.

   You'd better give up the idea altogether.

4. 死记 **sǐjì** memorize mechanically

   学习 要 思考, 不能 死记硬背。

   Xuéxí yào sīkǎo, bùnéng sǐjì-yìngbèi.

   You have to think about what you're learning, not just memorize it.

5. ···死了 **... sǐle** extremely

   走了 三 个 钟头, 把 我累死了。

   Zǒule sān ge zhōngtóu, bǎ wǒ lèisǐle.

   After walking for three hours, I'm completely exhausted.

Helpful tips: The horizontal stroke extends to accommodate the second component.　　　　**6 strokes**

死	一	丆	歹	歹	歼	死					

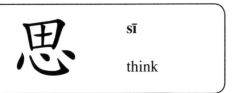

思   **sī**

think

Radical: 心 **# 76** "heart"

Compounds, sentences, and meanings

1. 思 **sī** think

   我思, 故我 在。

   Wǒ sī, gù wǒ zài.

   I think, therefore I am.

2. 思路 **sīlù** train of thought

   你的思路很 清楚。

   Nǐde sīlù hěn qīngchu.

   You think very clearly.

3. 思想 **sīxiǎng** thought

   美国 有 思想 自由。

   Měiguó yǒu sīxiǎng zìyóu.

   There is freedom of thought in the United States.

4. 思考 **sīkǎo** think deeply

   大学 主要 培养 独立思考。

   Dàxué zhǔyào péiyǎng dúlì sīkǎo.

   The main aim of a university education is to develop independent thinking.

5. 思索 **sīsuǒ** think deeply

   我一夜没 睡着, 反复思索这 个问题。

   Wǒ yí yè méi shuìzháo, fǎnfù sīsuǒ zhè ge wèntí.

   I lay awake all night, turning the problem over and over in my mind.

Helpful tips: The vertical stroke does not cross the enclosing box.									**9 strokes**		
思	丨	冂	冃	田	田	田	思	思	思		

理　**lǐ**

reason

Radical: 王 # 79 "king"

Compounds, sentences, and meanings

1. **理 lǐ** reason

   他 讲 的 句句 是 理。

   Tā jiǎng de jùju shì lǐ.

   There is truth in everything he says.

2. **理发 lǐfa** haircut

   她 去 理发。

   Tā qù lǐfa.

   She's going to have her hair done.

3. **理解 lǐjiě** understand

   你的 意思 我 完全 理解。

   Nǐde yìsi wǒ wánquán lǐjiě.

   I understand you completely.

4. **理想 lǐxiǎng** ideal

   这 天气 出去 郊游 太 理想 了。

   Zhè tiānqì chūqu jiāoyóu tài lǐxiǎng le.

   This weather is ideal for an outing.

5. **理由 lǐyóu** reason

   他 没有 理由 抱怨。

   Tā méiyǒu lǐyóu bàoyuàn.

   He has no grounds for complaint.

Helpful tips: Each horizontal stroke is evenly spaced.　　**11 strokes**

| 理 | ⁻₁ | ⁼₂ | 廾₃ | 王₄ | 玑⁵ | 玑⁶ | 玾₇ | 珇₈ | 珇⁹ | 理₁₀ | 理₁₁ | |

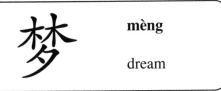

梦   **mèng**

dream

夢

Radical: 夕 # 56 "sunset"

Compounds, sentences, and meanings

1. 做梦 **zuòmèng** dream

   睡觉 的 时候, 我们 做 梦。
   Shuìjiào de shíhou, wǒmen zuò mèng.
   When we sleep, we dream.

2. 好梦 **hǎomèng** sweet dreams

   晚安, 祝你 好 梦!
   Wǎn'ān, zhùnǐ hǎo mèng!
   Good night, may you have sweet dreams!

3. 梦想 **mèngxiǎng** wish, dream

   有 安宁 的 家庭 是 许多 人 的
   Yǒu ān'níng de jiātíng shì xǔduō rén de
   梦想。
   mèngxiǎng.
   To have a peaceful home is many people's dream.

4. 梦见 **mèngjiàn** envision, see in a dream

   昨晚 我 梦见 我的老 朋友。
   Zuòwǎn wǒ mèngjiàn wǒ de lǎo péngyou.
   Last night I saw my old friend in a dream.

Helpful tips: The top components should be identical.										**11 strokes**

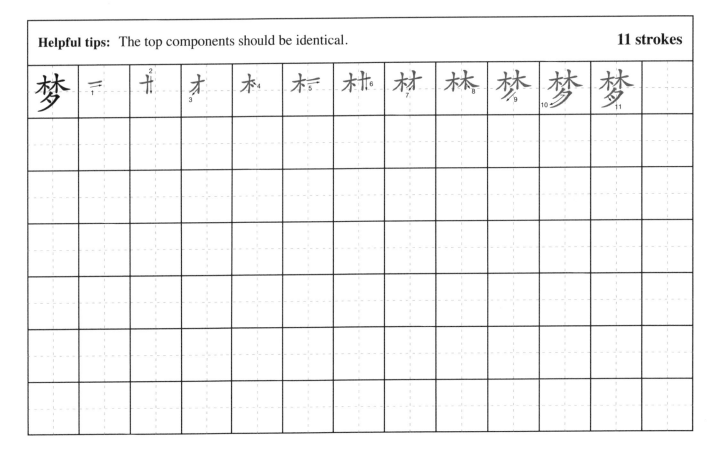

CHARACTER 306

重

chóng/zhòng

repeat; heavy

Radical: 丿 # 4 "downward-left stroke"

Compounds, sentences, and meanings

1. 重 **chóng** again

   把 生词 重 抄 一 遍。

   Bǎ shēngcí chóng chāo yí biàn.

   Copy the new words out again.

2. 重复 **chóngfù** repeat

   避免 不 必要 的 重复。

   Bìmiǎn bú bìyào de chóngfù.

   Avoid unnecessary repetition.

3. 重点 **zhòngdiǎn** focal point, key

   北京 大学 是 重点 大学。

   Běijīng Dàxué shì zhòngdiǎn dàxué.

   Beijing University is an elite university.

4. 重视 **zhòngshì** emphasize

   大家 都 很 重视 这 件 事。

   Dàjiā dōu hěn zhòngshì zhè jiàn shì.

   Everyone takes the matter seriously.

5. 重要 **zhòngyào** important

   学 语言 最 重要 是 能 记住 生词。

   Xué yǔyán zuì zhòngyào shì néng jìzhù shēngcí.

   The most important thing in learning a language is to be able to remember the new words.

Helpful tips: The second stroke is the longest.　　　　**9 strokes**

重	一	二	三	三	盲	盲	重	重	重		

A. Vocabulary Identification

Please write Chinese phrases to express the conditions in the illustrations.

_____ _____ _____ _____

B. Sentence Creation

Create a sentence that provides a context for each action proposed. Notice that for each of the actions a context allows for understanding, and these contexts can be expressed utilizing a 的时候 statement.

1. 你应该帮朋友的忙。

_____

2. 你应该睡觉。

_____

3. 你应该给父母打电话。

_____

4. 你应该觉得很好。

_____

C. Short Descriptions

For each of the following emotions or physical situations please explain a resulting activity. A strong description would introduce both what should be undertaken in response, and the effects of that response.

1.（你很累）_____

_____

_____

2.（你饿死了）_____

_____

_____

3.（你非常高兴）_____

_____

_____

4.（你生病了）_____

_____

_____

惯 guàn

be used to

惯

Radical: 忄 # 33 "upright heart"

Compounds, sentences, and meanings

1. **惯 guàn** get used to

   我 惯 了 早 睡 早 起。

   Wǒ guànle zǎo shuì zǎo qǐ.

   I've gotten into the habit of going to bed early and getting up early.

2. **惯坏 guànhuài** spoil (a child)

   别 把 孩子 惯坏 了。

   Bié bǎ háizi guànhuài le.

   Don't spoil the child.

3. **惯例 guànlì** usual practice

   这样 做 会 打破 惯例。

   Zhèyàng zuò huì dǎpò guànlì.

   This is a break from the usual practice.

4. **习惯 xíguàn** be accustomed to

   这样 潮湿 的 天气 我 实在 不 习惯。

   Zhèyàng cháoshī de tiānqì wǒ shízài bù xíguàn.

   I just can't get used to this damp weather.

Helpful tips: End the last stroke firmly.

11 strokes

| 惯 | 忄 | 忄 | 忄 | 忄 | 忄 | 忄 | 惯 | 惯 | 惯 | 惯 | |

CHARACTER 308

洗

xǐ

wash, clean

Radical: 氵 # 32 "water"

Compounds, sentences, and meanings

1. 洗手 **xǐshǒu** wash hands

   吃饭 以前 你 应该 洗手。

   Chīfàn yǐqián nǐ yīnggāi xǐshǒu.

   Before eating you should wash your hands.

2. 洗衣 **xǐyī** wash clothes

   每 两 星期 我洗衣一次。

   Měi liǎng xīngqī wǒ xǐyī yícì.

   Every two weeks, I wash clothes once.

3. 洗澡 **xǐzǎo** shower, bathe

   每天 早上 我洗澡。

   Měitiān zǎoshàng wǒ xǐzǎo.

   Every morning I take a shower.

4. 洗雪 **xǐxuě** wipe clean, erase

   现在 中国 的 政府 打算 洗雪 腐败

   Xiànzài Zhōngguó de zhèngfǔ dǎsuan xǐxuě fǔbài

   的 污名。

   de wūmíng.

   Currently Chinese politicians are planning to erase the stain of corruption.

5. 洗刷 **xǐshuā** wash and scrub, clean

   每 个 星期 我们 洗刷家里的 马桶。

   Měi ge xīngqī wǒmen xǐshuā jiālǐ de mǎtǒng.

   Every week we scrub the toilets in the house.

Helpful tips: The right hand component should be equal in height top and bottom.

9 strokes

洗	丶	冫	氵	沪	汼	汼	浅	涉	洗			

ná

take

Radical: 手 # 96 "whole hand" or 人 # 18 "people"

Compounds, sentences, and meanings

1. 拿 **ná** take

   请 把 这些 东西 拿走。

   Qǐng bǎ zhèxiē dōngxi názǒu.

   Please take these things away.

2. 拿主意 **ná zhǔyi** make a decision

   究竟 去不去, 你拿 主意 吧。

   Jiùjìng qù buqù, nǐ ná zhǔyi ba.

   Please decide whether to go or not.

3. 拿不起来 **nábuqǐlái** cannot manage

   这样 的 工作 他拿不起来。

   Zhèyàng de gōngzuò tā nábuqǐlái.

   He can't handle this kind of work.

4. 拿定主意 **nádìng zhǔyi** make up one's mind

   她一直 拿不定 主意。

   Tā yìzhí nábudìng zhǔyi.

   She just can't make up her mind.

5. 拿手 **náshǒu** good at

   他 很 拿手 做饭。

   Tā hěn náshǒu zuòfàn.

   He's a good cook.

Helpful tips: The last stroke ends with a hook.   **10 strokes**

拿	⁄ ¹	𠆢 ²	今 ³	今 ⁴	令 ⁵	合 ⁶	合 ⁷	拿 ⁸	拿 ⁹	拿 ¹⁰		

CHARACTER 310

Traditional Form

關

关

guān

connection, relationship; close

Radical: 丷 # 17 "inverted eight"

Compounds, sentences, and meanings

1. 关系 **guānxi** connection, relationship

   你的 想法 跟你的 说法 有 关系。

   Nǐ de xiǎngfǎ gēn nǐ de shuōfǎ yǒu guānxi.

   Your thinking and speaking are connected.

2. 关联 **guānlián** relationship

   欧洲 的国家 有 很 紧密的 关联。

   Ōuzhōu de guójiā yǒu hěn jǐnmì de guānlián.

   The countries of Europe have a very close relationship.

3. 关灯 **guāndēng** switch off the light

   要 睡觉 的 时候，需要 关灯。

   Yào shuìjiào de shíhou, xūyào guāndēng.

   When one wants to go to sleep, it is necessary to turn out the light.

4. 关心 **guānxīn** care about

   好人 关心 他们的 朋友。

   Hǎorén guānxīn tāmen de péngyou.

   Good people care about their friends.

5. 关门 **guānmén** shut a door

   今天 天气 很 冷，请 关门。

   Jīntiān tiānqì hěn lěng, qǐng guānmén.

   Today's weather is very cold, please close the door.

6. 关于 **guānyú** concerning

   关于 全球 暖化，每 个 国家 都 有 责任。

   Guānyú quánqiú nuǎnhuà, měi ge guójiā dōu yǒu zérèn.

   Concerning global warming, every country has responsibility.

Helpful tips: The second horizontal stroke is longer.

6 strokes

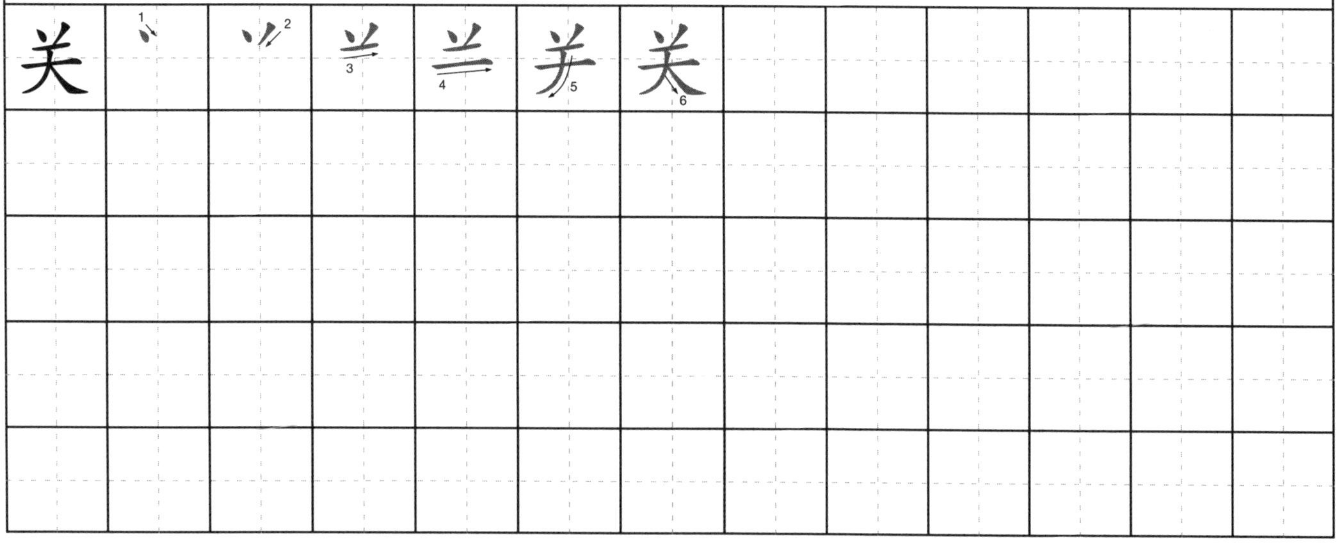

bǎ

handle; with regard to

Radical: 扌 # 48 "hand"

Compounds, sentences, and meanings

1. 把 **bǎ** preposition (used to shift the object before the verb)

   我把这件事忘了。

   Wǒ bǎ zhè jiàn shì wàng le.

   I forgot all about it.

2. 一把刀子 **yì bǎ dāozi** a knife (**bǎ** is used as a measure word)

   请 给我一把 刀子。

   Qǐng gěi wǒ yì bǎ dāozi.

   Please give me a knife.

3. 把柄 **bǎbìng** handle

   不要 给 人 留下 把柄。

   Búyào gěi rén liúxià bǎbìng.

   Don't do anything that people can hold against you.

4. 把握 **bǎwò** certainty

   他 有 把握 通过 考试。

   Tā yǒu bǎwò tōngguò kǎoshì.

   He's confident that he will pass the exam.

5. 把戏 **bǎxì** cheap trick, game

   他 玩 的 把戏 我 都　看穿 了。

   Tā wán de bǎxì wǒ dōu kànchuān le.

   I saw through his game.

Helpful tips: The last stroke ends with a hook.											**7 strokes**
把	一₁	才₂₃	才	扌₄	扌₅	扌₆	把₇				

发   **fā/fà**

     develop/hair

發/髮
(for "hair")

Radical: 又 # 24 "again"

Compounds, sentences, and meanings

1. 发 **fā** develop

   她 从来 没 发过脾气。

   Tā cónglái méi fāguo píqi.

   She has never lost her temper.

2. 发火 **fāhuǒ** lose one's temper

   你别 发火, 咱们 慢慢儿 谈。

   Nǐ bié fāhuǒ, zánmen mànmànr tán.

   Don't get angry. Let's talk it over calmly.

3. 发热 **fārè** run a temperature

   你 好像 有点儿 发热。

   Nǐ hǎoxiàng yǒudiǎnr fārè.

   You look as if you are running a temperature.

4. 发生 **fāshēng** happen

   前面 发生了 事故。

   Qiánmiàn fāshēngle shìgù.

   There's an accident ahead of us.

5. 发言 **fāyán** make a statement

   他在 会 上 发言了吗?

   Tā zài huì shàng fāyán le ma?

   Did he speak at the meeting?

6. 理发 **lǐfà** haircut

   她去理发。

   Tā qù lǐfà.

   She's going to have her hair done.

Helpful tips: The first stroke is a slanting-horizontal-bend.   **5 strokes**

发	ゝ	少	发	发	发						

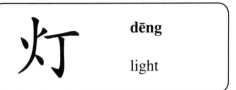

dēng

light

燈

Radical: 火 # 75 "fire"

Compounds, sentences, and meanings

1. 灯 **dēng** lamp

   突然 所有 的 灯 都 灭了。

   Tūrán suǒyǒu de dēng dōu miè le.

   Suddenly all the lights went out.

2. 灯光 **dēngguāng** lamplight

   这里 灯光 很暗。

   Zhèlǐ dēngguāng hěn àn.

   The light here is rather dim.

3. 灯火管制 **dēnghuǒ guǎnzhì** blackout

   这里 冬天 经常 有 灯火 管制。

   Zhèlǐ dōngtiān jīngcháng yǒu dēnghuǒ guǎnzhì.

   There are often blackouts here in winter.

4. 灯笼 **dēnglóng** lantern

   房子 前面 挂着 两个大 灯笼。

   Fángzi qiánmiàn guàzhe liǎng ge dà dēnglóng.

   In front of the house are two large lanterns.

5. 灯泡 **dēngpào** lightbulb

   有 没有 乳白 灯泡?

   Yǒu méiyǒu rǔbái dēngpào?

   Do you have a soft white lightbulb?

| Helpful tips: The final stroke ends in a hook. | | | | | | | | | | | 6 strokes |

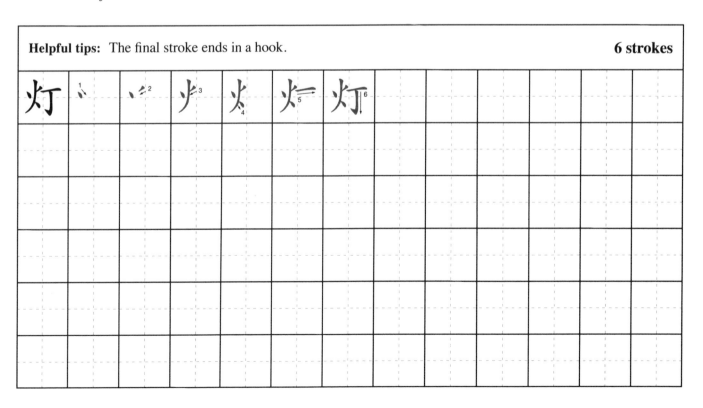

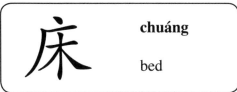

床   chuáng

bed

牀

Radical: 广 # 36 "broad"

Compounds, sentences, and meanings

1. 床 **chuáng** bed

   房间 里 放着 两 张 床。

   Fángjiān li fàngzhe liǎng zhāng chuáng.

   There are two beds in the room.

2. 床上 **chuángshang** in bed

   我 喜欢 躺 在 床上 看书。

   Wǒ xǐhuan tǎng zài chuángshang kànshū.

   I like to read in bed.

3. 床单 **chuángdān** bed sheet

   该 换 床单 了。

   Gāi huàn chuángdān le.

   The bedsheets need to be changed.

4. 单人床 **dānrénchuáng** single bed

   我 觉得 单人床 太 窄。

   Wǒ juéde dānrénchuáng tài zhǎi.

   I find that single beds are too narrow for me.

5. 双人床 **shuāngrénchuáng** double bed

   我 喜欢 睡 双人床。

   Wǒ xǐhuan shuì shuāngrénchuáng.

   I like to sleep on a double bed.

Helpful tips: The last stroke tapers off.   **7 strokes**

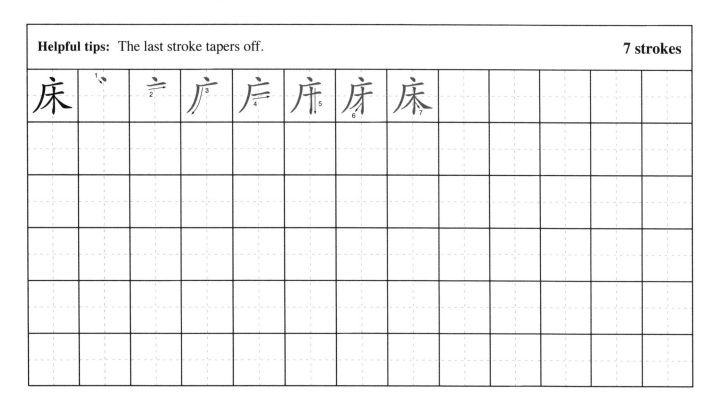

药 yào

medicine

藥

Radical: 艹 # 42 "grass"

Compounds, sentences, and meanings

1. 药 yào medicine

   你 吃过 药 了吗?

   Nǐ chīguo yào le ma?

   Have you taken your medicine?

2. 药材 yàocái medicinal materials

   人参 是一 种 补身 药材。

   Rénshēn shì yì zhǒng bǔshēn yàocái.

   Ginseng is a tonic.

3. 药方 yàofāng prescription

   这 是 治 感冒 的 药方。

   Zhè shì zhì gǎnmào de yàofāng.

   This is the prescription for the flu.

4. 药店 yàodiàn pharmacy, chemist

   这 种 药 在 大 药店 才 有。

   Zhè zhǒng yào zài dà yàodiàn cái yǒu.

   This medicine is only available at large pharmacies.

5. 药水 yàoshuǐ liquid medicine, mixture

   这 药水 吃下去 就 见效。

   Zhè yàoshuǐ chīxiàqu jiù jiànxiào.

   This medicine works immediately.

| Helpful tips: The eighth stroke ends with a hook. | | | | | | | | | 9 strokes |

药	一¹	艹²	艹³	艿⁴	苧⁵	芗⁶	药⁷	药⁸	药⁹		

shū

stretch

Radical: 人 # 18 "people"

Compounds, sentences, and meanings

1. 舒 **shū** stretch

   舒 筋 活 络。

   Shū jīn huó luò.

   Stretching stimulates blood circulation.

2. 舒畅 **shūchàng** be entirely free from worry

   山上 的 空气 使人 感到 舒畅。

   Shānshang de kōngqì shǐ rén gǎndào shūchàng.

   Mountain air is very refreshing.

3. 舒服 **shūfu** comfortable

   这 把椅子又 软 又 舒服。

   Zhè bǎ yǐzi yòu ruǎn yòu shūfu.

   This chair is soft and comfortable.

4. 舒散 **shūsàn** stretch and flex

   跑完步 应该 舒散 一下筋骨。

   Pǎowánbù yīnggāi shūsàn yíxià jīngǔ.

   After a run, you should do some stretching exercises.

5. 舒适 **shūshì** comfortable, cozy

   房间 不大,但 很 舒适。

   Fángjiān bú dà, dàn hěn shūshì.

   The room is not big, but it is very cozy.

Helpful tips: The last stroke ends with a hook.　　　　　　　　**12 strokes**

舒	ノ¹	𠂉²	𠂊³	亼⁴	今⁵	今⁶	舍⁷	舍⁸	舒⁹	舒¹⁰	舒¹¹	舒¹²

Lesson 29: Review Activities

A. Pronunciation and *Pinyin* Practice

Please transcribe the following questions into *pinyin*. For additional practice, say and then respond to these questions aloud.

1. 你有什么天天的习惯？

   _____

2. 晚上几点钟你常常关灯？

   _____

3. 你把我的课本放在哪里？

   _____

B. Sentence Completion

Please complete each of the following sentences with an appropriate verb. Then translate the resulting sentence into English.

1. 每天早上很多人_____澡。

   _____

2. 对不起, 我_____你的帽子在你的房间里。

   _____

3. 对你来说, 学生应该_____什么文具上课？

   _____

4. 我的朋友常常很累, 他不喜欢很早_____床。

   _____

5. 我不喜欢别人_____我的东西。

   _____

C. Short Description

Please write a short description of connected sentences on the following topic. Attempt to show accurate description of time and order of actions. Also, pay attention to expressing activity frequency and habits.

请介绍介绍你上床前的习惯。

_____

_____

_____

_____

_____

_____

_____

菜　cài

vegetables

Radical: 艹 # 42 "grass"

Compounds, sentences, and meanings

1. 菜 cài vegetables

妈妈　上街　买菜去了。

Māma shàngjiē mǎi cài qù le.

Mother has gone to the market to buy food. (Literally, vegetables)

2. 菜市场 càishìchǎng food market

菜市场　里面　卖　蔬菜、肉、水果、

Càishìchǎng lǐmiàn mài shūcài, ròu, shuǐguǒ,

什么的。

shénmede.

The food market sells vegetables, meat, fruits, and so on.

3. 菜单 càidān menu

请　给我　菜单。

Qǐng gěi wǒ càidān.

Please give me the menu.

4. 蔬菜 shūcài vegetables

多　吃　蔬菜　对　身体　有　好处。

Duō chī shūcài duì shēntǐ yǒu hǎochù.

Eat more vegetables, they're good for you.

5. 做菜 zuòcài cook

我　妈妈　很　会　做菜。

Wǒ māma hěn huì zuòcài.

My mother is a good cook.

Helpful tips: The vertical ninth stroke does not join the stroke above it.										**11 strokes**
菜	一	艹	艹	艹	艿	芗	莁	芟	芠	菜

酒　jiǔ

alcohol

Radical: 氵 # 32 "3 drops of water"

Compounds, sentences, and meanings

1. 酒 **jiǔ** alcoholic drink

   酒 不 醉 人 人 自 醉。

   Jiǔ bú zuì rén rén zì zuì.

   Alcohol doesn't make you drunk, you make yourself drunk.

2. 酒肉朋友 **jiǔròu péngyou** fair-weather friend
   (Literally, wine-and-meat friend)

   他 只是 酒肉 朋友，不会 帮助 你的。

   Tā zhǐ shì jiǔròu péngyou, búhuì bāngzhù nǐ de.

   He's only a fair-weather friend, he won't help you.

3. 酒后 **jiǔhòu** under the influence of liquor

   酒后 开车 是 犯法 的。

   Jiǔhòu kāichē shì fànfǎ de.

   Driving under the influence of drink is a crime.

4. 酒量 **jiǔliàng** capacity for liquor

   他 酒量 很 大。

   Tā jiǔliàng hěn dà.

   He can hold his liquor.

5. 啤酒 **píjiǔ** beer

   夏天 我 喜欢 喝啤酒。

   Xiàtiān wǒ xǐhuan hē píjiǔ.

   I like to drink beer in summer.

Helpful tips: The eighth stroke has a bend on the right.									**10 strokes**
酒	丶	丶	氵	沪	沔	洏	洒	酒	酒

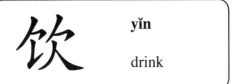

yǐn

drink

飲

Radical: 饣 # 59 "food"

Compounds, sentences, and meanings

1. 饮 **yǐn** drink

   饮 水 不忘 掘井人。

   Yǐn shuǐ búwàng juéjǐngrén.

   When you drink the water, think of those who dug the well.

2. 饮料 **yǐnliào** drinks

   你喝 什么 饮料?

   Nǐ hē shénme yǐnliào?

   What would you like to drink?

3. 饮食 **yǐnshí** food and drink

   要 注意 饮食 卫生。

   Yào zhùyì yǐnshí wèishēng.

   We have to pay attention to culinary hygiene.

4. 饮用水 **yǐnyòngshuǐ** drinking water

   这 不是 饮用水。

   Zhè búshì yǐnyòngshuǐ.

   This is not drinking water.

5. 冷饮 **lěngyǐn** cold drink

   天气 这么 热,要 点 冷饮 吗?

   Tiānqì zhème rè, yào diǎn lěngyǐn ma?

   It's so hot today, what about some cold drinks?

Helpful tips: The second and third strokes both end in a hook.　　　　**7 strokes**

饮	ノ¹	㇆²	饣³	饣⁴	饮⁵	饮⁶	饮⁷					

肉　**ròu**

meat

Radical: 冂 # 16 "border"

Compounds, sentences, and meanings

1. 肉 **ròu** meat

   许多 动物 的 肉 可以 吃。

   Xǔduō dòngwù de ròu kěyǐ chī.

   The flesh of many animals can be eaten.

2. 牛肉 **niúròu** beef

   我 喜欢 吃 牛肉 面。

   Wǒ xǐhuan chī niúròu miàn.

   I like beef noodles.

3. 肉片 **ròupiàn** sliced meat

   肉片、 肉丁、肉丝一般 都 是 猪肉。

   Ròupiàn, ròudīng, ròusī yìbān dōu shì zhūròu.

   Sliced meat, diced meat and shredded meat usually refer to pork.

4. 肉感 **ròugǎn** sexy

   她 穿起 那 条 短裙 非常 肉感。

   Tā chuānqǐ nà tiáo duǎnqún fēicháng ròugǎn.

   She looks very sexy in that short skirt.

5. 肉食 **ròushí** meat

   他 吃素, 从 不 吃 肉食。

   Tā chī sù, cóng bù chī ròushí.

   He's a vegetarian and never touches meat.

Helpful tips: End the second stroke of both 人 components firmly.									**6 strokes**
肉	冂	冂	内	肉	肉				

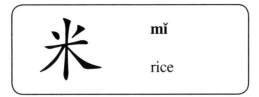

米	**mǐ**
	rice

Radical: 米 # 134 "rice"

Compounds, sentences, and meanings

1. 米 **mǐ** rice
   米 煮熟了 就是 米饭。
   Mǐ zhǔshúle jiù shì mǐfàn.
   When rice is cooked, it is called boiled rice.

2. 米饭 **mǐfàn** cooked rice
   我 每天 吃 两 顿 米饭。
   Wǒ měitiān chī liǎng dùn mǐfàn.
   I eat rice twice a day.

3. 米粉 **mǐfěn** rice-flour noodles
   我妻子喜欢 吃 米粉。
   Wǒ qīzi xǐhuan chī mǐfěn.
   My wife is fond of rice noodles.

4. 米酒 **mǐjiǔ** rice wine
   米酒要 暖了 才喝。
   Mǐjiǔ yào nuǎnle cái hē.
   Rice wine needs to be heated.

5. 一百米 **yībǎi mǐ** 100 meters
   我 家离 火车站 只有 一百米。
   Wǒ jiā lí huǒchēzhàn zhǐyǒu yībǎi mǐ.
   My home is only 100 meters from the train station.

| **Helpful tips:** The fifth stroke sweeps left, and the last stroke firms, then tapers off. | **6 strokes** |

米	丶	丷	兰	半	米	米					

zuò

sit

Radical: 土 # 40 "earth"

Compounds, sentences, and meanings

1. 坐 **zuò** sit

请 坐。

Qǐng zuò.

Please sit down.

2. 坐火车 **zuò huǒchē** travel by train

我 坐 火车 去 上海。

Wǒ zuò huǒchē qù Shànghǎi.

I'm traveling to Shanghai by train.

3. 坐位 **zuòwèi** seat

请 回到 你的 坐位 上 去。

Qǐng huídào nǐde zuòwèi shàng qù.

Please return to your seat.

4. 坐不下 **zuòbuxià** have not enough seats for

这 车 坐不下 这么 多 人。

Zhè chē zuòbuxià zhème duō rén.

This car can't seat so many people.

5. 坐班 **zuòbān** keep office hours

我的孩子还 小, 不 适合 干 坐班 的

Wǒde háizi hái xiǎo, bú shìhé gàn zuòbān de

工作。

gōngzuò.

My children are still small, it's not convenient for me to work in an office.

Helpful tips: The vertical stroke separates the two 人 components.								7 strokes

坐 | 人¹ | 人² | 人人³ | 人人⁴ | 坐⁵ | 坐⁶ | 坐⁷ |

CHARACTER 323

位　wèi

place, seat

Radical: 亻 # 19 "person"

Compounds, sentences, and meanings

1. 位 **wèi**　person, place

   今天 我 请 四位 客人 吃饭。

   Jīntiān wǒ qǐng sì wèi kèrén chīfàn.

   Today I invited four guests to a meal.

2. 座位 **zuòwèi**　seat

   这 张 桌子 有 六个 座位。

   Zhè zhāng zhuōzi yǒu liù ge zuòwèi.

   This table has six places.

3. 单位 **dànwèi**　work group, unit

   以前 每个 中国 工人 有 单位。

   Yǐqián měi ge Zhōngguó gōngrén yǒu dànwèi.

   Previously every Chinese worker had a work unit.

4. 位于 **wèiyú**　situated in

   广州 位于 中国 南方。

   Guǎngzhōu wèiyú Zhōngguó nánfāng.

   Canton is situated in the southern part of China.

5. 个位 **gèwèi**　digit, place, one's place in a number

   八十三 有 三 在 个位, 八 在 十位。

   Bā shí sān yǒu sān zài gèwèi, bā zài shíwèi.

   Eighty-three has three in the ones place, eight in the tens place.

Helpful tips: The small stroke should be centered over the first horizontal stroke.						**7 strokes**			
位	丿	亻	伫	俨	位	位	位		

bēi

glass, cup

盃

Radical: 木 # 81 "tree"

Compounds, sentences, and meanings

1. 杯 **bēi** [measure word (for drinks)]

我 喝了 两 杯 茶。

Wǒ hēle liǎng bēi chá.

I drank two cups of tea.

2. 杯子 **bēizi** cup, glass

这 杯子 还 没 洗干净 呢。

Zhè bēizi hái méi xǐgānjìng ne.

This glass hasn't been washed properly.

3. 茶杯 **chábēi** teacup

茶杯、酒杯 中文 都 叫 杯子。

Chábēi, jiǔbēi Zhōngwén dōu jiào bēizi.

Teacups and glasses are called "bēizi" in Chinese.

4. 干杯 **gānbēi** drink a toast (Literally, dry the cup)

为 我们 的 友谊 干杯!

Wèi wǒmen de yǒuyì gānbēi!

Let's drink to our friendship!

5. 世界杯 **Shìjièbēi** World Cup

中国 进入 2002年 世界杯

Zhōngguó jìnrù Èrlínglíngèrnián Shìjièbēi

足球 决赛。

Zúqiú Juésài.

China got into the finals of the 2002 World Cup Soccer.

Helpful tips: End the last stroke firmly.

8 strokes

杯	一	十	才	木	朾	杯	杯	杯				

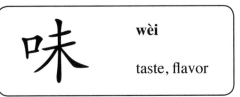

wèi

taste, flavor

Radical: 口 # 50 "mouth"

Compounds, sentences, and meanings

1. 味 **wèi** flavor

   这 糖 有 巧克力的 味儿。

   Zhè táng yǒu qiǎokèlì de wèir.

   The candy has a chocolate flavor.

2. 味道 **wèidao** taste, flavor

   这 个 菜 味道 很 好。

   Zhè ge cài wèidao hěn hǎo.

   This dish is delicious.

3. 味精 **wèijīng** gourmet powder (MSG)

   常 吃 味精 对 身体 不 好。

   Cháng chī wèijīng duì shēntǐ bù hǎo.

   It's bad for you to eat MSG too often.

4. 美味 **měiwèi** delicious

   北京 有 很多 美味 小吃。

   Běijīng yǒu hěnduō měiwèi xiǎochī.

   Beijing has a lot of delicious snacks.

5. 气味 **qìwèi** smell, odor

   有些 花儿 气味 浓郁。

   Yǒuxiē huār qìwèi nóngyù.

   The scent of some flowers is strong.

Helpful tips: The second horizontal stroke of 未 is longer.							**8 strokes**
味	丨	叮	吊	叶	吨	咔	味 味

够 **gòu**

sufficient, enough

夠

Radical: 夕 # 56 "evening"

Compounds, sentences, and meanings

1. 够了 **gòule** sufficient, enough

   够了! 我 同意 你的 意见。

   Gòule! Wǒ tóngyì nǐ de yìjiàn.

   Enough! I agree with your opinion.

2. 吃够 **chīgòu** have enough (food)

   我们 一起 吃了 很 多饭, 真的 吃 够了!

   Wǒmen yìqǐ chīle hěn duōfàn, zhēnde chī gòule!

   Together, we ate a lot of food, really we had enough!

3. 受够 **shòugòu** have enough

   我   常常   被 骗, 我 受够 了!

   Wǒ chángcháng bèi piàn, wǒ shòugòu le.

   I am often cheated; I've had enough!

4. 够大 **gòudà** quite big, big enough

   体育馆 够大, 可以 坐 一千 人。

   Tǐyùguǎn gòudà, kěyǐ zuò yīqiān rén.

   The gymnasium is quite big, it can seat 1,000 people.

5. 够格 **gòugé** quality, presentable

   德国 的汽车 真 的 够格。

   Déguó de qìchē zhēn de gòugé.

   German cars are really good quality.

Helpful tips: This character has two written forms: 够 and 夠. **11 strokes**

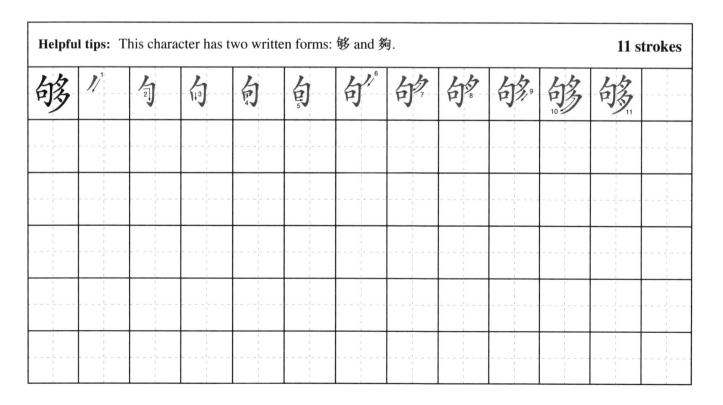

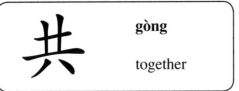

共 gòng

together

Radical: 八 # 17 "eight"

Compounds, sentences, and meanings

1. 共 **gòng** public

今天 很 高兴 能 有机会 跟老

Jīntiān hěn gāoxìng néng yǒu jīhuì gēn lǎo

朋友 共 聚一 堂。

péngyou gòng jù yì táng.

I'm very happy to have the opportunity to meet with old friends.

2. 一共 **yígòng** altogether

你们 一共 多少 人?

Nǐmen yígòng duōshao rén?

How many people are there altogether in your group?

3. 共同 **gòngtóng** common

他们 之间 没有 共同 的 语言。

Tāmen zhījiān méiyǒu gòngtóng de yǔyán.

They don't have a common language.

4. 公共 **gōnggòng** public

请 不要 在 公共 场所 吸烟。

Qǐng búyào zài gōnggòng chǎngsuǒ xīyān.

Please don't smoke in public places.

5. 共和国 **gònghéguó** republic

中华 人民 共和国

Zhōnghuá Rénmín Gònghéguó

The People's Republic of China

Helpful tips: The last stroke ends firmly.	6 strokes

共 一 卄 卅 共 共 共

A. Pronunciation and *Pinyin* Practice

Please transcribe in characters the prices shown on the menu. Be mindful of effective use of measure words in Chinese.

菜：	$
鱼香肉丝	8.50
红烧牛肉	12.00
家常豆腐	9.50
饭：	
白饭（碗）..........	1.50
饮：	
水（瓶）..........	2.00
茶（壶）..........	5.75
咖啡（杯）...	2.30

_____

_____

_____

_____

_____

_____

_____

B. Sentence Creation

Please create statements that introduce a combination of items from the menu above. Introduce the cost of each "meal" as composed of different food and drink combinations.

1. _____

2. _____

3. _____

4. _____

5. _____

C. Short Description

Write a short paragraph about the following topic that considers the different aspects of the situation.

你跟朋友一起去一家很好的饭店吃饭。对你来说，点什么菜就够了？

_____

_____

_____

_____

_____

_____

_____

_____

Traditional Form

節

jié

festival

Radical: ⺿ # 42 "grass"

Compounds, sentences, and meanings

1. 节 **jié** session [measure word]

   我 每个 星期 有 三节 中文 课。

   Wǒ měi ge xīngqī yǒu sān jié Zhōngwén kè.

   I have three Chinese lessons a week.

2. 节目 **jiémù** program

   你 想 看 什么 电视 节目?

   Nǐ xiǎng kàn shénme diànshì jiémù?

   Which TV program would you like to watch?

3. 节食 **jiéshí** on a diet

   要 保持 身材 苗条 就 得 节食。

   Yào bǎochí shēncái miǎotiáo jiù děi jiéshí.

   You have to diet if you want to stay slim.

4. 节假日 **jiéjiàrì** festivals and holidays

   每逢 节假日 黄山 有 很多 游人。

   Měiféng jiéjiàrì Huángshān yǒu hěnduō yóurén.

   During festivals and holidays, the Yellow Mountain has lots of tourists.

5. 中秋节 **Zhōngqiūjié** the Mid-Autumn Festival

   我 喜欢 中秋节 的 天气。

   Wǒ xǐhuan Zhōngqiūjié de tiānqì.

   I like the weather around the time of the Mid-Autumn Festival.

Helpful tips: The fourth stroke ends with a hook.

5 strokes

季 jì

season

Radical: 禾 # 124 "grain"

Compounds, sentences, and meanings

1. 季 **jì** season

   昆明 的 气候四季如 春。

   Kūmíng de qìhòu sìjì rú chūn.

   In Kunming it's like spring all year round.

2. 季节 **jìjié** season

   秋天 是 北京 最 好 的 季节。

   Qiūtiān shì Běijīng zuì hǎo de jìjié.

   Autumn is the loveliest season in Beijing.

3. 季节性 **jìjiéxìng** seasonal

   这 是 季节性 工作。

   Zhè shì jìjiéxìng gōngzuò.

   This is seasonal work.

4. 季候风 **jìhòufēng** monsoon

   这里的天气 受 季候风 影响。

   Zhìlǐ de tiānqì shòu jìhòufēng yǐngxiǎng.

   The monsoon has an influence on the climate here.

5. 冬季 **dōngjì** winter

   滑雪 是 冬季体育 运动。

   Huáxuě shì dōngjì tǐyù yùndòng.

   Skiing is a winter sport.

Helpful tips: The top stroke sweeps from right to left.								**8 strokes**				
季	一¹	二²	禾³	禾⁴	禾⁵	季⁶	季⁷	季⁸				

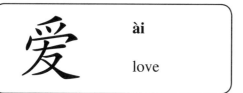

Traditional Form

爱 ài

love

愛

Radical: 爫 # 102 "claw"

Compounds, sentences, and meanings

1. 爱 ài love

   他 爱上 她了。

   Tā àishang tā le.

   He has fallen in love with her.

2. 爱情 àiqíng love

   他们 之间 已经 有了 很 深 的

   Tāmen zhījiān yǐjīng yǒule hěn shēn de

   爱情 了。

   àiqíng le.

   They are deeply in love.

3. 爱护 àihù take good care of

   请 爱护 公物。

   Qǐng àihù gōngwù.

   Please take care of public property.

4. 爱惜 àixī value highly and use prudently

   他 不 知道 爱惜 东西。

   Tā bù zhīdao àixī dōngxi.

   He doesn't know how to look after things.

5. 爱好 àihào hobby

   你 有 什么 爱好?

   Nǐ yǒu shénme àihào?

   What hobbies do you have?

Helpful tips: The last stroke firms and tapers off.										10 strokes	
爱	二₁	爫₂	爫₃	爫₄	爫₅	爫₆	爫₇	爫₈	爫₉	爱₁₀	

給/jǐ

give, supply

給

Radical: 纟 # 68 "silk"

Compounds, sentences, and meanings

1. 给 **gěi** for

   我 给 你 当 翻译。

   Wǒ gěi nǐ dāng fānyì.

   I'll act as interpreter for you.

2. 给了 **gěile** gave

   他 给 了 我 一 本 书 作为 礼物。

   Tā gěile wǒ yì běn shū zuòwéi lǐwù.

   He gave me a book as a present.

3. 供给 **gōngjǐ** supply

   教材 由 学校 供给。

   Jiàocài yóu xuéxiào gōngjǐ.

   Teaching materials are provided by the school.

4. 自给 **zìjǐ** self-sufficient

   现在 很少 国家 是 经济自给。

   Xiànzài hěnshǎo guójiā shì jīngjì zìjǐ.

   Nowadays very few countries are economically self-sufficient.

5. 给予 **jǐyǔ** (formal) give, render

   给予 难民 适当 的法律 保护。

   Jǐyǔ nànmín shìdàng de fǎlù bǎohù.

   Give appropriate legal protection to asylum seekers.

| **Helpful tips:** The third stroke rises. | | | | | | | | | | | **9 strokes** |

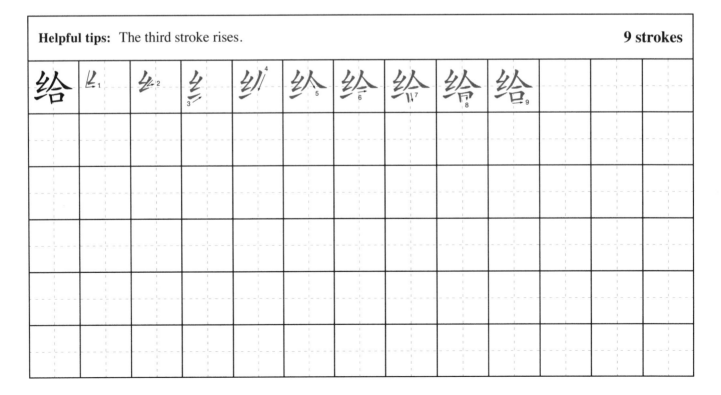

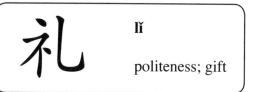

lǐ
politeness; gift

Traditional Form

禮

Radical: 礻 # 78 "ritual"

Compounds, sentences, and meanings

1. 礼 **lǐ** gift

   这 份礼很 重。

   Zhè fèn lǐ hěn zhòng.

   This is a generous gift.

2. 礼拜 **lǐbài** week

   今天 礼拜几?

   Jīntiān lǐbài jǐ?

   What day of the week is it today?

3. 礼拜三 **lǐbàisān** Wednesday

   今天 礼拜三。

   Jīntiān Lǐbàisān.

   Today is Wednesday.

4. 礼节 **lǐjié** etiquette

   中国 有 很多礼节跟 外国 不同。

   Zhōngguó yǒu hěnduō lǐjié gēn wàiguó bùtóng.

   In China a lot of the rules of etiquette are different.

5. 礼貌 **lǐmào** courteous

   我 觉得 这么 早 就 走 不大 礼貌。

   Wǒ juéde zhème zǎo jiù zǒu búdà lǐmào.

   I don't think it'd be polite for us to leave so soon.

Helpful tips: Note the difference between 礻 and 衤.   **5 strokes**

礼	㇇1	礻2	礻3	礻4	礼5							

物

wù

thing

Radical: 牛 # 95 "cattle"

Compounds, sentences, and meanings

1. 物 **wù** thing

   物以稀为贵。

   Wù yǐ xī wéi guì.

   Scarcity increases value.

2. 物价 **wùjià** commodity prices

   这 两 年 的 物价 稳定。

   Zhè liǎng nián de wùjià wěndìng.

   Prices in the last two years have remained stable.

3. 物品 **wùpǐn** goods

   不要 忘记 你 随身 携带 的 物品。

   Búyào wàngjì nǐ suíshēn xiédài de wùpǐn.

   Don't forget your personal belongings.

4. 食物 **shíwù** food

   他 住院 是 因为 食物 中毒。

   Tā zhùyuàn shì yīnwèi shíwù zhòngdú.

   He was hospitalized because of food poisoning.

5. 礼物 **lǐwù** gift

   他 送了 一份 很 重 的 礼物。

   Tā sòngle yí fèn hěn zhòng de lǐwù.

   His present was very generous.

Helpful tips: The sixth stroke is a horizontal-bend-hook.							**8 strokes**

玩　wán　play

Radical: 王 # 79 "king"

Compounds, sentences, and meanings

1. 玩 **wán** play

   我们 在 北京 玩了 三 天。

   Wǒmen zài Běijīng wánle sān tiān.

   We spent three days enjoying ourselves in Beijing.

2. 玩具 **wánjù** toy

   现在 小孩 的 玩具 花样 多极了。

   Xiànzài xiǎohái de wánjù huāyàng duōjíle.

   Nowadays, there are lots of different toys.

3. 玩笑 **wánxiào** joke

   他 是 开 玩笑, 你 别 认真。

   Tā shì kāi wánxiào, nǐ bié rènzhēn.

   He's only joking, don't take him seriously.

4. 玩意儿 **wányìr** thing

   他 手里拿的是 什么 玩意儿?

   Tā shǒulǐ ná de shì shénme wányìr?

   What's that thing in his hand?

5. 古玩 **gǔwán** antique

   这 是 古玩, 所以 这么 贵。

   Zhè shì gǔwán, suǒyǐ zhème guì.

   This is antique, that's why it's so expensive.

Helpful tips: The last stroke is a vertical-bend-hook.　　**8 strokes**

玩	一	二	干	王	玙	玡	玩	玩			

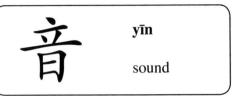

音

yīn

sound

Radical: 音 # 178 "sound"

Compounds, sentences, and meanings

1. 音 **yīn** sound

   美国 之 音
   Měiguó Zhī Yīn
   The Voice of America

2. 音响 **yīnxiǎng** stereo set

   这 套 音响 设备 比较 贵。
   Zhè tào yīnxiǎng shèbèi bǐjiào guì.
   This stereo is rather expensive.

3. 音乐 **yīnyuè** music

   你 喜欢 什么 音乐?
   Nǐ xǐhuan shénme yīnyuè?
   What kind of music do you like?

4. 声音 **shēngyīn** voice

   她的 声音 很 高。
   Tāde shēngyīn hěn gāo.
   She has a high-pitched voice.

5. 噪音 **zàoyīn** noise

   城市 里噪音 污染 是一个 严重
   Chéngshì lǐ zàoyīn wūrǎn shì yí ge yánzhòng
   问题。
   wèntí.
   Noise pollution in the city is a serious problem.

| **Helpful tips:** The second horizontal stroke is longer. | | | | | | | **9 strokes** |

音	丶	二	六	立	立	音	音	音		

乐 **lè/yuè**

joy/music

樂

Radical: ノ # 4 "downward-left stroke"

Compounds, sentences, and meanings

1. 乐 **lè** laugh, be amused

   他 说 的 笑话 把大家 都 逗 乐了。
   Tā shuō de xiàohuà bǎ dàjiā dōu dòu lè le.
   His joke made everyone laugh.

2. 快乐 **kuàilè** happy

   我的 童年 过得 很 快乐。
   Wǒde tóngnián guòde hěn kuàilè.
   I had a happy childhood.

3. 乐观 **lèguān** optimistic

   我 对 中国 的 将来 很 乐观。
   Wǒ duì Zhōngguó de jiānglái hěn lèguān.
   I'm optimistic about China's future.

4. 乐器 **yuèqì** musical instrument

   这 是 什么 乐器?
   Zhè shì shénme yuèqì?
   What sort of musical instrument is this?

5. 音乐 **yīnyuè** music

   我 喜欢 听 古典 音乐。
   Wǒ xǐhuan tīng gǔdiǎn yīnyuè.
   I like classical music.

Helpful tips: The second stroke is a slanting-bend-horizontal. **5 strokes**

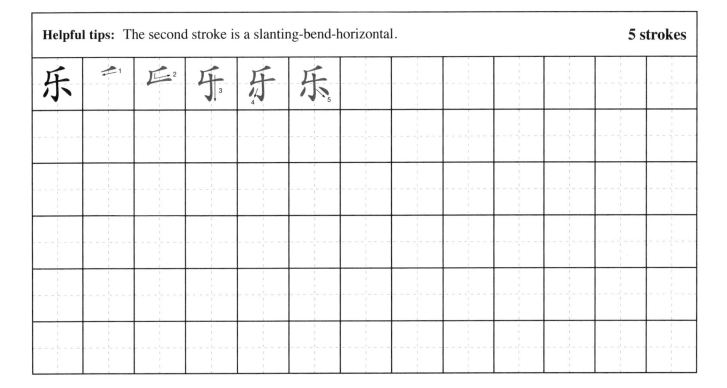

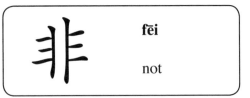

非 fēi

not

Radical: | # 3 "vertical stroke"

Compounds, sentences, and meanings

1. 非 **fēi** not

这 件 事 非 你 我 所 能 解决。

Zhè jiàn shì fēi nǐ wǒ suǒ néng jiějué.

This matter cannot be decided by you or me.

2. 非…不 **fēi ... bù** must, have to

要 学好 中文， 非下 苦工 不行。

Yào xuéhǎo Zhōngwén, fēi xià kǔgōng bùxíng.

You have to work hard to learn Chinese properly.

3. 非常 **fēicháng** extraordinary, very

街上 非常 热闹。

Jiēshàng fēicháng rè'nao.

The street is a hive of activity.

4. 非但 **fēidàn** not only

非但 学生 答不出 连 老师也

Fēidàn xuésheng dábuchū, lián lǎoshī yě

答不出。

dábuchū.

Not only the students, but the teacher too, didn't know the answer.

5. 非法 **fēifǎ** illegal

盗版 软件 被 宣布 为非法。

Dàobǎn ruǎnjiàn bèi xuānbù wéi fēifǎ.

Pirated software has been declared illegal.

Helpful tips: The two character components should be evenly balanced. **8 strokes**

非	丨¹	⌐²	⌐³	⌐⁴	非⁵	非⁶	非⁷	非⁸			

常

cháng

common

Radical: 小 # 49 "small" or 巾 # 52 "napkin"

Compounds, sentences, and meanings

1. 常 **cháng** constant

这 种 树 冬 夏 常 青。

Zhè zhǒng shù dōng xià cháng qīng.

This type of tree is evergreen.

2. 常常 **chángcháng** often

她 常常 工作 到 晚上

Tā chángcháng gōngzuò dào wǎnshang

十二点。

shí'èrdiǎn.

She often works until 12:00 midnight.

3. 常见 **chángjiàn** common

这儿 春天 风沙 是 常见 的。

Zhèr chūntiān fēngshā shì chángjiàn de.

Dust storms are common here in spring.

4. 常识 **chángshí** general knowledge

我的 科学 常识 不够。

Wǒde kēxué chángshí búgòu.

My general knowledge in science is weak.

5. 平常 **píngcháng** common

这 种 情况 很 平常。

Zhè zhǒng qíngkuàng hěn píngcháng.

This sort of thing is quite common.

Helpful tips: Write the short vertical stroke first, then the two side dots.　　**11 strokes**

| 常 | ⺌¹ | ⺌² | ⺌³ | ⺌⁴ | 尚⁵ | 尚⁶ | 常⁷ | 常⁸ | 常⁹ | 常¹⁰ | 常¹¹ | |

A. Character Practice

Please complete the two-character words that are provided, reflecting an understanding of character combinations.

 日   人   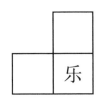 物   乐   节

B. Sentence Completion

Please match the following holidays with the season in which those holidays occur. Then, create a statement that describes an event or activity for each holiday.

中国国节   端午节   中秋节   春节

1. 春天 (   )

_____

2. 秋天 (   )

_____

3. 夏天 (   )

_____

4. 冬天 (   )

_____

C. Short Description

Please consider the following topic and then describe an appropriate example that would fulfill the topic requirements. A strong response would note both an appropriate item and the reasoning about your choice.

你要给一个小孩子礼物，什么东西是一个很好的礼物要给孩子？

_____

_____

_____

_____

_____

_____

_____

_____

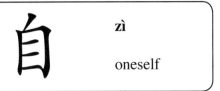

自 **zì**

oneself

Radical: 自 # 147 "oneself"

Compounds, sentences, and meanings

1. 自 **zì** naturally

现在 多 用功, 将来 自有 好处。

Xiànzài duō yònggōng, jiānglái zì yǒu hǎochù.

If you work hard now, you will reap the benefits later.

2. 自从 **zìcóng** since

我 自从 跳舞 以后, 身体 好 多 了。

Wǒ zìcóng tiàowǔ yǐhòu, shēntǐ hǎo duō le.

Since I took up dancing, my health has improved a lot.

3. 自己 **zìjǐ** self

我 觉得自己住 比较 方便。

Wǒ juéde zìjǐ zhù bǐjiào fāngbiàn.

I think it's easier to live alone.

4. 自行车 **zìxíngchē** bicycle

我 不会 骑 自行车。

Wǒ búhuì qí zìxíngchē.

I can't ride a bicycle.

5. 自由 **zìyóu** free, of one's choice

我 父母 是 自由 恋爱 结合 的。

Wǒ fùmǔ shì zìyóu liàn'ài jiéhé de.

My parents arranged their own marriage.

Helpful tips: There is equal spacing between the horizontal strokes.

6 strokes

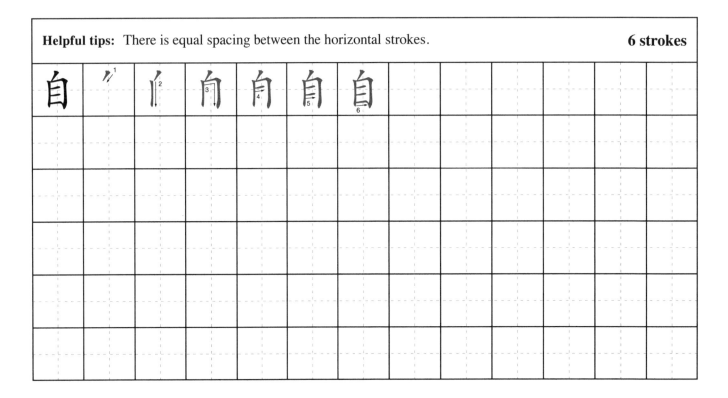

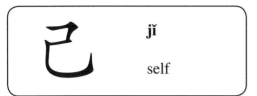

jǐ

self

Radical: 己 # 62 "self"

Compounds, sentences, and meanings

1. 己 **jǐ** self

   己 所 不 欲, 勿 施 于 人。

   Jǐ suǒ bú yù, wù shī yú rén.

   Don't treat others in a way you wouldn't like to be treated yourself.

2. 知己 **zhījǐ** close friend

   人生 难得 有 几个 知己。

   Rénshēng nándé yǒu jǐ ge zhījǐ.

   In life, it's rare to have more than a few close friends.

3. 我自己 **wǒ zìjǐ** myself

   放心 吧, 我 会 照顾 我自己的。

   Fàngxīn ba, wǒ huì zhàogu wǒ zìjǐ de.

   Don't worry, I'll look after myself.

4. 你自己 **nǐ zìjǐ** yourself

   你自己 想 办法 吧, 我 帮不了 你。

   Nǐ zìjǐ xiǎng bànfǎ ba, wǒ bāngbuliǎo nǐ.

   You work it out yourself, I can't help you.

5. 他自己 **tā zìjǐ** himself

   这 是 他自己的事, 我们 管不了。

   Zhè shì tā zìjǐ de shì, wǒmen guǎnbuliǎo.

   This is his affair, we shouldn't interfere.

Helpful tips: The top left corner is completely open.

3 strokes

己	己	己	己								

功　**gōng**

achievement

Radical: 工 # 39 "work" or 力 # 31 "strength"

Compounds, sentences, and meanings

1. 功 **gōng** achievement

   功 到 自然 成。

   Gōng dào zìrán chéng.

   Slow and steady wins the race.

2. 功课 **gōngkè** homework

   她 在 学校 里 门门 功课 都 很 好。

   Tā zài xuéxiào lǐ ménmén gōngkè dōu hěn hǎo.

   She does well in every subject at school.

3. 功能 **gōngnéng** function

   这 种 电脑 具有 多 种 功能。

   Zhè zhǒng diànnǎo jùyǒu duō zhǒng gōngnéng.

   This computer can perform many different functions.

4. 成功 **chénggōng** succeed; success

   你要 坚持 才会 成功。

   Nǐ yào jiānchí cái huì chénggōng.

   If you persevere, you will succeed.

5. 用功 **yònggōng** hardworking

   她还 在 图书馆 里 用功 呢。

   Tā hái zài túshūguǎn lǐ yònggōng ne.

   She is still working hard in the library.

Helpful tips: The last stroke of 工 lifts when written as a radical.

5 strokes

受 shòu

receive, endure

Radical: 爫 # 102 "claw"

Compounds, sentences, and meanings

1. 受不了 **shòubuliǎo** unbearable

又 上课 又 工作, 我 受不了!
Yòu shàngkè yòu gōngzuò, wǒ shòubuliǎo.
Going to class and having to work, I can't bear it!

2. 受伤 **shòushāng** injure, bear an injury

滑雪 是 很 危险 的 运动, 许多 人
Huáxuě shì hěn wēixiǎn de yùndòng, xǔduō rén

常常 受伤。
chángcháng shòushāng.
Skiing is a very dangerous activity, many people often get injured.

3. 受益 **shòuyì** receive benefit

慢慢 准备 自己受益。
Mànmàn zhǔnbèi zìjǐ shòuyì.
Those who prepare slowly enjoy benefits.

4. 受灾 **shòuzāi** bear a disaster

水灾 以后, 受灾 的 人 都 忙着
Shuǐzāi yǐhòu, shòuzāi de rén dōu mángzhe

重建 他们 的 房子。
chóngjiàn tāmen de fángzi.
After a flood, disaster survivors are all busily rebuilding their homes.

Helpful tips: There should be space between the sixth and seventh strokes.							8 strokes
受	爫¹	爫²	爫³	爫⁴	爫⁵	受⁶	受⁷ 受⁸

利
lì

sharp, benefit

Radical: 禾 # 124 "grain" or 刂 # 15 "upright knife"

Compounds, sentences, and meanings

1. 利 **lì** favorable

   文化 交流 对 两 国 都 有利。
   Wénhuà jiāoliú duì liǎng guó dōu yǒu lì.
   Cultural exchange benefits both countries.

2. 利害 **lìhai** terrible, formidable

   这 几 天 热 得 很 利害。
   Zhè jǐ tiān rède hěn lìhai.
   It's been terribly hot these last few days.

3. 利落 **lìluo** neat, orderly

   他 做事 干净 利落。
   Tā zuòshì gānjìng lìluo.
   He is a neat worker.

4. 利益 **lìyì** benefit

   我 这样 做 是 为 你的 利益 着想。
   Wǒ zhèyàng zuò shì wèi nǐde lìyì zhuóxiǎng.
   I did it out of consideration for your interests.

5. 利用 **lìyòng** make use of

   我们 应该 好好儿地 利用 空余 的
   Wǒmen yīnggāi hǎohāorde lìyòng kōngyú de

   时间。
   shíjiān.
   We should utilize our spare time properly.

Helpful tips: The vertical stroke of 禾 has no hook.						**7 strokes**
利	一¹	二²	千³	禾⁴	禾⁵	利⁶ 利⁷

较   jiào

to compare

較

Radical: 车 # 84 "vehicle"

Compounds, sentences, and meanings

1. 较 **jiào** relatively

你的汉语 有 较大 的进步。

Nǐde Hànyǔ yǒu jiàodà de jìnbù.

You have made considerable progress in your Chinese.

2. 相较 **xiāngjiào** compare

相较 实力,我方 优于 对方。

Xiāngjiào shílì, wǒfāng yōuyú duìfāng.

Using our strengths to compare, we are better than our opponent.

3. 比较 **bǐjiào** comparatively

我 最进比较 忙。

Wǒ zuìjìn bǐjiào máng.

I've been rather busy recently.

4. 较为 **jiàowéi** comparatively

这 本 词典 较为 便宜。

Zhè běn cídiǎn jiàowéi piányi.

This dictionary is comparatively cheap.

5. 较量 **jiàoliàng** measure one's strength with

你还是别 跟 这 个 小伙子 较量 了。

Nǐ háishì bié gēn zhè ge xiǎohuǒzi jiàoliàng le.

You'd be better off not to test your strength against this young guy.

Helpful tips: The last stroke comes down from left to right.										**10 strokes**

改 **gǎi**

change

Radical: 攵 # 99 "tap"

Compounds, sentences, and meanings

1. 改 **gǎi** change

几年 没来,这里 完全 改 样 了。

Jǐ nián méi lái, zhèlǐ wánquán gǎi yàng le.

I've been away for only a few years, but the place has changed completely.

2. 改变 **gǎibiàn** change

我 可以 改变 主意 吗?

Wǒ kěyǐ gǎibiàn zhǔyi ma?

Can I change my mind?

3. 改掉 **gǎidiào** give up, drop

他 决定 改掉 坏 习惯。

Tā juédìng gǎidiào huài xíguàn.

He has decided to give up his bad habits.

4. 改革 **gǎigé** reform

中国 还是 坚持 改革 开放。

Zhōngguó háishì jiānchí gǎigé kāifàng.

China is still continuing its reform and open-door policy.

5. 改正 **gǎizhèng** correct

老师 让 我们 在课 上 改正

Lǎoshī ràng wǒmen zài kè shàng gǎizhèng

错误。

cuòwù.

The teacher asks us to correct our mistakes in class.

Helpful tips: The last stroke of 改 is written as a vertical lift.									**7 strokes**
改	¹⁻ㄱ	²ㄹ	³ㄹ	⁴ㄹ′	⁵ㄹ′	⁶改	⁷改		

正 **zhèng**

right, correct

Radical: 一 # 2 "horizontal stroke" or 止 # 88 "stop"

Compounds, sentences, and meanings

1. 正 **zhèng** precisely

   这 双 鞋 大小 正 合适。

   Zhè shuāng xié dàxiǎo zhèng héshì.

   This pair of shoes is just the right size.

2. 正常 **zhèngcháng** normal

   这 几 天 天气 不 太 正常。

   Zhè jǐ tiān tiānqì bú tài zhèngcháng.

   The weather in the past few days has been quite abnormal.

3. 正好 **zhènghǎo** just in time

   你 来得 正好。

   Nǐ láide zhènghǎo.

   You've come just in time.

4. 正确 **zhèngquè** correct

   你 这样 做 是 正确 的。

   Ni zhèyàng zuò shì zhèngquè de.

   What you are doing is right.

5. 正在 **zhèngzài** right at the moment

   他们 正在 吃 晚饭。

   Tāmen zhèngzài chī wǎnfàn.

   They are having their dinner right now.

Helpful tips: The bottom horizontal stroke is slightly longer. **5 strokes**

正	一¹	丁²	下³	正⁴	正⁵							

记 jì
record

記

Radical: 讠 # 9 "word"

Compounds, sentences, and meanings

1. 记 jì jot down
   请 把 电话 号码 记下来。
   Qǐng bǎ diànhuà hàomǎ jìxiàlai.
   Please jot down the telephone number.

2. 记得 jìde remember
   我 完全 记不得了。
   Wǒ wánquán jíbude le.
   I simply don't remember it.

3. 记性 jìxìng memory
   她的 记性 很 好。
   Tāde jìxìng hěn hǎo.
   She has a good memory.

4. 记住 jìzhù learn by heart
   我 记不住 这么 多 汉字。
   Wǒ jìbuzhù zhème duō Hànzì.
   I can't remember so many characters.

5. 忘记 wàngjì forgotten
   他 紧张地 工作，忘记了 去 吃 晚饭。
   Tā jǐnzhāngde gōngzuò, wàngjìle qù chī wǎnfàn.
   He was working so hard that he forgot to go for dinner.

Helpful tips: Note the difference between 己 and 巳.　　　　**5 strokes**

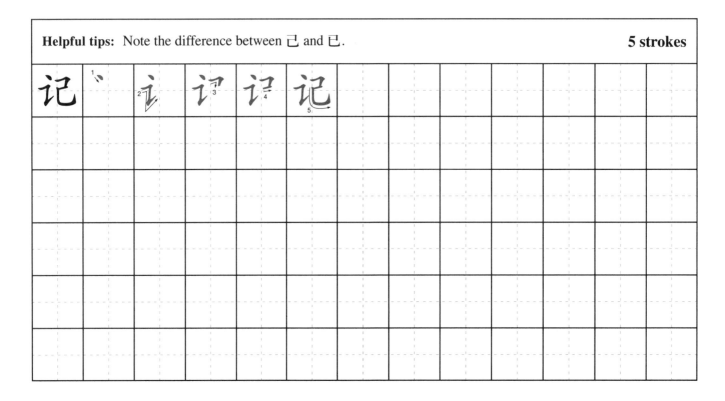

预   yù

beforehand

預

Radical: 页 # 140 "page"

Compounds, sentences, and meanings

1. 预 **yù** beforehand
   预 祝 你 取得 成功。
   Yù zhù nǐ qǔdé chénggōng.
   I wish you success.

2. 预报 **yùbào** forecast
   天气 预报 说 明天 会下雨。
   Tiānqì yùbào shuō míngtiān huì xiàyǔ.
   The weather forecast says it will rain tomorrow.

3. 预备 **yùbèi** get ready
   你们 预备好了吗?
   Nǐmen yùbèihǎo le ma?
   Are you ready?

4. 预订 **yùdìng** place an order
   我 预订 火车票 了。
   Wǒ yùdìng huǒchēpiào le.
   I've booked the train ticket.

5. 预约 **yùyuē** make an appointment
   你跟 医生 预约了吗?
   Nǐ gēn yīshēng yùyuē le ma?
   Have you made an appointment with the doctor?

Helpful tips: Finish the last stroke firmly.   **10 strokes**

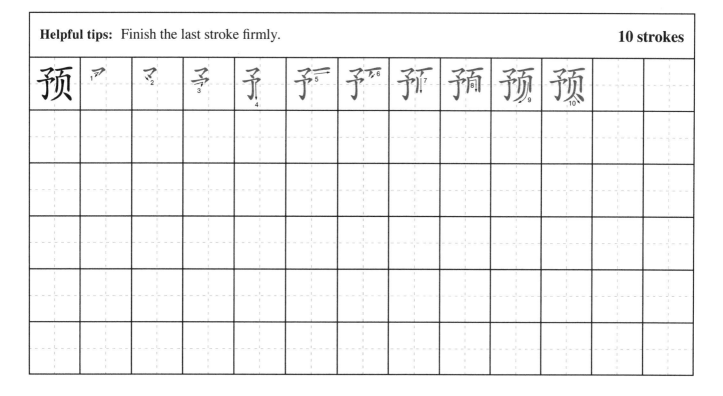

A. Pronunciation and *Pinyin* Practice

Please transcribe the following words in *pinyin*. Then practice saying these related terms clearly and accurately.

自己 _____   受利 _____   改变 _____

自动 _____   受伤 _____   改好 _____

自行 _____   受益 _____   改正 _____

B. Sentence Response

Suggest a response to each of the following circumstances. For each of these circumstances, express a change or revision of activities that should happen.

1. 你自己的情况比较好。

   _____

2. 你要准备受利。

   _____

3. 你常常生病。

   _____

4. 你天天不能睡好觉。

   _____

C. Focused Description

Consider the illustration. Write a description of it, noting down the key aspects of the illustration that make it remarkable and memorable.

_____

_____

_____

_____

_____

_____

_____

_____

_____

Section 7 Review (Lessons 28–32)

A. Character Practice

For each of the following general categories please provide 4 example terms in Chinese characters.

感觉	习惯	节日	礼物	菜

B. Short Description

In the spaces provided, sketch an illustration for each situation described. Then, create a short statement that describes a change to resolve the problem.

饿死了	很累	记不住

_____

_____

_____

_____

生病

要喝水

给别人很好的礼物

C. Holiday Description

Consider the following topic. Then create a description that demonstrates an understanding of a holiday and the cultural elements of celebration and activities. Express both the events and the order of those events. Additionally, a strong description will express cultural aspects of the different events and how events connect to expressing culture. Attempt to explore the topic with strong use of specific conjunctions and other constructions that allow for effective connected discourse.

每个人有自己最喜欢的节日, 请介绍你最喜欢的节日。

_____

_____

_____

_____

_____

D. Reflective Questions

Use these questions to both check the expressiveness of the previous section and to confirm your understanding of the previous topic. For additional practice, say and then respond to these questions aloud.

你很喜欢什么中国的节日？

你最喜欢的节目活动是什么？

你喜欢圣诞节，还是春节？

在圣诞节你要去哪里？

你在节日喜欢自己做什么饭？

什么时候你要给别人礼物？

什么节日你不太喜欢？为什么？

你有没有一个生日的故事？

每个人有自己的节日习俗，你有什么习俗？

有时候新的节日会开始，你想开始什么样的新节日？

楼　lóu

building

樓

Radical: 木 # 81 "tree"

Compounds, sentences, and meanings

1. 楼 **lóu** building

   大学 的 学院 大概 有 几个 大楼。

   Dàxué de xuéyuàn dàgài yǒu jǐ ge dàlóu.

   College campuses probably have several large buildings.

2. 一楼 **yīlóu** first floor, first story

   这个 大楼 的 一楼 只有 门厅 和 电梯,

   Zhège dàlóu de yīlóu zhǐyǒu méntīng hé diàntí,

   没有 办公室 或者 商店。

   méiyǒu bàngōngshì huǒzhe shāngdiàn.

   The first floor of this large building only has a lobby and elevators, there aren't offices or shops.

3. 楼上 **lóushàng** upstairs

   听一听, 楼上 的 邻居 好象 有

   Tīngyìtīng, lóushàng de línjū hǎoxiàng yǒu

   许多 客人。

   xǔduō kèrén.

   Take a listen, the neighbors upstairs seem to have a lot of guests.

4. 上楼 **shànglóu** go upstairs

   他 不在这里, 他 上楼 了。

   Tā búzài zhèlǐ, tā shànglóu le.

   He's not here, he went upstairs.

5. 楼台 **lóutài** staircase

   这个 房屋 的 楼台 很 漂亮。

   Zhège fángwù de lóutài hěn piàoliang.

   The staircase in this house is very pretty.

Helpful tips: The right hand component should be even top to bottom.　　**13 strokes**

楼	二¹	才²	才³	木⁴	术⁵	术⁶	桁⁷	村⁸	枕⁹	桦¹⁰	楼¹¹	楼¹²
楼¹³												

办

bàn

do, manage

辦

Radical: 力 # 31 "strength"

Compounds, sentences, and meanings

1. 办 **bàn** do, manage

   我 有 点 事 要 办。

   Wǒ yǒu diǎn shì yào bàn.

   There's something I have to do.

2. 办法 **bànfǎ** way, means

   你 要 想 办法 克服 困难。

   Nǐ yào xiǎng bànfǎ kèfú kùnnàn.

   You have to find a way to rise above your problems.

3. 办公室 **bàngōngshì** office

   我 十 点 以后 在 办公室。

   Wǒ shí diǎn yǐhòu zài bàngōngshì.

   I'll be in my office after 10:00.

4. 办理 **bànlǐ** handle, conduct

   请 到 那边 去办理离境 手续。

   Qǐng dào nàbiān qù bànlǐ líjìng shǒuxù.

   Please go over there to go through departure formalities.

5. 办事 **bànshì** handle affairs, work

   她 办事 很 认真。

   Tā bànshì hěn rènzhēn.

   She works conscientiously.

Helpful tips: The left dot ends firmly to the left, the right dot to the right.　　　　**4 strokes**

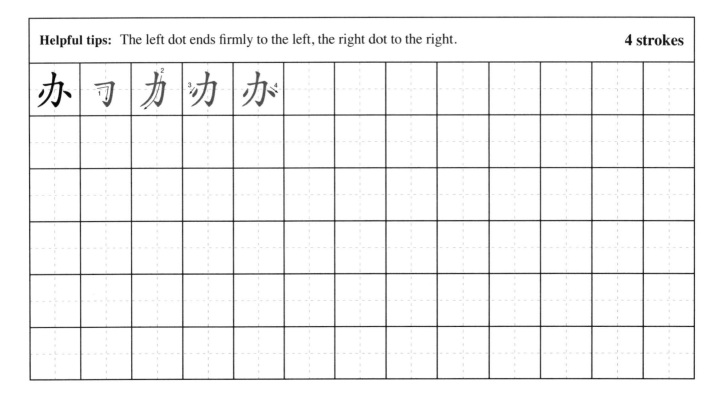

室

shì

room

Radical: 宀 # 34 "roof"

Compounds, sentences, and meanings

1. 办公室 **bàngōngshì** office

   每个 公司 需要 办公室。
   Měi ge gōngsi xūyào bàngōngshì.
   All companies need offices.

2. 休息室 **xiūxishì** break room, lounge

   大学 学生 宿舍 有 很好 的 休息室。
   Dàxué xuésheng sùshè yǒu hěnhǎo de xiūxishì.
   College dormitories have very nice lounges.

3. 室外 **shìwài** outside

   踢足球 是 一种 室外 的 运动。
   Tī zúqiú shì yìzhǒng shìwài de yùndòng.
   Playing soccer is a type of outside activity.

4. 室内 **shìnèi** inside, indoor

   冬天 的 时候, 许多 人 只想 做
   Dōngtiān de shíhou, xǔduō rén zhǐxiǎng zuò

   室内 的 活动。
   shìnèi de huódòng.
   During the winter, many people only want to do activities indoors.

Helpful tips: The radical and the final horizontal stroke should be of similar length.								**9 strokes**		
室	丶	宀	宀	宀	宕	宏	空	宰	室		

fáng

room, house

Radical: 户 # 77 "household"

Compounds, sentences, and meanings

1. 房间 **fángjiān** room

    房间 得 有 四道 墙。

    Fángjiān děi yǒu sì dào qiáng.

    A room must have four walls.

2. 房子 **fángzi** house, building

    现代 的 房子 很 方便。

    Xiàndài de fángzi hěn fāngbiàn.

    Modern buildings have convenient amenities.

3. 房客 **fángkè** tenant

    每 个 月, 房客 给 房东 租费。

    Měi ge yuè, fángkè gěi fángdōng zūfèi.

    Every month, tenants give landlords rent.

4. 客房 **kèfáng** guestroom

    这个 房子 很 大, 有 四个 客房。

    Zhège fángzi hěn dà, yǒu sì ge kèfáng.

    This house is large, it has four guestrooms.

Helpful tips: The horizontal stroke is slightly longer than the radical.

8 strokes

房	㇀¹	⼆	㇌	⼾⁴	⼾⁵	⼾⁶	房⁷	房⁸				

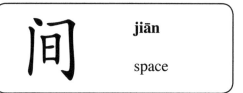

Traditional Form

間

jiān

space

Radical: 门 # 37 "door"

Compounds, sentences, and meanings

1. 间 **jiān** between, among

   朋友 之 间 不要 分得 太 清。

   Péngyou zhī jiān búyào fēnde tài qīng.

   Among friends, there should not be clear-cut distinctions.

2. 夜间 **yèjiān** at night

   很多 中国 城市 在 夜间 施工。

   Hěnduō Zhōngguó chéngshì zài yèjiān shīgōng.

   Many Chinese cities carry out construction work at night.

3. 时间 **shíjiān** time

   现在 是 北京 时间 二十点 整。

   Xiànzài shì Běijīng shíjiān èrshídiǎn zhěng.

   The time now is 20 hours Beijing time.

4. 中间 **zhōngjiān** middle

   他 是 我们 中间 最 年轻 的。

   Tā shì wǒmen zhōngjiān zuì niánqīng de.

   He's the youngest of us three.

5. 房间 **fángjiān** room

   这个 房间 又 大 又 亮。

   Zhè ge fángjiān yòu dà yòu liàng.

   This room is big and bright.

Helpful tips: The initial dot stroke ends firmly to the right.　　　**7 strokes**

间	丶	门	门	间	间	间	间					

táng

room

Radical: 小 # 49 "small"

1. 食堂 **shítáng** dining hall, cafeteria

   有 时候, 食堂 的 饭 不太 好吃。
   Yǒu shíhou, shítáng de fàn bútài hǎochī.
   At times, the food in the dining hall is not too good.

2. 会堂 **huìtáng** auditorium, meeting hall

   人民 大会堂 是 大陆 最 有名 的
   Rénmín Dàhuìtáng shì Dàlù zuì yǒumíng de
   会堂。
   huìtáng.
   The Great Hall of the People is the most famous meeting hall in Mainland China.

3. 课堂 **kètáng** classroom

   现代化 的 课堂 得 有 电脑。
   Xiàndàihuà de kètáng děi yǒu diànnǎo.
   Modern classrooms need to have computers.

4. 堂堂 **tángtáng** grand, regal

   堂堂 男子汉 怎么 可以 哭 呢?
   Tángtáng nánzǐhàn, zěnme kěyǐ kū ne?
   Such a macho man, how can he cry?

Helpful tips: The height between each horizontal stroke should be the same.										**11 strokes**
堂	⼩¹	⼩²	⼩³	⼩⁴	尚⁵	尚⁶	尚⁷	堂⁸	堂⁹	堂¹⁰ 堂¹¹

屋

wū

house, room

Radical: 尸 # 61 "dwelling"

Compounds, sentences, and meanings

1. 屋 **wū** house

   山上 有一座 小 屋。
   Shānshàng yǒu yí zuò xiǎo wū.
   There's a small house on the hill.

2. 屋顶 **wūdǐng** roof

   我们 家的 屋顶 要修理。
   Wǒmen jiā de wūdǐng yào xiūlǐ.
   The roof of our house needs to be repaired.

3. 屋里 **wūlǐ** inside the room

   请 到屋里坐。
   Qǐng dào wūlǐ zuò.
   Please come in and sit down.

4. 屋子 **wūzi** room

   这套 单元房 有三 间 屋子。
   Zhè tào dānyuánfáng yǒu sān jiān wūzi.
   This apartment has three rooms.

5. 房屋 **fángwū** housing

   这里高 质量的 房屋 短缺。
   Zhèlǐ gāo zhìliàng de fángwū duǎnquē.
   There's a shortage of quality housing here.

Helpful tips: Each horizontal stroke is evenly spaced.　　　　**9 strokes**

屋	一	三	尸	尸	居	层	屋	屋	屋			

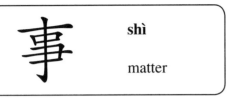

shì

matter

Radical: 一 **# 2** "horizontal stroke"

Compounds, sentences, and meanings

1. 事 **shì** matter

   我 把 这 件 事 忘 了。

   Wǒ bǎ zhè jiàn shì wàng le.

   I've forgotten all about it.

2. 事情 **shìqing** matter

   我 把 这 件 事情 忘 了。

   Wǒ bǎ zhè jiàn shìqing wàng le.

   I've forgotten all about it.

3. 事故 **shìgù** accident

   路 滑 慢 驶, 防止 发生 事故。

   Lù huá màn shǐ, fángzhǐ fāshēng shìgù.

   The road is slippery, try to avoid accidents.

4. 事后 **shìhòu** after the event

   不要 老是 作 事后 的 批评。

   Búyào lǎoshì zuò shìhòu de pīpíng.

   Don't get into the habit of criticizing after the event.

5. 事先 **shìxiān** in advance, beforehand

   应该 事先 作好 准备。

   Yīnggāi shìxiān zuòhǎo zhǔnbèi.

   We should get everything ready beforehand.

Helpful tips: Each horizontal stroke is evenly spaced. Also, the final stroke ends in a hook. **8 strokes**

事	一	一	写	写	写	写	事				

食

shí

food; eat

Radical: 食 # 181 "eat"

Compounds, sentences, and meanings

1. 食 **shí** eat (lit.)

   只 有 狂人 饿而不食。

   Zhǐ yǒu kuángrén è'ér bù shí.

   Only crazy people are hungry but don't eat.

2. 食品 **shípǐn** foodstuff

   市场 里有 许多 人买 食品。

   Shìchǎng lǐ yǒu xǔduō rén mǎi shípǐn.

   In the market a whole bunch of people are buying food.

3. 食粮 **shíliáng** grain

   米是 中国 最 重要 的 食粮。

   Mǐ shì Zhōngguó zuì zhòngyào de shíliáng.

   Rice is China's most important grain.

4. 食物 **shíwù** edible

   你 看一看, 这是 什么 食物?

   Nǐ kànyíkàn, zhè shì shénme shíwù?

   Take a look, what food is this?

5. 食言 **shíyán** eat one's words

   你不 要 食言。

   Nǐ bú yào shíyán.

   You don't want to eat your own words.

Helpful tips: The seventh stroke ends in a hook to the right.　　　　**9 strokes**

食	丿	𠆢	𠆢	今	今	食	食	食	食			

面 　 **miàn**

face

Radical: 一 # 2 "horizontal stroke"

Compounds, sentences, and meanings

1. 面 **miàn** face

   她 常常 面 带 笑容。

   Tā chángcháng miàn dài xiàoróng.

   She often has a smile on her face.

2. 面貌 **miànmào** features

   他们 的 面貌 十分 相似。

   Tāmen de miànmào shífēn xiāngsì.

   They look very much alike.

3. 面熟 **miànshú** look familiar

   这 人 看着 面熟。

   Zhè rén kànzhe miànshú.

   That person looks familiar.

4. 面积 **miànji** area

   这 套 房子的 使用 面积 是 五十

   Zhè tào fángzi de shǐyòng miànji shi wǔshí

   平方 公尺。

   píngfāng gōngchǐ.

   The usable area of this apartment is 50 square meters.

5. 面子 **miànzi** face

   他 是 老板, 给他 留 点 面子 吧。

   Tā shì lǎobǎn, gěi tā liú diǎn miànzi ba.

   He is our boss, show some respect.

Helpful tips: Note the difference between 面 and 而.									**9 strokes**		
面	一	丁	丆	而	而	面	面	面			

Lesson 33: Review Activities

A. Vocabulary and Pronunciation

Please complete this diagram of a multi-story building with different offices and other locations: first, supply the characters for each of the 3 unnamed locations. Then transcribe all of the locations in *pinyin*.

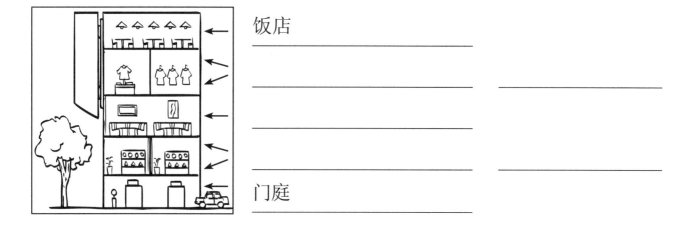

饭店 _____

_____   _____

_____

_____   _____

门庭 _____

B. Short Description

Use the small map to consider the following buildings. For each building, describe each of the locations in it. Note any differences in the contents of the various buildings.

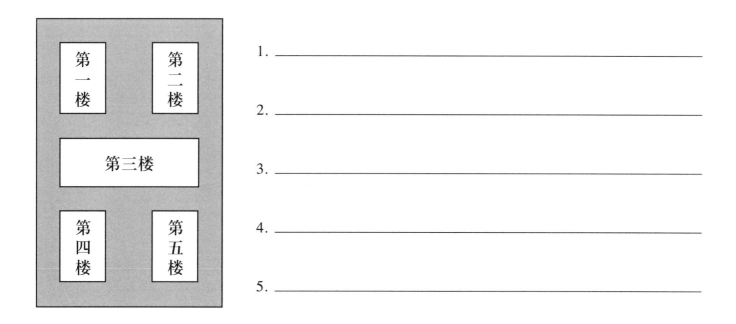

第一楼   第二楼

第三楼

第四楼   第五楼

1. _____

2. _____

3. _____

4. _____

5. _____

C. Location Description

For each of the following types of rooms and locations please create a small discussion that highlights the different specific items that one would find in each. Discuss similar items that each location would need and how that item would be used differently.

1. （办公室）

_____

_____

_____

_____

2. （食堂）

_____

_____

_____

_____

3. （学生宿舍房间）

_____

_____

_____

_____

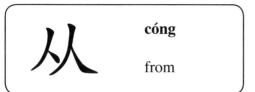

Traditional Form

从   cóng

from

從

Radical: 人 # 18 "person"

Compounds, sentences, and meanings

1. 从 **cóng** from

   你 从 哪儿 来?

   Nǐ cóng nǎr lái?

   Where do you come from?

2. 从…到 **cóng ... dào** from ... to

   她 从 早 到 晚 都 想着 跳舞。

   Tā cóng zǎo dào wǎn dōu xiǎngzhe tiàowǔ.

   She thinks of dancing day and night.

3. 从来 **cónglái** all along

   我 从来 没有 见过 他。

   Wǒ cónglái méiyǒu jiànguo tā.

   I've never seen him before.

4. 从前 **cóngqián** formerly

   这 是 从前, 现在 不 一样 了。

   Zhè shì cóngqián, xiànzài bù yíyàng le.

   That was in the past, now it is different.

5. 从小 **cóngxiǎo** from childhood

   我 从小 就 喜欢 运动。

   Wǒ cóngxiǎo jiù xǐhuan yùndòng.

   I've loved sports ever since I was a child.

Helpful tips: The last stroke tapers off.   **4 strokes**

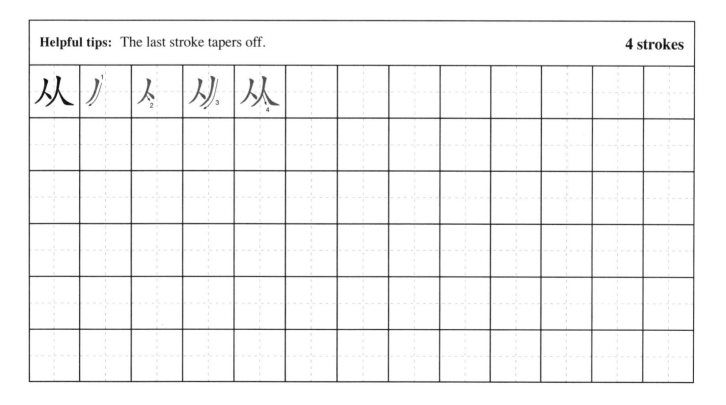

离
lí
depart

離

Radical: 亠 # 6 "top of 六"

Compounds, sentences, and meanings

1. 离 **lí** distance from

    公园　离学校　有一公里。

    Gōngyuán lí xuéxiào yǒu yì gōnglǐ.

    The park is one kilometer from the school.

2. 离婚 **líhūn** divorce

    离婚　以后他就　没有　再　结婚。

    Líhūn yǐhòu tā jiù méiyǒu zài jiēhūn.

    He hasn't remarried since his divorce.

3. 离开 **líkāi** depart

    离开　北京, 她坐　火车　去西安。

    Líkāi Běijīng, tā zuò huǒchē qù Xī'ān.

    Departing Beijing, she took the train to Xian.

4. 离别 **líbié** bid farewell

    我离别　故乡　已经十年了。

    Wǒ líbié gùxiāng yǐjīng shí nián le.

    It's been ten years since I left my hometown.

5. 离题 **lítí** digress from the subject

    发言　不要离题。

    Fāyán búyào lítí.

    Please keep to the subject when you speak.

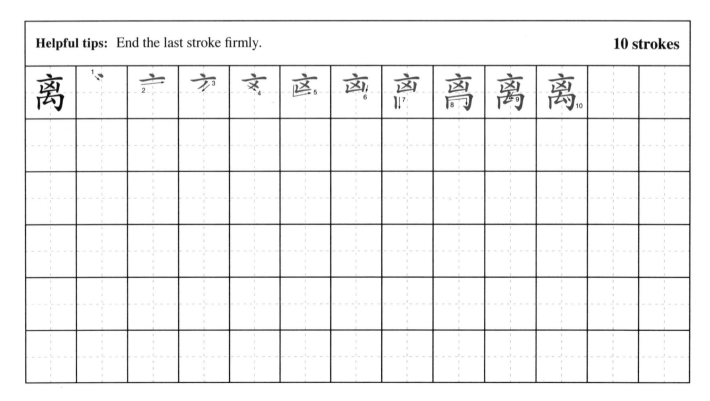

Helpful tips: End the last stroke firmly.

10 strokes

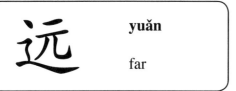

远　yuǎn

far

遠

Radical: 辶　# 38 "movement"

Compounds, sentences, and meanings

1. 远 **yuǎn** far

   公园　离 学 校　有 多　远?

   Gōngyuán lí xuéxiào yǒu duō yuǎn?

   How far is the park from the school?

2. 远处 **yuǎnchù** distant point or place

   我　看见 几个人 从　远处　走来。

   Wǒ kànjiàn jǐ ge rén cóng yuǎnchù zǒulái.

   I saw a few people coming towards me from a distance.

3. 远近 **yuǎnjìn** distance

   这　两　条 路 远近　差不多。

   Zhè liǎng tiáo lù yuǎnjìn chàbuduō.

   The distance is about the same by either road.

4. 远大 **yuǎndà** long-range, lofty

   年青人　应该　有　远大 的　理想。

   Niánqīngrén yīnggāi yǒu yuǎndà de lǐxiǎng.

   Young people ought to have lofty ideals.

5. 长远 **chángyuǎn** long-term

   从　长远　的　观点　看 问题。

   Cóng chángyuǎn de guāndiǎn kàn wèntí.

   Look at problems from a long-term view.

Helpful tips: The last stroke of 元 ends with a hook.　　　　**7 strokes**

远	二	二	厃	元	元	沅	远				

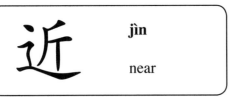

jìn

near

Radical: 辶 # 38 "movement"

Compounds, sentences, and meanings

1. 近 **jìn** near

   我 家 离 火车站 很 进。

   Wǒ jiā lí huǒchēzhàn hěn jìn.

   My house is near the rail station.

2. 近来 **jìnlái** recently

   近来他的身体 不太 好。

   Jìnlái tāde shēntǐ bú tài hǎo.

   He has been rather unwell recently.

3. 近视 **jìnshì** nearsighted

   她 有点 近视。

   Tā yǒudiǎn jìnshì.

   She is slightly nearsighted.

4. 近便 **jìnbiàn** close and convenient

   我们 找 个 近便 的 饭馆 吃

   Wǒmen zhǎo ge jìnbiàn de fànguǎn chī

   午饭 吧。

   wǔfàn ba.

   Let's have lunch at the nearest restaurant.

5. 附近 **fùjìn** nearby

   学校 附近 有 一个 公园。

   Xuéxiào fùjìn yǒu yí ge gōngyuán.

   There is a park near the school.

Helpful tips: The last stroke tapers off.							**7 strokes**
近	丿¹	厂²	斤³	斤⁴	斤⁵	近⁶	近⁷

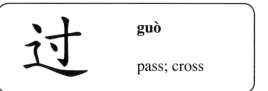

guò

pass; cross

過

Radical: 辶 # 38 "movement"

Compounds, sentences, and meanings

1. 过 **guò** pass, cross

   过 两 条 街 就 是。

   Guò liǎng tiáo jiē jiù shì.

   Cross two streets and you are there.

2. 过敏 **guòmǐn** allergy

   我 对 牛奶 过敏。

   Wǒ duì niúnǎi guòmǐn.

   I'm allergic to milk.

3. 过去 **guòqù** formerly

   他 比 过去 瘦 多 了。

   Tā bǐ guòqù shòu duō le.

   He's much thinner than he used to be.

4. 过时 **guòshí** out of date

   这 件 衣服 早 就 过时 了。

   Zhè jiàn yīfu zǎo jiù guòshí le.

   This garment is long out of fashion.

5. 不过 **búguò** but, however

   爸爸的 身体 还 不错, 不过 有点儿 胖。

   Bàba de shēntǐ hái búcuò, búguò yǒudiǎnr páng.

   My dad's heath is quite good, but he is a bit overweight.

Helpful tips: End the fourth stroke firmly.

6 strokes

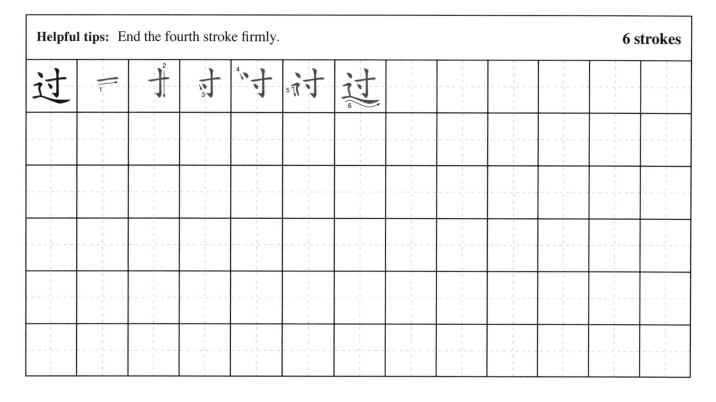

往 **wǎng**

toward

Radical: 彳 # 54 "double-person"

Compounds, sentences, and meanings

1. 往 **wǎng** toward
   你 往 东 走 去 就 是 了。
   Nǐ wǎng dōng zǒu qù jiù shì le.
   Go east and you'll get there.

2. 往往 **wǎngwǎng** often
   这里 春天　往往　刮 大 风。
   Zhèlǐ chūntiān wǎngwǎng guā dà fēng.
   It's often windy here in spring.

3. 往常 **wǎngcháng** habitually in the past
   她　往常　不 这样。
   Tā wǎngcháng bú zhèyàng.
   She wasn't like that before.

4. 往返 **wǎngfǎn** journey there and back
   往返 要 多 长　时间?
   Wǎngfǎn yào duō cháng shíjiān?
   How long does it take to get there and back?

5. 往来 **wǎnglái** contact, dealings
   他们　两 家 人　往来　很 密切。
   Tāmen liǎng jiā rén wǎnglái hěn mìqiè.
   The two families are in close contact.

Helpful tips: Note the difference between 往 and 住. **8 strokes**

往	⼃¹	⼻²	彳³	彳⁴	行⁵	徍⁶	徍⁷	往⁸				

向   xiàng

toward

Radical: 丿 # 4 "downward-left stroke" or 口 # 50 "mouth"

Compounds, sentences, and meanings

1. 向 **xiàng** toward

   河水 向 东 流去。

   Héshuǐ xiàng dōng liú qù.

   The river flows east.

2. 向导 **xiàngdǎo** act as a guide

   我 来 给 你们 做 向导， 怎么样?

   Wǒ lái gěi nǐmen zuò xiàngdǎo, zěnmeyàng?

   Why don't I come as your guide?

3. 向来 **xiànglái** always, all along

   他 向来 做事 认真。

   Tā xiànglái zuòshì rènzhēn.

   He's always been conscientious in his work.

4. 向例 **xiànglì** usual practice

   我们 这里 向例 起得 早。

   Wǒmen zhèlǐ xiànglì qǐde zǎo.

   Here, we get up early as a rule.

5. 向往 **xiàngwǎng** yearn for, look forward to

   我 终于 登上了 向往 已久

   Wǒ zhōngyú dēngshàngle xiàngwǎng yǐ jiǔ

   的 长城。

   de Chángchéng.

   I finally climbed the Great Wall, which I had wanted to do for a long time.

Helpful tips: The first stroke sweeps down from right to left.											**6 strokes**
向	丿	亻	向	向	向	向					

回

huí

return

Radical: 囗 # 51 "4-sided frame"

Compounds, sentences, and meanings

1. 回 **huí** return

今天　晚上　你几点　回家？

Jīntiān wǎnshang nǐ jǐ diǎn huíjiā?

What time will you go home tonight?

2. 回答 **huídá** reply

请 你 回答 我的 问题。

Qǐng nǐ huídá wǒde wèntí.

Answer my question, please.

3. 回来 **huílái** come back

请 你 稍　等, 她 马上　就 回来。

Qǐng nǐ shāo děng, tā mǎshàng jiù huílái.

Please wait a while, she'll be back shortly.

4. 回去 **huíqù** go back

天　太　晚 了, 你 今天　回不去 了。

Tiān tài wǎn le, nǐ jīntiān huíbuqù le.

It's too late; you can't go back home today.

5. 回头 **huítóu** turn one's head

他 回头　往　后　看。

Tā huítóu wǎng hòu kàn.

He turned his head and looked back.

Helpful tips: The rectangular frame is taller than it is wide.												**6 strokes**
回	丨	冂	冂	冋	回	回						

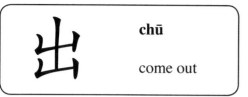

出   chū

come out

Radical: 凵 **# 29** "3-sided frame, open top"

Compounds, sentences, and meanings

1. 出 **chū** put up

   你 给 我 出 个 主意, 好 吗?

   Nǐ gěi wǒ chū ge zhǔyi, hǎo ma?

   How about giving me a suggestion?

2. 出差 **chūchāi** go on a business trip

   我 这次 去 北京 是 出差。

   Wǒ zhè cì qù Běijīng shì chūchāi.

   I'm going to Beijing on business.

3. 出错 **chūcuò** make mistakes

   她 做事 很少 出错。

   Tā zuòshì hěnshǎo chūcuò.

   She seldom makes a mistake.

4. 出发 **chūfā** start off

   我们 明天 几点 出发?

   Wǒmen míngtiān jǐ diǎn chūfā?

   When do we set out tomorrow?

5. 出去 **chūqu** go out

   我们 出去 走走, 好 不 好?

   Wǒmen chūqu zǒuzou, hǎo bù hǎo?

   Why don't we go for a walk?

Helpful tips: The vertical stroke in the middle does not cross the lower horizontal stroke.   **5 strokes**

入 rù

enter, come in

Radical: 人 # 18 "people"

Compounds, sentences, and meanings

1. 入口 **rùkǒu** entrance

   博物馆 的 入口 在那里。

   Bówùguǎn de rùkǒu zài nàlǐ.

   The entrance to the museum is there.

2. 进入 **jìnrù** enter, come inside

   你的 房间 太 小 啊, 只有 一个人

   Nǐ de fángjiān tài xiǎo ā, zhǐyǒu yí ge rén

   可以进入!

   kěyǐ jìnrù!

   Your room is too small, only one person can come inside.

3. 入神 **rùshén** be entranced

   他看他爱人 的 照片 看 得 入神。

   Tā kàn tā ài'rén de zhàopiān kàn de rùshén

   He is entranced when he looks at a picture of his loved one.

4. 入学 **rùxué** start school, enter school

   什么 年龄 的孩子可以入学?

   Shénme niánlíng de háizi kěyǐ rùxué?

   At what age can children start school?

Helpful tips: The first stroke begins below the second stroke.

2 strokes

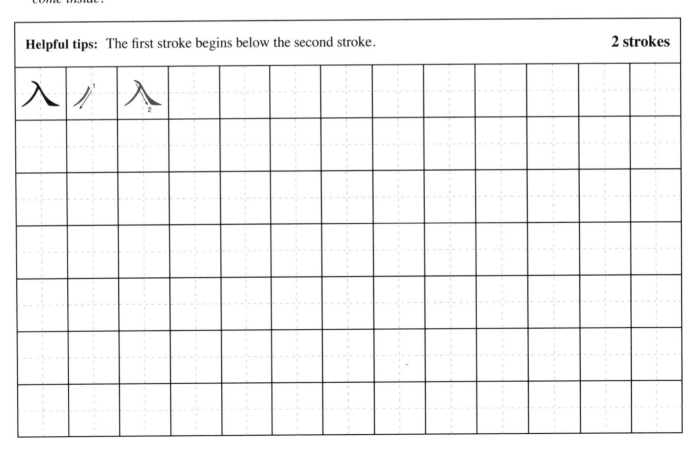

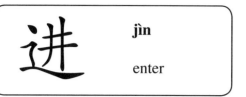

jìn

enter

進

Radical: 辶 # 38 "movement"

Compounds, sentences, and meanings

1. 进 **jìn** enter

   请 进！

   Qǐng jìn!

   Please come in!

2. 进来 **jìnlai** enter

   让 他进来。

   Ràng tā jìnlai.

   Let him come in.

3. 进行 **jìnxíng** be in progress

   工作 进行得 怎么样？

   Gōngzuò jìnxíngde zěnmeyàng?

   How are you getting on with your work?

4. 进步 **jìnbù** make progress

   你 写 汉字 很 有 进步。

   Nǐ xiě Hànzì hěn yǒu jìnbù.

   You are making great progress in your Chinese character writing.

5. 进出口 **jìnchūkǒu** import and export

   她 在一家 进出口 公司 工作。

   Tā zài yì jiā jìnchūkǒu gōngsī gōngzuò.

   She works in an import and export company.

Helpful tips: The left vertical stroke slants to the left.

7 strokes

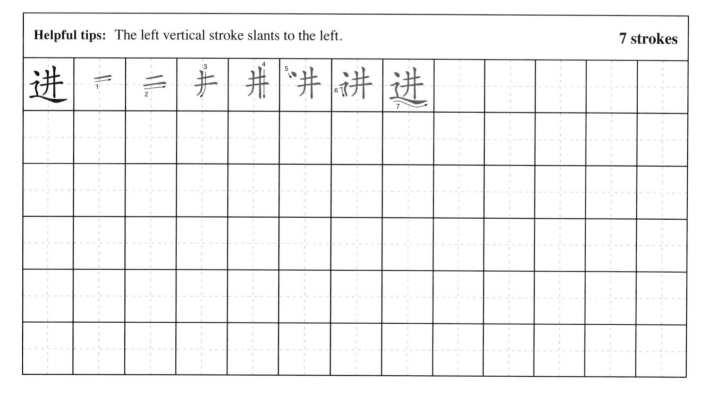

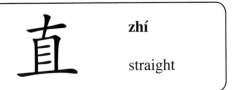

直　　zhí

straight

Radical: 十 # 11 "ten"

Compounds, sentences, and meanings

1. 直 **zhí** straight

   这里的 街道 又 宽 又 直。

   Zhèlǐ de jiēdào yòu kuān yòu zhí.

   The streets are wide and straight.

2. 一直 **yìzhí** all the way

   你 从 这儿一直 走 就 是 了。

   Nǐ cóng zhèr yìzhí zǒu jiù shì le.

   Go straight ahead and you'll be there.

3. 直到 **zhídào** until

   我 直到 昨晚 才 接到 通知。

   Wǒ zhídào zuówǎn cái jiēdào tōngzhī.

   I was not informed until last night.

4. 直接 **zhíjiē** direct

   你 应该 直接 跟 我 说。

   Nǐ yīnggāi zhíjiē gēn wǒ shuō.

   You should speak to me directly.

5. 直来直去 **zhílái-zhíqù** blunt, frank and outspoken

   她 是 个 直来 直去 的人， 说话

   Tā shì ge zhílái-zhíqù de rén, shuōhuà

   有口 无心。

   yǒukǒu-wúxīn.

   She's a blunt woman, often speaking sharply, but she means well.

Helpful tips: The three short horizontals are in the middle.								8 strokes

Lesson 34: Review Activities

A. Vocabulary Identification

Please identify each of the following movement terms based on the illustrations.

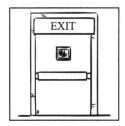  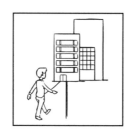  

_____ _____ _____ _____ _____

B. Sentence Completion

Please complete each of the following sentences with one of the movement terms provided. For each statement, be mindful of the grammatical differences between the various terms.

从　　　离　　　直　　　进　　　向

1. 请_____。请坐, 你要不要喝茶?

_____

2. 饭店在那里, _____右拐吧。

_____

3. 我想家人, 我_____他们太远啊!

_____

4. 你不可能_____这里走路到城市中心。

_____

5. 如果一个人不知道路线, 他会常常说"一_____走五分钟。"

_____

C. Route Description

Using the map, create a route that will go from the starting location (the school) back to your home. Then, based on the route created, accurately describe these locations and the different locations along the route.

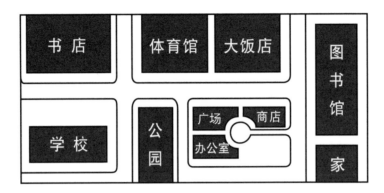

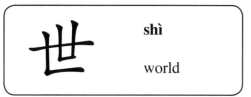

世

shì

world

Radical: 一 **# 2** "horizontal stroke"

Compounds, sentences, and meanings

1. 世 **shì** world

   北京 烤鸭举世 闻名。

   Běijīng kǎoyā jǔshì wénmíng.

   Beijing duck is world-famous.

2. 世故 **shìgù** ways of the world

   老 王 于世故。

   Lǎo Wáng yú shìgù.

   Wang is a man of the world.

3. 世纪 **shìjì** century

   现在 是二十一世纪的 开始。

   Xiànzài shì èrshíyī shìjì de kāishǐ.

   Now is the beginning of the twenty-first century.

4. 世界 **shìjiè** world

   他打破了男子一百米世界记录。

   Tā dǎpòle nánzi yìbǎi mǐ shìjiè jìlù.

   He broke the men's 100 meter world record.

5. 世上 **shìshàng** in the world

   世上 无 难事,只怕 有心人。

   Shìshàng wú nánshì, zhǐ pà yǒuxīnrén.

   Nothing in the world is difficult if you set your mind to it.

Helpful tips: Each vertical stroke should be evenly spaced.											**5 strokes**

世 一 十 卅 世 世

界

jiè

boundary

Radical: 田 # 119 "field"

Compounds, sentences, and meanings

1. 界 **jiè** boundary

   山西 和 陕西 以 黄河 为界。
   Shānxī hé Shǎnxī yǐ Huánghé wéi jiè.
   The boundary between Shanxi and Shaanxi is the Yellow River.

2. 眼界 **yǎnjiè** field of vision

   这个 展览 使 我们 大 开 眼界。
   Zhè ge zhǎnlǎn shǐ wǒmen dà kāi yǎnjiè.
   This exhibition has been a real eye-opener.

3. 外界 **wàijiè** external world, outside

   我们 应该 向 外界 征求 意见。
   Wǒmen yīnggāi xiàng wàijiè zhēngqiú yìjiàn.
   We should seek comments and suggestions from external sources.

4. 界限 **jièxiàn** dividing line

   朋友 之 间 界限 最好 不要
   Péngyou zhī jiān jièxiàn zuìhǎo búyào
   分得太 清。
   fēnde tài qīng.
   Among friends, it is best that limits are not too rigid.

5. 新闻界 **xīnwénjiè** press circles

   今天 的 会议 邀请了 新闻界 人士
   Jīntiān de huìyì yāoqǐngle xīnwénjiè rénshì
   参加。
   cānjiā.
   People from the press were invited to today's meeting.

Helpful tips: The eighth stroke ends with a sweep to the left.									**9 strokes**
界									

旅

lǚ

travel; journey

Radical: 方 # 74 "direction"

Compounds, sentences, and meanings

1. 旅 lǚ travel

   这次 北京 之旅 愉快 吗?

   Zhè cì Běijīng zhī lǚ yúkuài ma?

   Did you enjoy your trip to Beijing?

2. 旅程 lǚchéng route, itinerary

   去 中国 的 旅程 你 安排好了吗?

   Qù Zhōngguó de lǚchéng nǐ ānpáihǎo le ma?

   Have you arranged the itinerary for your China trip?

3. 旅馆 lǚguǎn hotel

   这家 旅馆离市区 比较 远。

   Zhè jiā lǚguǎn lí shìqū bǐjiào yuǎn.

   This hotel is quite a distance from the city.

4. 旅途 lǚtú journey

   祝你旅途愉快!

   Zhù nǐ lǚtú yúkuài!

   Bon voyage!

5. 旅行 lǚxíng travel

   假期里你打算 去哪儿旅行?

   Jiàqīli nǐ dǎsuàn qù nǎr lǚxíng?

   Where do you plan to go for your holidays?

| Helpful tips: The last stroke tapers off. | | | | | | | | | | **10 strokes** |

旅	`	二	亍	方	方	方	方	旅	旅	旅		

游　yóu

swim; tour

遊

(for meanings associated with "tour, travel")

Radical: 氵 # 32 "3 drops of water"

Compounds, sentences, and meanings

1. 游 **yóu** swim

   这 条 河 太 宽，我 游 不 过去。

   Zhè tiáo hé tài kuān, wǒ yóu bu guòqu.

   This river is too wide, I can't swim across it.

2. 游泳 **yóuyǒng** swim

   夏天 很多 人 去 海边 游泳。

   Xiàtiān hěnduō rén qù hǎibian yóuyǒng.

   Many people go to the seaside to swim in summer.

3. 游戏 **yóuxì** game

   孩子们 喜欢 玩 游戏。

   Háizimen xǐhuan wán yóuxì.

   Children love to play games.

4. 游人 **yóurén** tourist, traveler

   游人 止步。

   Yóurén zhǐbù

   No entrance. (literally, travelers stop)

5. 游览 **yóulǎn** go sight-seeing

   明天 我们 去 游览 故宫。

   Míngtiān wǒmen qù yóulǎn Gùgōng.

   Tomorrow we are touring the Imperial Palace.

Helpful tips: The last stroke of 氵 goes up.											12 strokes
游											

假

jiǎ/jià

false/holiday

Radical: 亻 # 19 "upright person"

Compounds, sentences, and meanings

1. **假 jiǎ** fake

   以 假 乱 真。
   Yǐ jiǎ luàn zhēn
   Create confusion by passing off the fake as genuine.

2. **假造 jiǎzào** counterfeit

   这 张 钞票 是 假造 的。
   Zhè zhāng chāopiào shì jiǎzào de.
   This is a forged banknote.

3. **假如 jiǎrú** if, supposing

   假如 我 忘 了, 请 提醒 我。
   Jiǎrú wǒ wàng le, qǐng tíxǐng wǒ.
   Please remind me if I forget.

4. **假期 jiàqī** holiday

   假期 你 想 到 哪儿 去 玩儿?
   Jiàqī nǐ xiǎng dào nǎr qù wánr?
   Where would you like to go for your holidays?

5. **请假 qǐngjià** ask for leave

   她 请 病假 回家 了。
   Tā qǐng bìngjià huíjiā le.
   She's gone home sick.

Helpful tips: Each of the three character components should be evenly balanced. **11 strokes**

先 **xiān**

first

Radical: 儿 # 21 "child"

Compounds, sentences, and meanings

1. 先 **xiān** first

   他 比 我 先 到。

   Tā bǐ wǒ xiān dào.

   He arrived before me.

2. 先后 **xiānhòu** priority

   这些 事 都 该 办, 不过 得 有 个 先后。

   Zhèxiē shì dōu gāi bàn, búguò děi yǒu ge xiānhòu.

   All these matters should be tackled, but they should be taken up in order of priority.

3. 先前 **xiānqián** previously

   这 孩子 比 先前 高 多 了。

   Zhè háizi bǐ xiānqián gāo duō le.

   This child is much taller than before.

4. 先生 **xiānsheng** mister, gentleman

   女士们, 先生们。

   Nǚshìmen, xiānshengmen.

   Ladies and gentlemen.

5. 先头 **xiāntóu** formerly

   你 先头 没 说过 这 件 事。

   Nǐ xiāntóu méi shuōguo zhè jiàn shì.

   You didn't mention this before.

Helpful tips: The last stroke is a vertical-bend-hook.   **6 strokes**

先	ノ	上	牛	生	先	先					

rán

right, correct

Radical: 灬 # 71 "fire"

Compounds, sentences, and meanings

1. 然 **rán** right, correct

   他 不 以 为 然。

   Tā bù yǐ wéi rán.

   He doesn't think so.

2. 然而 **rán'ér** but, however

   这 篇 文章 写得 不错, 然而

   Zhè piān wénzhāng xiěde búcuò, rán'ér

   还 可以 改进。

   hái kěyǐ gǎijìn.

   The essay is all right, but there is room for improvement.

3. 果然 **guǒrán** sure enough

   他 说 要 下雪, 果然 就 下 了。

   Tā shuō yào xiàxuě, guǒrán jiù xià le.

   He said it would snow, and sure enough it did.

4. 然后 **ránhòu** then, afterwards

   我们 看了 一 场 电影, 然后 就

   Wǒmen kànle yì chǎng diànyǐng, ránhòu jiù

   回家 了。

   huíjiā le.

   We saw a movie, and after that we went home.

5. 忽然 **hūrán** suddenly

   我 正 要 出去, 忽然 下起 大雨 来了。

   Wǒ zhèng yào chūqu, hūrán xiàqǐ dàyǔ lái le.

   I was about to go out when suddenly it started to rain heavily.

Helpful tips: The top left component slants slightly to the left.											**12 strokes**
然	丿	夕	夕	夕	夕	外	然	然	然	然	然	然

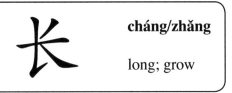

CHARACTER 378

Traditional Form

长　cháng/zhǎng
long; grow

長

Radical: ノ # 4 "downward-left stroke"

Compounds, sentences, and meanings

1. 长 cháng long
   这 条 河 很 长。
   Zhè tiáo hé hěn cháng.
   This river is quite long.

2. 长处 chángchù strong points
   她 有 很多 长处。
   Tā yǒu hěnduō chángchù.
   She has many good qualities.

3. 长大 zhǎngdà grow up
   他们的 孩子 长大 了。
   Tāmende háizi zhǎngdà le.
   Their children have grown up.

4. 长辈 zhǎngbèi elder, senior
   对 长辈 要 有 礼貌。
   Duì zhǎngbèi yào yǒu lǐmào.
   Show respect for one's elders.

5. 长江 Chángjiāng the Yangtze river (literally, long river)
   长江 是世界第三 长 河。
   Chángjiāng shì shìjiè dìsān cháng hé.
   The Yangtze is the third longest river in the world.

Helpful tips: Write the downward-right stroke last.　　　**4 strokes**

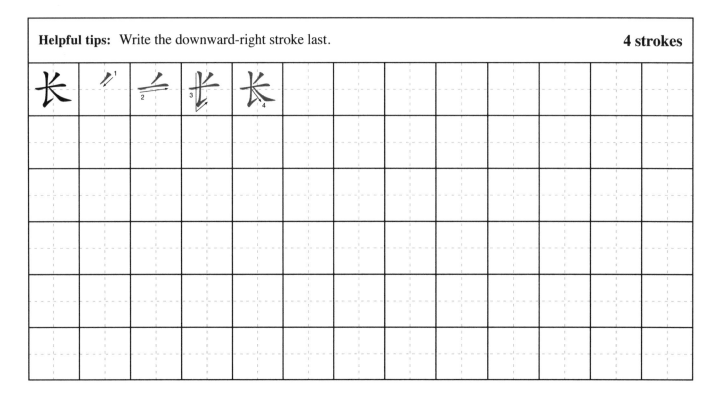

短

duǎn

short, brief

Radical: 矢 # 123 "arrow"

Compounds, sentences, and meanings

1. 短 **duǎn** short

   她的头发 很 短。

   Tā de tóufa hěn duǎn.

   Her hair is very short.

2. 短期 **duǎnqī** a short time

   你的 办法 只 有 短期 的 好处。

   Nǐ de bànfǎ zhǐ yǒu duǎnqī de hǎochu.

   Your method only has the benefit of being quick.

3. 短浅 **duǎnqiǎn** lacking, shallow

   小 孩子的 生活 经历比较 短浅。

   Xiǎo háizi de shēnghuó jīnglì bǐjiào duǎnqiǎn.

   The life experience of small children is comparatively shallow.

4. 长短 **chángduǎn** length

   这 件 裤子很 好看, 裤子 长短

   zhè jiàn kùzi hěn hǎokàn, kùzi chángduǎn

   好吗?

   hǎoma?

   These pants are nice, is the length okay?

5. 短处 **duǎnchù** shortcoming

   每 个 人 都 有自己的 短处。

   Měi ge rén dōu yǒu zìjǐ de duǎnchù.

   Everyone has their own shortcomings.

Helpful tips: The height of the two components should be equal.											**12 strokes**
短	⼁	⼆	⼷	矢	矢	矢	矢	矩	矩	短	短

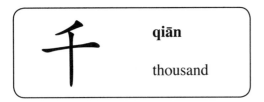

千 qiān

thousand

Radical: 丿 # 4 "downward-left stroke"

Compounds, sentences, and meanings

1. **千 qiān** thousand

   这 是 一千 块 钱，请 你 点一点。

   Zhè shì yìqiān kuài qián, qǐng nǐ diǎnyidiǎn.

   This is altogether 1,000 dollars, please check it.

2. **千里 qiānlǐ** a long distance (literally, a thousand miles)

   千里 之 行, 始于 足 下。

   Qiānlǐ zhī xíng, shǐ yú zú xià.

   A thousand-li journey begins with the first step.

3. **千万 qiānwàn** be sure to

   千万 要 小心 啊！

   Qiānwàn yào xiǎoxīn a!

   Do be careful!

4. **千方百计 qiānfāng-bǎijì** in a thousand and one ways

   他 千方 百计地 请 好 大夫 看病。

   Tā qiānfāng-bǎijì de qǐng hǎo dàifu kànbìng.

   He goes all out to find good doctors to treat his illness.

5. **千篇一律 qiān piān yí lù** following the same pattern

   那些 文章 千 篇 一律, 没有

   Nàxiē wénzhāng qiān piān yí lù, méiyǒu

   什么 新 东西。

   shénme xīn dōngxi.

   Those articles are like the rest; they offer nothing new.

Helpful tips: The top stroke sweeps down to the left.　　　　　**3 strokes**

千	⺄¹	⼆₂	千₃								

万

wàn

ten thousand

萬

Radical: 一 # 2 "horizontal stroke"

Compounds, sentences, and meanings

1. 万 **wàn** ten thousand

   买 一 辆 小 汽车 要 八 万 元。

   Mǎi yì liàng xiǎo qìchē yào bā wàn yuán.

   It costs ¥80,000 to buy a small car.

2. 百万 **bǎiwàn** million

   她 想 嫁给 百万 富翁。

   Tā xiǎng jià gěi bǎiwàn fùwēng.

   She wants to marry a millionaire.

3. 一千万 **yì qiānwàn** 10 million

   北京 的 人口 超过 一千万。

   Běijīng de rénkǒu chāoguò yìqiānwàn.

   Beijing's population exceeds 10 million.

4. 万事 **wànshì** all things

   万事 起头 难。

   Wànshì qǐtóu nán.

   Everything is difficult in the beginning.

5. 万一 **wànyī** just in case

   万一 有 人 找 我, 就 请 他 留 个 条。

   Wànyī yǒu rén zhǎo wǒ, jiù qǐng tā liú ge tiáo.

   If someone looks for me, please ask him to leave a message.

| Helpful tips: The last stroke ends with a hook. | | | | | | | | | | 3 strokes |

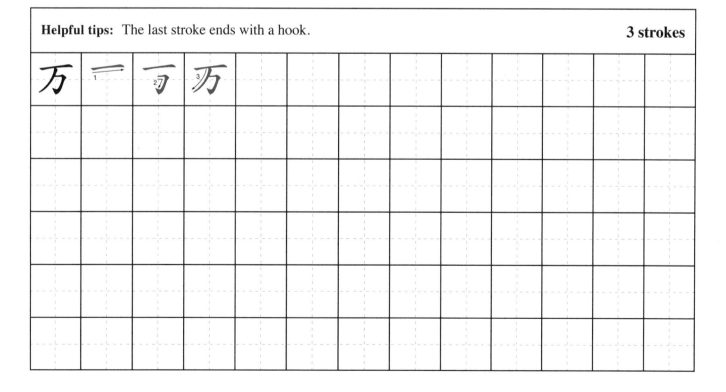

Lesson 35: Review Activities

A. Vocabulary Identification

Please identify eight countries on the map. Then, provide the Chinese characters for the countries' names.

1. _____

2. _____

3. _____

4. _____

5. _____

6. _____

7. _____

8. _____

B. Sentence Completion and Translation

Please complete each of the following sentences with one of the number words provided. Then, translate the resulting sentence into English.

一　　　十　　　百　　　千　　　万

1. _____言万语也不能形容一幅好的画。

_____

2. 天天做的事，_____来二去地也就变成习惯了。

_____

3. 好老师_____问不烦。

_____

4. 一个有道德的人_____夫莫当。

_____

5. 水灾之后地区_____室九空。

_____

C. Short Description

Consider the following topic and create a short discussion. Your discussion should demonstrate clear expression of order of events.

你的学校放很长的暑假，你可以选很多地方去旅游。你要去哪个国家旅游，要去哪个城市？

_____

_____

_____

_____

_____

_____

_____

飞　fēi

fly

飛

Radical: 飞 # 5 "horizontal-slanting-hook"

Compounds, sentences, and meanings

1. 飞 **fēi** fly

   我 从 北京 直飞 广州。

   Wǒ cóng Běijīng zhí fēi Guǎngzhōu.

   I'm flying directly from Beijing to Guangzhou.

2. 飞机 **fēijī** airplane

   飞机很 快 就要 着陆 了。

   Fēijī hěn kuài jiù yào zhuólù le.

   The plane will be landing soon.

3. 飞快 **fēikuài** very fast

   汽车以飞快 的速度 前进。

   Qìchē yǐ fēikuài de sùdù qiánjìn.

   The car is going at a breakneck speed.

4. 飞速 **fēisù** at full speed

   中国 的经济 正在 飞速 发展。

   Zhōngguó de jīngjì zhèngzài fēisù fāzhǎn.

   The Chinese economy is developing rapidly.

5. 飞机场 **fēijīchǎng** airport

   最好 提前 两 个 钟头 到 飞机场。

   Zuìhǎo tíqián liǎng ge zhōngtóu dào fēijīchǎng.

   It's a good idea to get to the airport two hours before the flight.

Helpful tips: The first stroke ends with a hook.										3 strokes
飞	飞	飞	飞							

jī

machine; opportunity

機

Radical: 木 # 81 "tree"

Compounds, sentences, and meanings

1. 机 **jī** opportunity

   机不可失, 时不再来。
   Jī bù kě shī, shí bú zài lái.
   Opportunity only knocks once.

2. 机动 **jīdòng** motorized

   我 买了 一 辆 机动 自行车。
   Wǒ mǎile yí liàng jīdòng zìxíngchē.
   I bought a moped.

3. 机会 **jīhuì** opportunity

   能 有机会去 中国 旅行就 好了。
   Néng yǒu jīhuì qù Zhōngguó lǚxíng jiù hǎo le.
   It would be wonderful if I could visit China.

4. 机器 **jīqì** machine

   这 是 什么 机器?
   Zhè shì shénme jīqì?
   What kind of machine is this?

5. 机灵 **jīlíng** clever

   这个人 办事 挺 机灵 的。
   Zhè ge rén bànshì tǐng jīlíng de.
   This person manages things quite cleverly.

Helpful tips: The last stroke ends with a hook.　　**6 strokes**

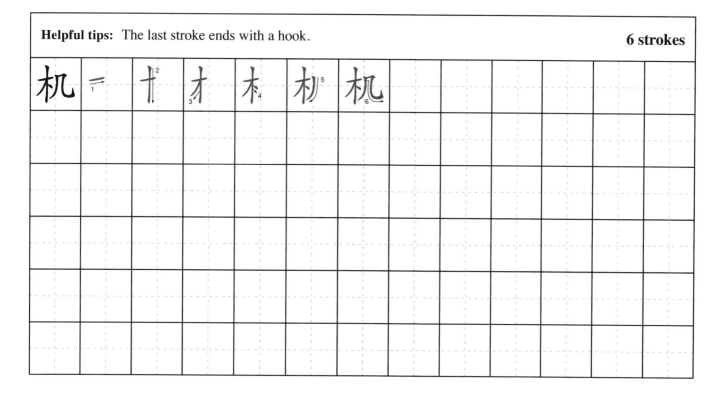

场　cháng/chǎng

[measure word]/field

場

Radical: 土 # 40 "earth"

Compounds, sentences, and meanings

1. 场 **cháng** [measure word]

昨晚 下了一 场 大雨。

Zuówǎn xiàle yì cháng dà yǔ.

It rained heavily last night.

2. 广场 **guǎngchǎng** public square

天安门　广场　在 北京市　中心。

Tiān'ānmén Guǎngchǎng zài Běijīngshì zhōngxīn.

Tiananmen Square is in the center of Beijing.

3. 商场 **shāngchǎng** arcade/commercial bazaar

商场　里面 有　小吃店。

Shāngchǎng lǐmiàn yǒu xiǎochīdiàn.

There are snack bars in the arcade.

4. 剧场 **jùchǎng** theater

今晚　剧场 有 杂技 表演。

Jīnwǎn jùchǎng yǒu zájì biǎoyǎn.

There's an acrobatic performance at the theater tonight.

5. 市场 **shìchǎng** market

他们 去　市场 买 东西 了。

Tāmen qù shìchǎng mǎi dōngxi le.

They went shopping at the market.

Helpful tips: The fourth stroke has 3 bends, ending with a hook.　　　　**6 strokes**

场	一	圠	土	圬	场	场					

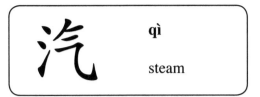

qì

steam

Radical: 氵 # 32 "3 drops of water"

Compounds, sentences, and meanings

1. 汽 **qì** vapor

   汽船 用 蒸汽 开动。
   Qìchuán yòng zhēngqì kāidòng.
   Steamships are driven by steam.

2. 汽油 **qìyóu** gasoline

   最近 汽油 涨价 了。
   Zuìjìn qìyóu zhǎngjià le.
   Recently the price of gasoline has risen.

3. 汽水 **qìshuǐ** soft drinks

   这 是 什么 汽水?
   Zhè shì shénme qìshuǐ?
   What is this soft drink?

4. 汽车 **qìchē** automobile

   路上 有 很多 汽车。
   Lùshang yǒu hěnduō qìchē.
   There are lots of cars on the road.

5. 汽船 **qìchuán** steamship

   现在 很少 有 汽船 了。
   Xiànzài hěnshǎo yǒu qìchuán le.
   Nowadays steamships are rare.

Helpful tips: The last stroke ends in a hook.   **7 strokes**

汽	丶	冫	氵	汒	汽	汽	汽				

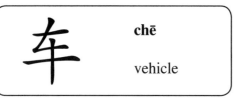

車 chē

vehicle

車

Radical: 车 # 84 "vehicle"

Compounds, sentences, and meanings

1. 车 chē vehicle

   路上 有 很多 车。

   Lùshang yǒu hěnduō chē.

   There are many vehicles on the road.

2. 车费 chēfèi (passenger's) fare

   到 颐和园 的 车费 多少?

   Dào Yíhéyuán de chēfèi duōshao?

   How much is the fare to the Summer Palace?

3. 火车 huǒchē train

   中国 的 火车 比较 慢。

   Zhōngguó de huǒchē bǐjiào màn.

   Trains in China are rather slow.

4. 公共气车 gōnggòngqìchē bus

   中国 的 公共汽车 很挤。

   Zhōngguó de gōnggòngqìchē hěn jǐ.

   Buses in China are packed.

5. 车祸 chēhuò traffic accident

   前面 好像 发生了 车祸。

   Qiánmian hǎoxiàng fāshēngle chēhuò.

   It seems that there's an accident ahead.

Helpful tips: The last stroke doesn't meet the top horizontal stroke.										**4 strokes**
车	一	左	车	车						

火

huǒ

fire

Radical: 火 # 75 "fire"

Compounds, sentences, and meanings

1. 火 **huǒ** fire

   不要 让 小孩子 玩火。

   Búyào ràng xiǎoháizi wánhuǒ.

   Don't let children play with fire.

2. 火车 **huǒchē** train

   她 明天 坐 火车 去西安。

   Tā míngtiān zuò huǒchē qù Xī'ān.

   She will be taking a train to Xian tomorrow.

3. 火柴 **huǒchái** matches

   请问, 有 没有 火柴?

   Qǐngwèn, yǒu méiyǒu huǒchái?

   Excuse me, do you have a match?

4. 火候 **huǒhou** duration and degree of heating

   炒菜 的 时候, 掌握 火候 很

   Chǎocài de shíhou, zhǎngwò huǒhou hěn

   重要。

   zhòngyào.

   Heat control is very important in stir-frying.

5. 火气 **huǒqì** temper

   他的 火气 很 大。

   Tāde huǒqì hěn dà.

   He has a bad temper.

Helpful tips: The last stroke tapers off.   **4 strokes**

火	丶	丷	少	火								

站

zhàn

stand

Radical: 立 # 111 "stand"

Compounds, sentences, and meanings

1. 站 **zhàn** train/bus stop

   我 下 个 站 下车。

   Wǒ xià ge zhàn xiàchē.

   I get off at the next stop.

2. 火车站 **huǒchēzhàn** train station

   我 家 离 火车站 不 远。

   Wǒ jiā lí huǒchēzhàn bù yuǎn.

   My house is not far from the railway station.

3. 站立 **zhànlì** be on one's feet

   他 腿 疼, 不能 站立。

   Tā tuǐ téng, bùnéng zhànlì.

   His leg was so sore that he couldn't stand up.

4. 站稳 **zhànwěn** come to a stop

   等 车 站稳了 再 下。

   Děng chē zhànwěnle zài xià.

   Wait till the bus/train stops completely before getting out.

5. 站住 **zhànzhù** stop, halt

   风 刮 得 人 都 站不住 了。

   Fēng guāde rén dōu zhànbuzhù le.

   The wind was so strong that you could hardly stand.

Helpful tips: The fifth stroke lifts slightly.									10 strokes
站	丶	亠	亠	立	立	壮	站	站	站

船

chuán

boat, ship

Radical: 舟 # 149 "boat"

Compounds, sentences, and meanings

1. 船 **chuán** boat, ship

   可以 坐 船 去 大连。

   Kěyǐ zuò chuán qù Dàlián.

   One can get to Dalian by ship.

2. 船票 **chuánpiào** steamer ticket

   我 预订 去 大连 的 船票。

   Wǒ yùdìng qù Dàlián de chuánpiào.

   I'd like to book a passage to Dalian.

3. 帆船 **fānchuán** sailing boat

   海湾 里有 很多 帆船。

   Hǎiwān lǐ yǒu hěnduō fānchuán.

   There are lots of sailing boats in the harbor.

4. 货船 **huòchuán** cargo ship

   现在 的 货船 很 大。

   Xiànzài de huòchuán hěn dà.

   Modern cargo ships are very big.

5. 客船 **kèchuán** oceanliner

   这 是 六星级的 豪华 客船。

   Zhè shì liùxīngjí de háohuá kèchuán.

   This is a 6-star luxury oceanliner.

Helpful tips: The eighth stroke is a horizontal-bend-vertical-bend.											*11 strokes*
船	⸌¹	⺁₂	⺇₃	月₄	甪₅	舟₆	舟⁷	舟⁸	船₉	船₁₀	船₁₁

票   piào

ticket

Radical: 西 # 139 "west" or 示 # 114 "show"

Compounds, sentences, and meanings

1. 票 **piào** ticket

你买了 火车票 没有?

Nǐ mǎile huǒchēpiào méiyǒu?

Have you bought your train ticket?

2. 票房 **piàofáng** box office

这个 电影 打破了今年 的 票房

Zhè ge diànyǐng dǎpòle jīnnián de piàofáng

记录。

jìlù.

This movie has smashed this year's box office record.

3. 票价 **piàojià** price of ticket

音乐会 的 票价 是 多少?

Yīnyuèhuì de piàojià shì duōshao?

What's the price of a ticket to the concert?

4. 绑票 **bǎngpiào** kidnap (for ransom)

他的儿子被 绑票了。

Tāde érzi bèi bǎngpiàole.

His son was held for ransom.

5. 投票 **tóupiào** vote

这 是 无记名 投票。

Zhè shì wújìmíng tóupiào.

This is a secret ballot.

Helpful tips: The second horizontal stroke of 示 is longer.										**11 strokes**
票	一	一	一	西	西	西	西	西	票	票	票

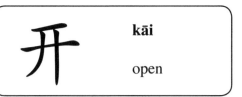

kāi

open

開

Radical: 一 # 2 "horizontal stroke" or 廾 # 44 "bottom of 开"

Compounds, sentences, and meanings

1. 开 **kāi** open

   这 把 钥匙 开不了 这 个 锁。

   Zhè bǎ yàoshi kāibuliǎo zhè ge suǒ.

   This key doesn't open this lock.

2. 开车 **kāichē** drive or start a vehicle

   快 开车了, 大家 上车 吧。

   Kuài kāchē le, dàjiā shàngchē ba.

   The bus is going to start. Hurry up, everybody.

3. 开放 **kāifàng** open to public use

   星期天 图书馆 照常 开放。

   Xīngqītiān túshūguǎn zhàocháng kāifàng.

   The library is always open on Sundays.

4. 开口 **kāikǒu** start to talk

   没 等 我 开口, 他就 抢先 替我

   Méi děng wǒ kāikǒu, tā jiù qiǎngxiān tì wǒ

   说 了。

   shuō le.

   Before I could open my mouth, he jumped in and spoke on my behalf.

5. 开始 **kāishǐ** begin

   舞会 什么 时候 开始?

   Wǔhuì shénme shíhou kāishǐ?

   What time does the dance start?

Helpful tips: The first left vertical stroke of 开 ends with a sweep to the left.   **4 strokes**

开	一	二	开	开							

chéng

ride, be a passenger

Radical: 丿 # 4 "downward-left stroke"

Compounds, sentences, and meanings

1. 乘车 **chéngchē** ride in a vehicle

   欧洲 人 习惯 乘 火车 旅游。

   Ōuzhōu rén xíguàn chéng huŏchē lǚyóu.

   Europeans have the habit of riding trains on trips.

2. 乘客 **chéngkè** passenger

   这 辆 汽车可以 有 五个 乘客。

   Zhè liàng qìchē kěyǐ yǒu wǔ ge chéngkè.

   This car can have five passengers.

3. 乘机 **chéngjī** seize an opportunity

   父母 不在 的 时候, 孩子 乘机 开 派对。

   Fùmǔ búzài de shíhou, hàizi chéngjī kāi pàiduì.

   When parents aren't around their children seize the opportunity to throw a party.

Helpful tips: The vertical stroke should not be noticeably longer than the left and right downward sweeping strokes.										10 strokes	
乘	二¹	二²	千³	千⁴	千⁵	乖⁶	乖⁷	乖⁸	乘⁹	乘¹⁰	

Lesson 36: Review Activities

A. Vocabulary Identification and Pronunciation

Please identify each of the following vocabulary terms by sketching a small illustration. Then provide the *pinyin* for each of the vocabulary terms.

汉字/拼音	画	汉字/拼音	画	汉字/拼音	画
汽车		飞机		火车	
船		自行车			

B. Answer Selection

In the chart below, mark *X*'s to indicate for each of the following modes of transportation how one would travel by that mode of transportation. If one does not drive the given mode of transportation, indicate if a ticket is necessary.

	开	乘	要票		开	乘	要票
汽车				马车			
出租汽车				地铁			
飞机				自行车			
火车				公共汽车			

C. Location Comparison

Create a comparison between the two locations provided. Attempt to describe both what is similar between the two locations and what is different between the two.

比一比火车站和飞机场，它们有什么地方不一样？

_____

_____

_____

_____

_____

_____

_____

_____

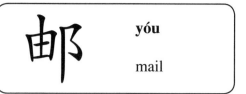

yóu

mail

郵

Radical: 阝 # 28 "right earlobe"

Compounds, sentences, and meanings

1. 邮 **yóu** mail

我 上 月 给 家里 邮 去了 一千 元。

Wǒ shàng yuè gěi jiālǐ yóu qù le yìqiān yuán.

I sent 1,000 yuan home last month.

2. 邮包 **yóubāo** postal parcel

你 觉得 需要 买 邮包 保险 吗?

Nǐ juéde xūyào mǎi yóubāo bǎoxiǎn ma?

Do you think postal insurance is necessary?

3. 邮递员 **yóudìyuán** postman

今天 邮递员 来过 没有?

Jīntiān yóudìyuán láiguo méiyǒu?

Has the postman been by today?

4. 邮寄 **yóujì** send by mail

我 想 邮寄 书籍。

Wǒ xiǎng yóujì shūjí.

I'd like to post these books.

5. 邮票 **yóupiào** stamp

寄 美国 的 明信片 要 贴

Jì Měiguó de míngxìnpiàn yào tiē

多少 邮票?

duōshao yóupiào?

What's the postage on a postcard to the United States?

Helpful tips: Each of the two character components should be evenly balanced.

7 strokes

邮	丨	冂	冃	曲	由	由3	邮				

局

jú

bureau

Radical: 尸 # 61 "dwelling"

Compounds, sentences, and meanings

1. 局 **jú** game, set, innings

   第一局 谁 赢了?

   Dìyī jú shéi yíng le?

   Who won the first set?

2. 局部 **júbù** part

   局部地区 下雪。

   Júbù dìqū xiàxuě.

   It snows in some places.

3. 邮局 **yóujú** post office

   邮局 里面 有 公用 电话。

   Yóujú lǐmiàn yǒu gōngyòng diànhuà.

   There are public phones inside the post office.

4. 局势 **júshì** situation

   最近 国际局势不太 稳定。

   Zuìjìn guójì júshì bú tài wěndìng.

   The international situation has been very unstable lately.

5. 公安局 **gōng'ānjú** police station

   公安局 就 是 警察局。

   Gōng'ānjú jiù shì jǐngchájú.

   The Public Security Bureau is the same as the Police.

Helpful tips: The fourth stroke is a horizontal-bend-hook.										**7 strokes**
局	一	弓	尸	局	局	局	局			

安 **ān**

peaceful, tranquil, stable

Radical: 宀 # 34 "roof"

Compounds, sentences, and meanings

1. 安静 **ānjìng** calm, still, peaceful

   老人 都 喜欢 安静 的 地方。

   Lǎorén dōu xǐhuan ānjìng de dìfang.

   Elderly people all enjoy peaceful places.

2. 安全 **ānquán** safety, security

   电影 院 有 很 多 安全 出口。

   Diànyǐng yuàn yǒu hěn duō ānquán chūkǒu.

   Movie theaters have many emergency exits.

3. 平安 **píng'ān** serene, safe, secure

   我 希望 一生 平安。

   Wǒ xīwàng yìshēng píng'ān.

   I wish to have a life of peace and serenity.

4. 安心 **ānxīn** carefree

   星期六， 工人 可以 安心 休息。

   Xīngqīliù, gōngrén kěyǐ ānxīn xiūxi.

   On Saturdays, workers can rest without concerns.

5. 安危 **ānwēi** safety

   要是 孩子 还没 回家 父母 担心 小

   Yàoshì háizi háiméi huíjiā fùmǔ dānxīn xiǎo

   孩子 的 安危。

   háizi de ānwēi.

   If their children still haven't returned home, parents worry for the safety of their children.

Helpful tips: The final stroke should be longer than the radical. **6 strokes**

安	丶	丷	宀	㝉	安	安					

mén

[measure word]; door

門

Radical: 门 # 37 "door"

Compounds, sentences, and meanings

1. 门 **mén** [measure word]

她 在 学校 里 门门 功课 都 很 好。

Tā zài xuéxiào lǐ ménmén gōngkè dōu hěn hǎo.

She does well in every subject at school.

2. 门口 **ménkǒu** entrance

我 在 门口 等候。

Wǒ zài ménkǒu děnghòu.

I'll wait at the gate.

3. 门牌 **ménpái** street number; house number

你家 门牌 几号?

Nǐ jiā ménpái jǐ hào?

What's the number of your house?

4. 门路 **ménlù** social connections (Literally, doors and roads)

办 这 种 事,他 有 门路。

Bàn zhè zhǒng shì, tā yǒu ménlù.

He knows where to go to get this kind of job done.

5. 门外汉 **ménwàihàn** layman

对于 美术, 我 是 门外汉。

Duìyú měishù, wǒ shì ménwàihàn.

Where the fine arts are concerned, I am only a layman.

Helpful tips: The final stroke should end in a hook.										**3 strokes**

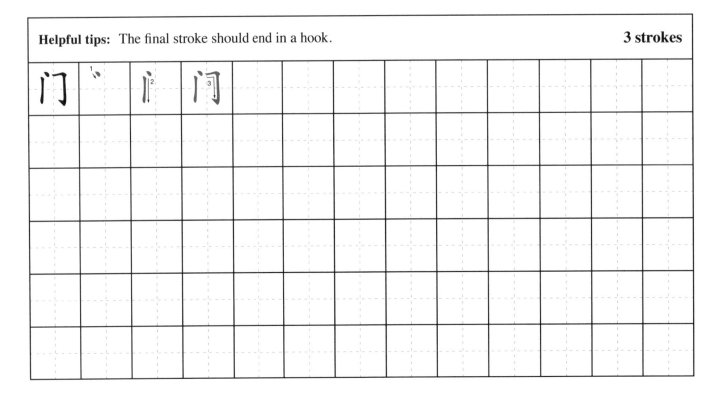

厕   cè

lavatory

厠

Radical: 厂 # 12 "building"

Compounds, sentences, and meanings

1. 厕 **cè** toilet

   如厕 后 请 冲水。

   Rúcè hòu qǐng chōngshuǐ.

   Please flush the toilet after use.

2. 厕所 **cèsuǒ** toilet

   这里的厕所 很 干净。

   Zhèlǐ de cèsuǒ hěn gānjìng.

   The toilets here are quite clean.

3. 女厕 **nǔcè** ladies' toilet

   女厕要 排队。

   Nǔcè yào páiduì.

   You have to queue for the women's toilet.

4. 坐厕 **zuòcè** seated toilet

   坐厕比 蹲厕 舒服。

   Zuòcè bǐ dūncè shūfu.

   It's more comfortable to sit than to squat when on the toilet.

Helpful tips: The first stroke is horizontal, the next is a downward sweep.   **8 strokes**

厕	一	厂	厂	厈	厔	厔	厕	厕				

带

dài

carry, bear; belt

带

Radical: 巾 # 52 "cloth"

Compounds, sentences, and meanings

1. 带 **dài** carry, bring

   旅游 的 时候, 你 带 行李 还是 背包?

   Lǚyóu de shíhou, nǐ dài xíngli háishì bēibāo?

   When traveling, do you bring luggage or a backpack?

2. 带子 **dàizi** belt

   这 条 带子 很 好看。

   Zhè tiáo dàizi hěn hǎokàn.

   This belt is very nice.

3. 带领 **dàilǐng** lead, guide

   去 很 远 的 地方 要 有 人 带领 你。

   Qù hěn yuǎn de dìfang yào yǒu rén dàilǐng nǐ.

   When going to a faraway place, someone should guide you.

4. 带头 **dàitóu** pioneer, start

   社会 需要 好人 带头 做 好事。

   Shèhuì xūyào hǎorén dàitóu zuò hǎoshì.

   Society needs good people to start doing good work.

Helpful tips: The vertical stroke does not cross the horizontal sixth stroke.   **9 strokes**

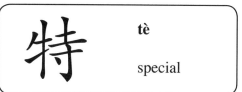

特　tè

special

Radical: 牛 # 95 "cattle"

Compounds, sentences, and meanings

1. 特 **tè** especially

   这 种 药 治咳嗽特灵。

   Zhè zhǒng yào zhì késou tè líng.

   This medicine is especially good for coughs.

2. 特长 **tècháng** special skill

   他 有 什么 特长?

   Tā yǒu shénme tècháng?

   What is he skilled in?

3. 特点 **tèdiǎn** special features

   日本菜 有 什么 特点?

   Rìběncài yǒu shénme tèdiǎn?

   What are the distinctive features of Japanese cooking?

4. 特色 **tèsè** characteristic

   这 是一个 富有 民族特色的 歌舞 节目。

   Zhè shì yí ge fùyǒu mínzú tèsè de gēwǔ jiémù.

   This musical performance is very characteristic of the ethnic group.

5. 特有 **tèyǒu** peculiar

   这 是 广东人 特有的一 种 说法。

   Zhè shì Guǎngdōngrén tèyǒu de yì zhǒng shuōfǎ.

   This is an expression peculiar to people from Guangdong.

Helpful tips: The seventh stroke is longer than the ones above and below it.　**10 strokes**

特	丿	느	牜	牛	牛	牜	特	特	特	特		

別　bié

other

Radical: 刂 # 15 "upright knife"

Compounds, sentences, and meanings

1. 别 **bié** don't
   别 忘 了。
   Bié wàng le.
   Don't forget.

2. 别的 **biéde** other
   还 要 别的 吗?
   Hái yào biéde ma?
   Would you like something else?

3. 别致 **biézhì** unique
   天坛 的 建筑 结构 非常 别致。
   Tiāntán de jiànzhù jiégòu fēicháng biézhì.
   The architecture of the Temple of Heaven is unique.

4. 别人 **biéren** other people
   认真 考虑 别人 的 意见。
   Rènzhēn kǎolù biéren de yìjiàn.
   Give other people's suggestions serious consideration.

5. 特别 **tèbié** special, peculiar
   他的 口音 很 特别。
   Tāde kǒuyīn hěn tèbié.
   He has a peculiar accent.

| **Helpful tips:** The last stroke is a vertical hook. | | | | | | **7 strokes** |

民   mín

people

Radical: 乙 # 5 "horizontal-bend"

Compounds, sentences, and meanings

1. 民 **mín** people

   连 年 内战, 民 不 聊 生。

   Lián nián nèizhàn mín bù liáo shēng.

   Years of civil war made life impossible for the people.

2. 人民 **rénmín** people

   中华   人民   共和国

   Zhōnghuá Rénmín Gònghéguó

   The People's Republic of China

3. 民歌 **mín'gē** folk songs

   《茉莉花》是 一 首 民歌。

   "Mòlìhuā" shì yì shǒu mín'gē.

   "Jasmine" is a folk song.

4. 民主 **mínzhǔ** democratic

   美国 是 一个 民主 国家。

   Měiguó shì yí ge mínzhǔ guójiā.

   The United States is a democratic country.

5. 民族 **mínzú** nation, ethnic group

   中国   是 一个 多 民族 国家。

   Zhōngguó shì yí ge duō mínzú guójiā.

   China is a multi-ethnic country.

Helpful tips: The last stroke is a slanting hook.											**5 strokes**
民	一	二	尸	民	民						

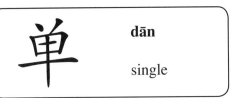

単 **dān**

single

Traditional Form

單

Radical: ` ` # 17 "inverted eight"

Compounds, sentences, and meanings

1. 单 **dān** only, alone

   不要 单 凭 热情 去 工作。

   Búyào dān píng rèqíng qù gōngzuò.

   In work, enthusiasm alone is not enough.

2. 单程 **dānchéng** one way

   我 只 买了 单程 票。

   Wǒ zhǐ mǎile dānchéng piào.

   I only bought a one-way ticket.

3. 单单 **dāndān** only

   别人 都 来 了, 单单 他 没 来。

   Biéren dōu lái le, dāndān tā méi lái.

   Everyone else is here. He's the only one missing.

4. 单独 **dāndú** alone

   我 要 和他 单独 谈一谈。

   Wǒ yào hé tē dāndú tányitán.

   I want to talk privately with him.

5. 单身 **dānshēn** single (not married)

   她 今年 虽然 三十八, 但 还 是 单身。

   Tā jīnnián suīrán sānshíbā, dàn hái shì dānshēn.

   Although she's 38, she's still single.

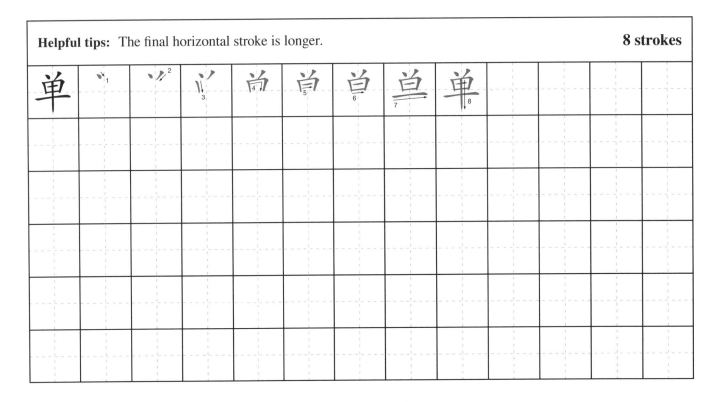

Helpful tips: The final horizontal stroke is longer.

8 strokes

Lesson 37: Review Activities

A. Pronunciation and *Pinyin* Practice

Please transcribe the following questions into *pinyin*. For additional practice, say and then respond to these questions aloud.

1. 对不起，厕所在哪儿？

_____

2. 请问，你的城市有没有公安局？

_____

3. 你在邮局可以买什么东西？

_____

B. Sentence Creation

Based on the map provided, accurately describe the location of each place given. Show your understanding of the multiple methods for describing location.

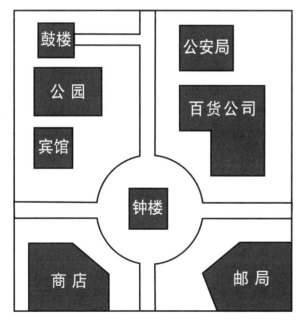

1. 邮局

_____

2. 宾馆

_____

3. 钟楼

_____

4. 公园

_____

5. 公安局

_____

C. Short Description

Please sketch an example of each item. Then describe the important features for each of the illustrations. A strong demonstration of understanding will note those features that are special for this particular example and what features are necessary for normal operation.

（手机）

_____

_____

_____

_____

（电视）

_____

_____

_____

_____

A. Vocabulary Identification

For each of the following locations, write the mode of transportation that you would take to get to that city. Then, in the space provided, also write the mode of transportation that you would then use when inside of that city.

中国   来：   英国   来：   美国   来：
北京   内：   伦敦   内：   纽约   内：

中国   来：   德国   来：   美国   来：
上海   内：   巴林   内：   洛杉矶   内：

B. Short Description

Using the map, describe a route to get from the starting location to the destination. Attempt to clearly express both the beginning and ending locations but also the other locations along the route.

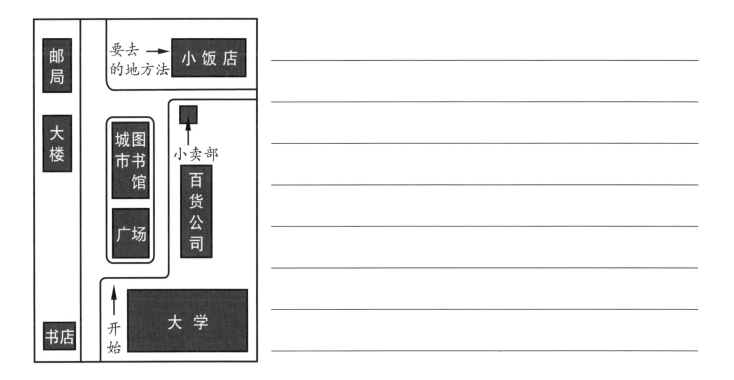

C. Travel Description

Consider the following topic. Then write a description that demonstrates an understanding of travel and expresses the different concerns of a trip. A strong description will express events and the order of those events, and it will express reasoning for the locations visited. Attempt to show strong use of specific conjunctions and other constructions that allow for effective connected discourse.

你的家人要去一个很有趣的旅游地方；对你来说，什么亚洲的地方人人都应该去旅游旅游？

_____

_____

_____

_____

_____

_____

_____

D. Reflective Questions

Use these questions to both check the expressiveness of the previous section and to confirm your understanding of the previous topic. For additional practice, say and then respond to these questions aloud.

请问，你常常去旅游，还是你喜欢留在家里休息？
你去过亚洲的城市吗？
哪个亚洲的城市很有名？
在很大的城市你可以做什么？
你要旅游很多国家，为什么？
从哪个国家开始旅游最好？
然后你要去别的城市，还是去自然环境的地方？
哪个亚洲的自然环境地方很有名？
人们都应该去长城吗？你去过吗？
你计划什么时候旅游亚洲？

yán

color; face

颜

Radical: 页 # 140 "page"

Compounds, sentences, and meanings

1. 颜 yán face

他 犯了 大 错误, 觉得 无 颜 见 人。
Tā fànle dà cuòwù, juéde wú yán jiàn rén.
He made a grave mistake and felt that he couldn't face people.

2. 颜面 yánmiàn face, prestige

说话 请 客气点儿, 要 顾全
Shuōhuà qǐng kèqi diǎnr, yào gùquán
他的 颜面。
tāde yánmiàn.
Please speak politely so that he doesn't lose face.

3. 颜料 yánliào pigment

这 是 天然 颜料。
Zhè shì tiānrán yánliào.
This is a natural pigment.

4. 颜色 yánsè color

你 最 喜欢 什么 颜色?
Nǐ zuì xǐhuan shénme yánsè?
What color do you like most?

5. 五颜六色 wǔyán-liùsè of various (or all) colors

五颜六色 的 云霞 真 好看。
Wǔyán-liùsè de yúnxiá zhēn hǎokàn.
The multi-colored clouds are really beautiful.

Helpful tips: The three strokes of 彡 taper down from right to left.

15 strokes

颜											
颜	颜	颜									

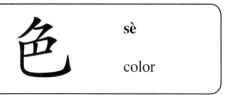

色   sè

color

Radical: 刀 # 30 "knife"

Compounds, sentences, and meanings

1. 色 **sè** color (as a suffix)

   这 道 菜色, 香, 味俱佳。

   Zhè dào cài sè, xiāng, wèi jù jiā.

   This dish looks good, smells good, and tastes good.

2. 色彩 **sècǎi** characteristic quality, flavor

   这 种 服装 富有 民族色彩。

   Zhè zhǒng fúzhuāng fùyǒu mínzú sècǎi.

   This costume is rich in ethnic flavor.

3. 色情 **sèqíng** pornographic

   色情 杂志在 中国 是非法的。

   Sèqíng zázhì zài Zhōngguó shì fēifǎ de.

   Pornographic magazines are illegal in China.

4. 色泽 **sèzé** color and luster

   我 喜欢 这 幅画儿, 它的色泽 鲜明。

   Wǒ xǐhuan zhè fú huàr, tāde sèzé xiānmíng.

   I like this painting for its bright luster.

5. 黄色 **huángsè** yellow, pornographic

   中国 严禁 黄色 书刊。

   Zhōngguó yánjìn huángsè shūkān.

   China strictly forbids pornographic books and magazines.

Helpful tips: The last stroke ends with a hook.

6 strokes

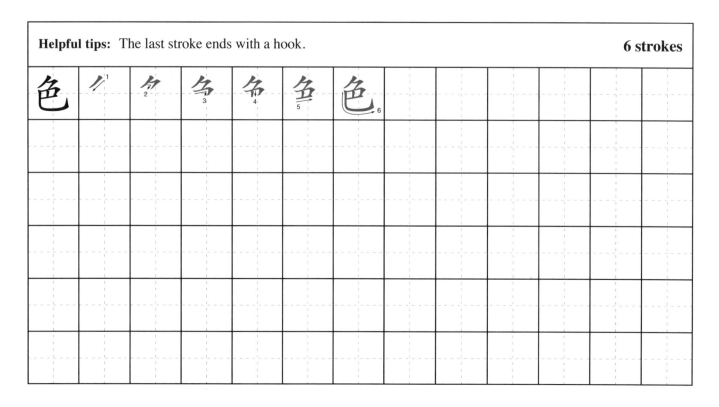

白

bái

white

Radical: 白 # 125 "white"

Compounds, sentences, and meanings

1. 白 **bái** white
   她的皮肤很白。
   Tāde pífū hěn bái.
   She has a fair complexion.

2. 白白 **báibái** in vain, for nothing
   不要 让 时光 白白 过去。
   Búyào ràng shíguāng báibái guòqù.
   Don't let time slip by.

3. 白菜 **báicài** Chinese cabbage
   白菜 做 汤 好喝。
   Báicài zuò tāng hǎohē.
   Chinese cabbage soup is delicious.

4. 白费 **báifèi** waste
   再 等下去 是 白费 时间。
   Zài děngxiàqù shì báifèi shíjiān.
   It's a waste of time to wait any longer.

5. 白天 **báitiān** daytime
   白天 我 睡不着。
   Báitiān wǒ shuìbuzháo.
   I can't sleep in the daytime.

Helpful tips: There should be equal spacing between the horizontal lines.   **5 strokes**

CHARACTER 406

黑　**hēi**

black

Radical: 黑 # 187 "black"

Compounds, sentences, and meanings

1. 黑 **hēi** dark, black

   天 黑 了。
   Tiān hēi le.
   It is already dark.

2. 黑暗 **hēi'àn** darkness

   山洞 里一片 黑暗。
   Shāndòng lǐ yí piàn hēi'àn.
   It's all darkness in the cave.

3. 黑白 **hēibái** black and white

   这 个 电视 是 黑白 的。
   Zhè ge diànshì shì hēibái de.
   This is a black-and-white television.

4. 黑板 **hēibǎn** blackboard

   黑板 上 写着 什么?
   Hēibǎn shàng xiězhe shénme?
   What's written on the blackboard?

5. 黑人 **hēirén** black people

   黑人 在 美国 的 社会 地位 提高 了。
   Hēirén zài Měiguó de shèhuì dìwèi tígāo le.
   The social status of blacks in America has improved.

Helpful tips: The bottom horizontal stroke is longer.　　**12 strokes**

| 黑 | 1 | 2 | 3 | 4 | 5 | 6 | 7 | 8 | 9 | 10 | 11 | 12 |

黄

huáng

yellow

Radical: 艹 # 42 "grass"

Compounds, sentences, and meanings

1. 黄 **huáng** yellow

   树叶 开始 发黄 了。

   Shùyè kāishǐ fāhuáng le.

   The leaves are beginning to turn yellow.

2. 黄金 **huángjīn** gold

   最近 黄金 价格 涨 了。

   Zuìjìn huángjīn jiàgé zhǎng le.

   The price of gold has risen recently.

3. 黄油 **huángyóu** butter

   请 递给 我 黄油。

   Qǐng dì gěi wǒ huángyóu.

   Please pass me the butter.

4. 黄河 **Huánghé** the Yellow River

   黄河 是 中国 文化 的 摇篮。

   Huánghé shì Zhōngguó wénhuà de yáolán.

   The Yellow River is the cradle of Chinese civilization.

Helpful tips: The central vertical stroke crosses through the line above.　　**11 strokes**

| 黄 | 一 | 艹 | 艹 | 共 | 昔 | 昔 | 昔 | 苗 | 黄 | 黄 | 黄 | |

红　hóng

red

红

Radical: 纟 # 68 "silk"

Compounds, sentences, and meanings

1. 红 **hóng** red

   他的 眼睛 都 熬红 了。

   Tāde yǎnjing dōu áohóng le.

   His eyes are bloodshot from staying up late all night.

2. 红包 **hóngbāo** red envelope containing money

   小孩 喜欢 过年, 因为 能 拿到

   Xiǎohái xǐhuan guònián, yīnwèi néng nádào

   很多 红包。

   hěnduō hóngbāo.

   Children love Chinese New Year because they get lots of red packages.

3. 红绿灯 **hónglǜdēng** traffic lights

   在 红绿灯 右 拐弯。

   Zài hónglǜdēng yòu guǎiwān.

   Turn right at the lights.

4. 红薯 **hóngshǔ** sweet potato

   烤 红薯 很 好吃。

   Kǎo hóngshǔ hěn hǎochī.

   Roasted sweet potatoes are delicious.

5. 红眼 **hóngyǎn** be jealous

   他 红眼 别人 收入 比他 多。

   Tā hóngyǎn biéren shōurù bǐ tā duō.

   He is jealous of people who earn more than him.

Helpful tips: The bottom horizontal stroke is slightly longer.　　　　**6 strokes**

红	纟	纟	纟	纟	纟	红					

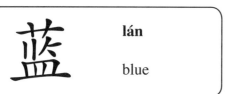

lán

blue

藍

Radical: 艹 # 42 "grass"

Compounds, sentences, and meanings

1. 蓝 **lán** blue

   这里的天很蓝。

   Zhèlǐ de tiān hěn lán.

   The sky here is blue.

2. 蓝宝石 **lánbǎoshí** sapphire

   蓝宝石戒指很贵。

   Lánbǎoshí jièzhǐ hěn guì.

   Sapphire rings are expensive.

3. 蓝鲸 **lánjīng** blue whale

   蓝鲸是最大的鲸鱼。

   Lánjīng shì zuìdà de jīngyú.

   The blue whale is the largest whale.

4. 蓝领 **lánlǐng** blue collar

   他是蓝领工人。

   Tā shì lánlǐng gōngrén.

   He is a blue-collar worker.

5. 蓝色 **lánsè** blue color

   这个湖的水是蓝色的。

   Zhè ge hú de shuǐ shì lánsè de.

   The water in the lake is blue.

Helpful tips: The bottom horizontal stroke is longer.											**13 strokes**
藍	一	十	艹	艹	芷	苏	莎	萨	萨	菡	蓝	蓝
蓝											

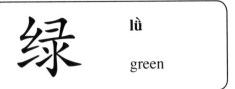

绿　lù　green

綠

Radical: 纟 # 68 "silk"

Compounds, sentences, and meanings

1. 绿 lù green
   他的 毛衣 是 绿的。
   Tāde máoyī shì lù de.
   His woolen sweater is green.

2. 绿茶 lùchá green tea
   我 喜欢 喝绿茶。
   Wǒ xǐhuan hē lùchá.
   I like green tea.

3. 绿灯 lùdēng approval (literally, green light)
   他 给 我 开 绿灯。
   Tā gěi wǒ kāi lùdēng.
   He gave me the go-ahead.

4. 绿豆芽 lùdòuyá mung bean sprouts
   绿豆芽 很 嫩。
   Lùdòuyá hěn nèn.
   Mung bean sprouts are very tender.

5. 绿化 lùhuà greening
   市民 热烈地 参与 绿化 城市 的 工作。
   Shìmín rèliède cānyù lùhuà chéngshì de gōngzuò.
   The people are very positive about the greening of the city.

Helpful tips: The last stroke slants to the right, then tapers off.										11 strokes
绿	ㄥ₁	纟₂	纟₃	纟₄	纟₅	绉₆	绿₇	绿₈	绿₉	绿₁₀ 绿₁₁

fěn

pink; powder, chalk

Radical: 米 # 134 "rice"

Compounds, sentences, and meanings

1. 米粉 **mǐfěn** rice noodles

    米粉 汤 很 好吃。

    Mǐfěn táng hěn hǎochī.

    Rice noodle soup is really good.

2. 粉红 **fěnhóng** pink

    粉红色 的 裤子 很 难看。

    Fěnhóngse de kùzi hěn nánkàn.

    Pink pants are really ugly.

3. 粉碎 **fěnsuì** break, shatter

    哎呀, 我的 眼镜 粉碎了。

    Āiyā, wǒde yǎnjìng fěnsuìle!

    Oh no, my glasses broke!

4. 粉笔 **fěnbǐ** chalk

    请 用 粉笔在 黑板 上 写字。

    Qǐng yǒng fěnbǐ zài hēibǎn shàng xiězi.

    Please use chalk to write on the blackboard.

Helpful tips: The seventh and eighth strokes are separated.									**10 strokes**
粉	⼂¹	⼍²	⺍³	半⁴	米⁵	米⁶	米⁷	粉⁸	粉⁹	粉¹⁰		

深   **shēn**

deep, dark

Radical: 氵 # 32 "water"

Compounds, sentences, and meanings

1. 深沉 **shēnchén** deep, low

   他的 声音 比我的还 深沉。

   Tā de shēngyīn bǐ wǒ de hái shēnchén.

   His voice is deeper than mine.

2. 深深 **shēnshēn** deep, profound

   你的故事给我 深深 的 印象。

   Nǐ de gùshì gěi wǒ shēnshēn de yìnxiàng.

   Your story had a profound impression on me.

3. 深水 **shēnshuǐ** deep water

   美国 有 一些 重要 的 深水 港。

   Měiguó yǒu yìxiē zhòngyào de shēnshuǐ gǎng.

   The United States has some important deep water ports.

4. 深蓝色 **shēnlánse** deep blue

   有 些 地方 的 天空 是 深蓝色 的,

   Yǒu xiē dìfang de tiānkōng shì shēnlánse de,

   很 漂亮。

   hěn piàoliang.

   There are some places where the sky is a deep blue; it is very pretty.

5. 深思 **shēnsì** think deeply

   哲学 让 人 深思 人生 的 大问题。

   Zhéxué ràng rén shēnsì rénshēng de dà wèntí.

   Philosophy allows people to think deeply on the problems of one's life.

| **Helpful tips:** The sixth and seventh strokes should be inside of the fourth and fifth strokes. | **11 strokes** |

深	丶	冫	氵	汀	沪	浐	浬	浬	浲	深	

Lesson 38: Review Activities

A. Vocabulary Identification

Identify the following items in Chinese characters. Then write the major color associated with that item.

（东西）

_____   _____   _____   _____   _____

（颜色）

_____   _____   _____   _____   _____

B. Short Description

Colors have considerable cultural connections. For the following colors, introduce your own cultural understanding. Then, if possible, discuss these cultural connotations in Chinese with a speaker from another culture.

1. （红色） _____

2. （白色） _____

3. （黑色） _____

4. （黄色） _____

5. （粉红色） _____

C. Example Description

Consider a color that you find enjoyable and sketch three examples to show your choice. Then write a short description of these items and the color that you enjoy. Convey how the illustrations show the ways the color is understood across various items.

#1	#2	#3

_____

_____

_____

_____

_____

_____

_____

Traditional Form

环

huán

surround

環

Radical: 王 # 79 "king"

Compounds, sentences, and meanings

1. 环 **huán** link

这 是 最 薄弱 的 一 环。

Zhè shì zuì bóruò de yì huán.

This is the weakest link.

2. 环境 **huánjìng** environment

环境 污染 是 一个 严重 问题。

Huánjìng wūrǎn shì yí ge yánzhòng wèntí.

Environmental pollution is a serious problem.

3. 环节 **huánjié** link, sector

减少 环节, 提高 效率。

Jiǎnshǎo huánjié, tígāo xiàolù.

Streamlining increases efficiency.

4. 环保 **huánbǎo** environmental protection

环保 就是 环境 保护。

Huánbǎo jiù shì huánjìng bǎohù.

"Huánbǎo" is the acronym for environmental protection.

5. 环城 **huánchéng** around the city

这 是 环城 公路, 自行车

Zhè shì huánchéng gōnglù, zìxíngchē

不许 驶入。

bùxǔ shǐrù.

This is a ring road. Bicycles are not allowed.

Helpful tips: The last stroke of 王 lifts when written as a radical.   **8 strokes**

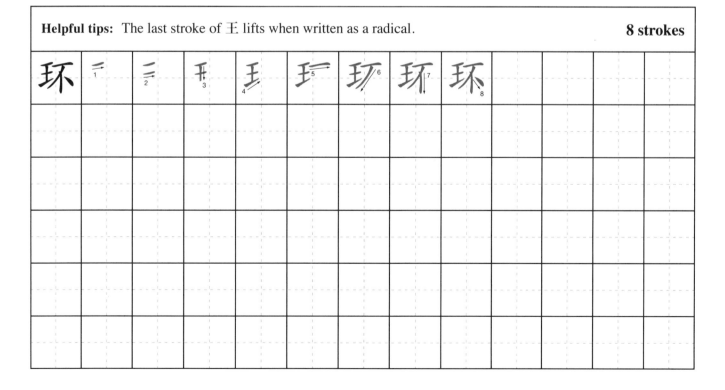

境　jìng

territory

Radical: 土 # 40 "earth"

Compounds, sentences, and meanings

1. 境 **jìng** territory

少林寺 在 河南省 境内。

Shàolínsì zài Hénánshěng jìng nèi.

Shaolin Temple is in Henan Province.

2. 境地 **jìngdì** circumstances

他把自己陷入 完全 孤立的境地。

Tā bǎ zìjǐ xiànrù wánquán gūlì de jìngdì.

He has completely isolated himself.

3. 境况 **jìngkuàng** (financial) condition

我 最近的 境况 不错。

Wǒ zuìjìn de jìngkuàng búcuò.

My financial situation is not bad right now.

4. 境遇 **jìngyù** one's lot

我 很 同情 她悲惨的境遇。

Wǒ hěn tóngqíng tā bēicǎn de jìngyù.

I'm truly sympathetic to her difficult circumstances.

5. 困境 **kùnjìng** difficult position

你要 想 办法 摆脱 困境。

Nǐ yào xiǎng bànfǎ bǎituō kùnjìng.

You must think of a way out of this predicament.

Helpful tips: The last stroke is a vertical-bend-hook.　　　　**14 strokes**

境	二1	土2 3	土	土4	土5	土6	土7	垃8	垃9	培10	培11	培12
境13	境14											

空

kōng/kòng

empty; leisure time

Radical: 穴 # 110 "cave"

Compounds, sentences, and meanings

1. 空 **kōng** empty

屋里是 空 的,一个人也 没有。

Wūli shì kōng de, yí ge rén yě méiyǒu.

The room is empty; there's no one there.

2. 空气 **kōngqì** air

城里 空气 污染 很 严重。

Chéngli kōngqì wūrǎn hěn yánzhòng.

Air pollution is very serious in the city.

3. 空儿 **kòngr** free time

今天 下午 我 有 空儿。

Jīntiān xiàwǔ wǒ yǒu kòngr.

I'm free this afternoon.

4. 空调 **kōngtiáo** air conditioning

进来, 外面 很 热,屋里有 空调。

Jìnlai, wàimian hěn rè, wūli yǒu kōngtiáo.

Come in, it's hot outside, there's air conditioning inside the room.

5. 空闲 **kòngxián** leisure time

等 你 空闲 的 时候, 我们 聊聊天。

Děng nǐ kòngxián de shíhou, wǒmen liáoliaotiān.

The next time you're free, let's chat.

Helpful tips: The bottom horizontal stroke is longer.								**8 strokes**
空	丶	八	宀	空	穴	空	空	空

晴

qíng

fine, sunny

Radical: 日 # 90 "sun"

Compounds, sentences, and meanings

1. 晴 **qíng** fine day

   天 晴 了。

   Tiān qíng le.

   It's clearing up.

2. 晴朗 **qínglǎng** fine, sunny

   今天 天气 晴朗。

   Jīntiān tiānqì qínglǎng.

   Today is sunny.

3. 晴天 **qíngtiān** sunny day

   昨天 是 晴天。

   Zuótiān shì qíngtiān.

   Yesterday was a fine day.

4. 晴间多云 **qíng jiān duōyún** fine with occasional clouds

   预报 说 明天 晴 间 多云。

   Yùbào shuō míngtiān qíng jiān duōyún.

   The weather forecast says tomorrow will be fine with occasional clouds.

5. 晴转阴 **qíng zhuǎn yīn** fine changing to overcast

   下午 晴 转 阴。

   Xiàwǔ qíng zhuǎn yīn.

   It will cloud over in the afternoon.

Helpful tips: The third horizontal stroke of 青 is the longest.											**12 strokes**
晴											

shān

mountain

Radical: 山 # 53 "mountain"

Compounds, sentences, and meanings

1. 山 **shān** mountain

   中国 有 很多 山。

   Zhōngguó yǒu hěnduō shān.

   There are many mountains in China.

2. 山城 **shānchéng** mountain city

   重庆 是一座 山城。

   Chóngqìng shì yí zuò shānchéng.

   Chongqing is a mountain city.

3. 山区 **shānqū** mountain area

   很多 农民 住 在 山区。

   Hěnduō nóngmín zhù zài shānqū.

   Many peasants live in the mountains.

4. 山顶 **shāndǐng** hilltop

   从 山顶 往 下 看，风景 美极了。

   Cóng shāndǐng wǎng xià kàn, fēngjǐng měijíle.

   Looking down from the peak, the scenery is really beautiful.

5. 黄山 **Huángshān** the Yellow Mountain

   黄山 风景 美极了。

   Huángshān fēngjǐng měijíle.

   The Yellow Mountain is a really beautiful spot.

Helpful tips: The first vertical stroke is slightly longer.													**3 strokes**
山	丨	山	山										

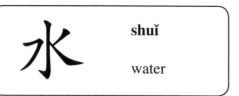

shuǐ

water

Radical: 水 # 109 "water"

Compounds, sentences, and meanings

1. 水 **shuǐ** water

这里 水 平 如 镜。

Zhèlǐ shuǐ píng rú jìng.

The water here is as smooth as a mirror.

2. 水果 **shuǐguǒ** fruit

多 吃 水果 对 身体 有 好处。

Duō chī shuǐguǒ duì shēntǐ yǒu hǎochù.

Eating fruit is good for you.

3. 水龙头 **shuǐlóngtóu** tap

用 后 将 水龙头 关紧。

Yòng hòu jiāng shuǐlóngtóu guānjǐn.

Please turn off the tap tightly after use.

4. 水平 **shuǐpíng** standard, level

中国 人民 的 生活 水平

Zhōngguó rénmín de shēnghuó shuǐpíng

提高了。

tígāo le.

The living standard of the Chinese people has improved.

5. 山水画 **shānshuǐhuà** landscape painting

她 送 我 一 副 山水画。

Tā sòng wǒ yí fù shānshuǐhuà.

She gave me a landscape painting.

Helpful tips: The vertical stroke ends with a hook.					**4 strokes**
水	亅	刁	氺	水	

海

hǎi

sea

Radical: 氵 # 32 "3 drops of water"

Compounds, sentences, and meanings

1. 海 **hǎi** sea

   台湾 四面 环海。

   Táiwān sìmiàn huánhǎi.

   Taiwan is surrounded by sea.

2. 海边 **hǎibian** seaside

   我 常 去 海边 游泳。

   Wǒ cháng qù hǎibian yóuyǒng.

   I often go to the seaside to swim.

3. 海外 **hǎiwài** overseas

   他是 海外 华侨。

   Tā shì hǎiwài Huáqiáo.

   He is an overseas Chinese.

4. 海拔 **hǎibá** above sea level

   这里的 山 比较 高, 平均 海拔

   Zhèlǐ de shān bǐjiào gāo, píngjūn hǎibá

   四千 米。

   sìqiān mǐ.

   The mountains here are quite high, averaging 4,000 meters above sea level.

5. 上海 **Shànghǎi** Shanghai

   她 是 上海人

   Tā shì Shànghǎirén.

   She's a native of Shanghai.

Helpful tips: Write the horizontal stroke before the final two dots.										**10 strokes**	
海	丶	冫	氵	汐	汇	洈	海	海	海	海	

CHARACTER 420

河　　hé

river

Radical: 氵 # 32 "3 drops of water"

Compounds, sentences, and meanings

1. 河 **hé** river

   前面　有一条河。

   Qiánmiàn yǒu yì tiáo hé.

   There's a river ahead.

2. 河流 **héliú** river

   中国　有　很多　河流。

   Zhōngguó yǒu hěnduō héliú.

   There are many rivers in China.

3. 河鱼 **héyú** freshwater fish

   我 不 喜欢 吃河鱼。

   Wǒ bù xǐhuan chī héyú.

   I don't like the taste of freshwater fish.

4. 河北 **Héběi** Hebei Province

   河北 在　黄河　　北边。

   Héběi zài Huánghé běibiān.

   Hebei Province is situated north of the Yellow River.

5. 黄河 **Huánghé** the Yellow River

   黄河 是　中国　文化 的 摇篮。

   Huánghé shì Zhōngguó wénhuà de yáolán.

   The Yellow River is the cradle of the Chinese civilization.

Helpful tips: The final stroke ends in a hook.											**8 strokes**
河	丶	冫	氵	汀	沪	沪	沪	河			

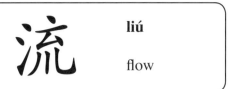

流　liú

flow

Radical: 氵 # 32 "three drops of water"

Compounds, sentences, and meanings

1. 流 **liú** flow

   中国 的河大都 向 东 流。

   Zhōngguó de hé dà dōu xiàng dōng liú.

   Most of the rivers in China flow to the east.

2. 流传 **liúchuán** hand down

   这 是 个 古代 流传下来 的 寓言。

   Zhè shì ge gǔdài liúchuánxiàlai de yùyán.

   This is a fable handed down from ancient times.

3. 流动 **liúdòng** on the move

   中国 有 很多 流动 人口。

   Zhōngguó yǒu hěnduō liúdòng rénkǒu.

   China has a large floating population.

4. 流利 **liúlì** fluent

   他 说 一 口 流利的法语。

   Tā shuō yì kǒu liúlì de Fǎyǔ.

   He speaks fluent French.

5. 流行 **liúxíng** popular

   这 首 歌在 台湾 很 流行。

   Zhè shǒu gē zài Táiwān hěn liúxíng.

   This song is very popular in Taiwan.

Helpful tips: The last stroke is a vertical-bend-hook.　　　　　**10 strokes**

流	1	2	3	4	5	6	7	8	9	10		

Traditional Form

丽   lì

beautiful, pretty

麗

Radical: 一 # 2 "horizontal stroke"

Compounds, sentences, and meanings

1. 美丽 **měilì** beautiful

   法国 的 艺术 博物馆 有 许多 美丽

   Fǎguó de yìshù bówùguǎn yǒu xǔduō měilì

   的 画。

   de huā.

   Art museums in France have many beautiful paintings.

2. 华丽 **huálì** resplendent, gorgeous

   他 为 女儿 建了 一座 华丽的 房子。

   Tā wèi nǔr jiànle yízuò huálì de fángzi.

   He built a magnificent house for his daughter.

Helpful tips: The small strokes inside of the bottom components do not cross any other strokes.   **7 strokes**

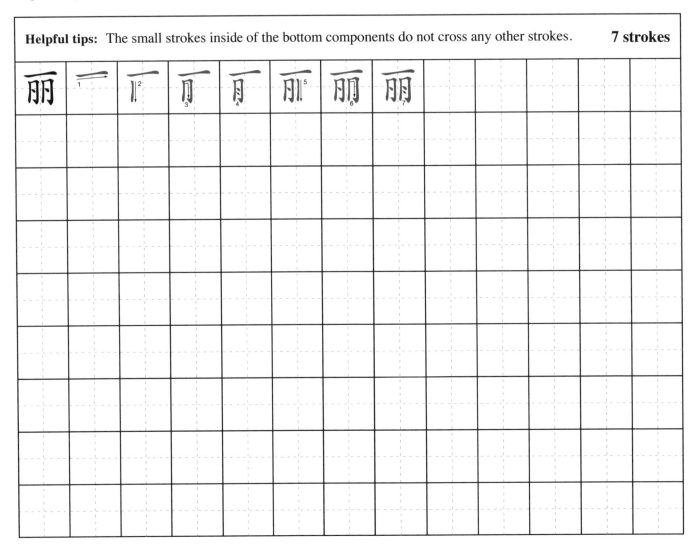

Traditional Form

树   shù

     tree

樹

Radical: 木 # 81 "tree"

Compounds, sentences, and meanings

1. 树 **shù** tree

这 是 什么 树?

Zhè shì shénme shù?

What kind of tree is this?

2. 树立 **shùlì** set up

当 老师要树立好 榜样。

Dāng lǎoshī yào shùlì hǎo bǎngyàng.

A teacher has to set a good example.

3. 树林 **shùlín** forest

前面 是 树林，走不过去。

Qiánmiàn shì shùlín, zǒubuguòqu.

There's a forest ahead, we can't get through.

4. 树阴 **shùyīn** the shade of a tree

树阴 下面 凉快， 坐下来 歇 会儿。

Shùyīn xiàmiàn liángkuài, zuòxiàlai xiē huìr.

It's nice and cool under the tree, let's sit down and have a rest.

5. 树枝 **shùzhī** branch

这 树枝可以 用 来做 拐杖。

Zhè shùzhī kěyǐ yòng lái zuò guǎizhàng.

This branch can be used as a walking stick.

Helpful tips: The eighth stroke ends with a hook.									9 strokes		
树	一	十	才	木	杓	权	权	树	树		

云   yún

cloud; say

雲

Radical: 二 # 10 "two"

Compounds, sentences, and meanings

1. 云 **yún** clouds

   今天 的 天气 不 太好, 云 很 多。
   Jīntiān de tiānqì bú tàihǎo, yún hěn duō.
   Today the weather isn't so good, there are many clouds.

2. 云 **yún** say (lit.)

   你要 有自己的看法, 别 人云 亦云。
   Nǐ yào yǒu zìjǐ de kànfǎ, bié rényún yìyún.
   You want to have your own opinions, don't just repeat what others have said.

3. 云层 **yúncéng** cloud layer

   云层 很低的日子, 让 人 觉得世界
   Yúncéng hěn dī de rìzi, ràng rén juéde shìjiè

   很 小。
   hěn xiǎo.
   On days when the cloud layer is low, people feel that the world is very small.

4. 云彩 **yúncai** cloud, cloud shapes

   孩子 喜欢 想象 云彩 是 动物。
   Háizi xǐhuan xiǎngxiàng yúncai shì dòngwù.
   Children enjoy imagining the shapes of clouds are animals.

Helpful tips: The second horizontal stroke is longer.				**4 strokes**

云　二　二　云　云

Lesson 39: Review Activities

A. Vocabulary Identification and Pronunciation

Identify the vocabulary terms listed below by writing each term in the appropriate place on the illustration, to label it. Then transcribe each of the vocabulary terms in *pinyin*.

山 ＿＿＿＿＿＿＿   河 ＿＿＿＿＿＿＿   云 ＿＿＿＿＿＿＿

水 ＿＿＿＿＿＿＿   石 ＿＿＿＿＿＿＿   天空 ＿＿＿＿＿＿＿

树 ＿＿＿＿＿＿＿   雪 ＿＿＿＿＿＿＿   环境 ＿＿＿＿＿＿＿

B. Sentence Creation

Create a sentence that connects the location given with an activity. Each of the different locations should be connected to a different activity.

1. （山）＿＿＿＿＿＿＿＿＿＿＿＿＿＿＿＿＿＿＿＿＿＿＿＿＿＿＿＿＿＿

2. （海）＿＿＿＿＿＿＿＿＿＿＿＿＿＿＿＿＿＿＿＿＿＿＿＿＿＿＿＿＿＿

3. （河）＿＿＿＿＿＿＿＿＿＿＿＿＿＿＿＿＿＿＿＿＿＿＿＿＿＿＿＿＿＿

4. （花园）＿＿＿＿＿＿＿＿＿＿＿＿＿＿＿＿＿＿＿＿＿＿＿＿＿＿＿＿

5. （自然环境）＿＿＿＿＿＿＿＿＿＿＿＿＿＿＿＿＿＿＿＿＿＿＿＿＿

C. Short Description

In a clear and concise paragraph, describe a location that you enjoy. Include clear reasoning for why the location is an enjoyable one, including activities and other important aspects of the location.

你喜欢什么样的地方：自然环境的地方，还是城市里？

_____

_____

_____

_____

_____

_____

_____

_____

养

yǎng

provide for

養

Radical: 羊 # 133 "sheep"

Compounds, sentences, and meanings

1. 养 **yǎng** provide for

他 从小 没有 父母, 是 姑姑 把

Tā cóngxiǎo méiyǒu fùmǔ, shì gūgu bǎ

他 养 大 的。

tā yǎng dà de.

He lost his parents when he was a child, and was brought up by his aunt.

2. 养神 **yǎngshén** rest to attain mental tranquility

不要 打搅 他, 他 在 闭目 养神。

Búyào dǎjiǎo tā, tā zài bìmù yǎngshén.

Don't disturb him, he's resting.

3. 保养 **bǎoyǎng** take good care of one's health

他 很 会 保养。

Tā hěn huì bǎoyǎng.

He knows how to take care of himself.

4. 修养 **xiūyǎng** accomplishment

他 在 文学 上 很 有 修养。

Tā zài wénxué shàng hěn yǒu xiūyǎng.

He has a wide knowledge of literature.

5. 营养 **yíngyǎng** nutrition

牛奶 的 营养 价值 很 高。

Niúnǎi de yíngyǎng jiàzhí hěn gāo.

Milk has a high nutritional value.

Helpful tips: Each horizontal stroke is evenly spaced.　　　　**9 strokes**

养	`	`	兰	兰	兰	羊	美	养	养			

鸡　**jī**

chicken

雞

Radical: 又 # 24 "again" or 鸟 # 127 "bird"

Compounds, sentences, and meanings

1. 鸡 **jī** chicken

   我 爱 吃 鸡, 不 爱 吃 鸭子。
   Wǒ ài chī jī, bú ài chī yāzi.
   I like chicken, but not duck.

2. 鸡毛蒜皮 **jīmáo-suànpí** trifles (Literally, chicken feathers and garlic skin)

   你何苦为 这 点 鸡毛蒜皮 的 事 跟
   Nǐ hékǔ wèi zhè diǎn jīmáo-suànpí de shì gēn
   他 吵 呢?
   tā chǎo ne?
   Why argue with him over such trifles?

3. 鸡犬不宁 **jī-quǎn bù níng** general turmoil
   (Literally, chickens and dogs in upheaval)

   他们 经常 吵架, 闹得家里
   Tāmen jīngcháng chǎojià, nàode jiāli
   鸡犬 不 宁。
   jī-quǎn bù níng.
   They fight all the time, turning the whole family upside down.

4. 公鸡 **gōngjī** rooster

   他 连 公鸡 和母鸡 都 分不清。
   Tā lián gōngjī hé mǔjī dōu fēnbuqīng.
   He can't even tell the difference between a rooster and a hen.

Helpful tips: Note the difference between 鸟 and 乌.										**7 strokes**
鸡	又	又	又	鸡	鸡	鸡	鸡			

216

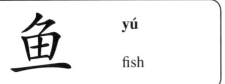

CHARACTER 427

Traditional Form

鱼 yú fish

魚

Radical: 鱼 # 176 "fish"

Compounds, sentences, and meanings

1. 鱼 yú fish
这 小 池里 有 几 条鱼。
Zhè xiǎo chílǐ yǒu jǐ tiáoyú.
This little pool has a couple of fish.

2. 钓鱼 diàoyú fish; fishing
我 的 爷爷 很 喜欢 钓鱼。
Wǒ de yéye hěn xǐhuan diàoyú.
My grandfather enjoys fishing.

3. 鱼竿 yúgān fishing pole
这 支 鱼竿 长 两 米。
Zhè zhī yúgān cháng liǎng mǐ.
This fishing pole is two meters in length.

4. 鱼龙混杂 yúlóng hùnzá good and bad mixed together
每个 现代 大 城市 鱼龙 混杂。
Měi ge xiàndài dà chéngshì yúlóng hùnzá.
In every modern large city good and bad are mixed together.

5. 鱼目混珠 yúmù hùnzhū confuse worthless for value
别 去 那个 商店 买 东西, 他们
Bié qù nà ge shāngdiàn mǎi dōngxi, tāmen
用 假货 鱼目 混珠。
yòng jiǎhuò yúmù hùnzhū.
Don't go to that store to buy things, they use fake goods to mislead customers.

Helpful tips: The final stroke is the longest.　　　**8 strokes**

217

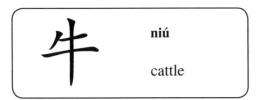

niú

cattle

Radical: 牛 # 95 "cattle"

Compounds, sentences, and meanings

1. 牛 **niú** cattle

   我 是 一九七三年 出生 的,我 属 牛。
   Wǒ shì Yījiǔqīsānián chūshēng de, wǒ shǔ niú.
   I was born in 1973, in the year of the Ox.

2. 牛劲 **niújìn** great strength

   我 费了 牛劲 才 把 门 打开。
   Wǒ fèile niújìn cái bǎ mén dǎkāi.
   I had to exert all my strength to open the door.

3. 牛油 **niúyóu** butter

   面包 上 放 点 牛油 才 好吃。
   Miànbāo shàng fàng diǎn niúyóu cái hǎochī.
   Bread doesn't taste good without butter.

4. 牛脾气 **niúpíqi** stubbornness

   他 有 股 牛脾气,干 什么 事 一定 要
   Tā yǒu gǔ niúpíqi, gàn shénme shì yídìng yào
   干 到底。
   gàn dào dǐ.
   He's very stubborn, once he starts something he must finish it.

5. 吹牛 **chuīniú** brag, talk big

   他 就 爱 吹牛。
   Tā jiù ài chuīniú.
   He blows his own trumpet.

Helpful tips: Note the difference between 牛 and 午.										**4 strokes**
牛	丿	仁	仨	牛						

轻

qīng

light, easy

輕

Radical: 车 # 84 "vehicle"

Compounds, sentences, and meanings

1. 轻重 **qīngzhòng** weight

这 两 个 包 轻重 不 一样。

Zhè liǎng ge bāo qīngzhòng bù yíyàng.

The weights of these two bags are not the same.

2. 轻信 **qīngxìn** gullible; easily believe

我们 都 有 一个 朋友 轻信 我们

Wǒmen dōu yǒu yí ge péngyou qīngxìn wǒmen

的 话。

de huà.

We all have a friend who easily believes whatever we say.

3. 轻快 **qīngkuài** sprightly, easily

我 的 父亲 心情 很好, 走路 走路 得

Wǒ de fùqīn xīnqíng hěnhǎo, zǒulù zǒulù de

很 轻快。

hěn qīngkuài.

My father is fine, he is walking easily.

4. 年轻 **niánqīng** young, youth

年轻 人 常常 以为 他们 的 问题

Niánqīng rén chángcháng yǐwèi tāmen de wèntí

都 是 新的。

dōu shì xīnde.

Young people often believe that their problems are all new.

Helpful tips: The seventh stroke fits beneath the two previous strokes.

9 strokes

轻	一₁	七₂ 夕₃	车₄	轩₅	轩₆	轻₇	轻₈	轻₉		

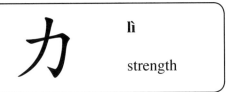

力 lì

strength

Radical: 力 # 31 "strength"

Compounds, sentences, and meanings

1. 力 **lì** power, strength

   我 想 帮 你,可是 恐怕 力不从心。

   Wǒ xiǎng bāng nǐ, kěshì kǒngpà lì bù cóng xīn.

   I wanted to help but I'm afraid I don't have the ability.

2. 力量 **lìliang** strength

   我 一定 尽 我的 力量 帮忙。

   Wǒ yídìng jìn wǒde lìliang bāngmáng.

   I'll certainly do everything in my power to help.

3. 力气 **lìqi** physical strength

   他的力气不 小。

   Tāde lìqi bù xiǎo.

   He's very strong.

4. 力求 **lìqiú** make every effort to

   我们 力求取得一致 意见。

   Wǒmen lìqiú qǔdé yízhì yìjiàn.

   We'll do our best to reach a consensus.

5. 力争 **lìzhēng** work hard for

   力争 上游。

   Lìzhēng shàngyóu.

   Try hard to come first.

Helpful tips: The first stroke ends with a hook.											**2 strokes**
力	フ	力									

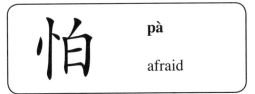

怕　pà

afraid

Radical: 忄 # 33 "upright heart"

Compounds, sentences, and meanings

1. 怕 **pà**　be afraid of

   我 怕 黑。

   Wǒ pà hēi.

   I'm afraid of the dark.

2. 怕事 **pàshì**　be afraid of getting into trouble

   她 胆小 怕事。

   Tā dǎnxiǎo pàshì.

   She's timid and overcautious.

3. 怕冷 **pàlěng**　be afraid of the cold

   我 从小 就 不 怕冷。

   Wǒ cóngxiǎo jiù bú pàlěng.

   Since my youth, I have not been afraid of the cold.

4. 怕羞 **pàxiū**　bashful

   我 小 时候 很 怕羞。

   Wǒ xiǎo shíhou hěn pàxiū.

   I was very shy when I was small.

5. 恐怕 **kǒngpà**　be afraid of

   这样 做, 恐怕 不行。

   Zhèyàng zuò, kǒngpà bùxíng.

   I'm afraid this won't work.

Helpful tips: The fourth stroke tapers down from right to left.									**8 strokes**

怕	忄	忄	忄	忄	怕	怕	怕		

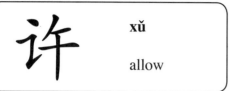

xǔ

allow

許

Radical: 讠 # 9 "word"

Compounds, sentences, and meanings

1. 许 **xǔ** allow

   每组只许去一个人。

   Měi zǔ zhǐ xǔ qù yí ge rén.

   Only one person is allowed from each group.

2. 许多 **xǔduō** many

   家里有许多事情要干。

   Jiālǐ yǒu xǔduō shìqing yào gàn.

   There are lots of things to do at home.

3. 许久 **xǔjiǔ** for a long time

   我们 商量了 许久了。

   Wǒmen shāngliangle xǔjiǔ le.

   We talked things over for a long time.

4. 不许 **bùxǔ** not allowed

   对不起, 这里不许吸烟。

   Duìbuqǐ, zhèlǐ bùxǔ xīyān.

   I'm sorry, you can't smoke here.

5. 也许 **yěxǔ** perhaps, maybe

   也许我不应该告诉她。

   Yěxǔ wǒ bù yīnggāi gàosu tā.

   Perhaps I shouldn't have told her.

Helpful tips: The second horizontal stroke is longer.

6 strokes

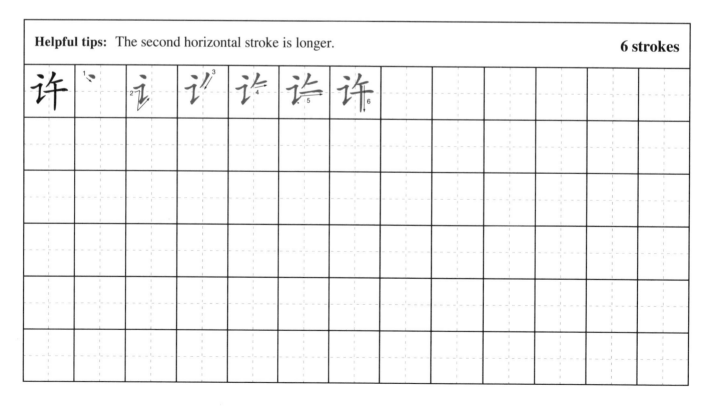

优　yōu

excellent

優

Radical: 亻 # 19 "upright person"

Compounds, sentences, and meanings

1. **优 yōu** excellence

优 胜 劣 败。

Yōu shèng liè bài.

Survival of the fittest. (Literally, the superior wins and the inferior loses)

2. **优先 yōuxiān** have priority

这 是 必须 优先 考虑 的 问题。

Zhè shì bìxū yōuxiān kǎolù de wèntí.

This is a question which takes precedence over all others.

3. **优待 yōudài** preferential treatment

我们 受到了 特别 的 优待。

Wǒmen shòudàole tèbié de yōudài.

We were given preferential treatment.

4. **优点 yōudiǎn** merit, strong point

每个 人 都 有自己的 优点。

Měi ge rén dōu yǒu zìjǐ de yōudiǎn.

Each person has their own strong points.

5. **优美 yōuměi** graceful, beautiful

这里 一带 风景 优美。

Zhèlǐ yídài fēngjǐng yōuměi.

The scenery around here is beautiful.

Helpful tips: The fifth stroke is a vertical-bend-hook.　　　　**6 strokes**

优	ノ	亻	仁	仇	优	优							

liáng/liàng

measure/quantity

Radical: 日 # 90 "sun"

Compounds, sentences, and meanings

1. 量 **liáng** measure

   我 给 你 量量 体温 吧。

   Wǒ gěi nǐ liángliang tǐwēn ba.

   Let me take your temperature.

2. 量词 **liàngcí** measure word, quantifier

   中文 量词 很多。

   Zhōngwén liàngcí hěnduō.

   There are many measure words in Chinese.

3. 量力 **liànglì** estimate strength or ability

   我们 应该 量力而行。

   Wǒmen yīnggāi liànglì ér xíng.

   We should do what we are capable of.

4. 气量 **qìliàng** tolerance, forbearance

   气量 大 的 人 对 这 点 小事 是

   Qìliàng dà de rén duì zhè diǎn xiǎoshì shì

   不会 介意 的。

   búhuì jièyì de.

   Broad-minded people don't bother about such trifles.

5. 力量 **lìliang** power, force

   我 一定 尽 我的 力量 帮忙。

   Wǒ yídìng jìn wǒde lìliang bāngmáng.

   I'll certainly do everything in my power to help.

Helpful tips: Each horizontal stroke is evenly spaced.　　　　**12 strokes**

量											

Lesson 40: Review Activities

A. Vocabulary Identification

Write the characters for each of the illustrations below. Also write the weight of each item in Chinese.

	(1 kg)	(10 g)	(100 lbs)	(500 lbs)	(1000 kg)
东西：					
重量：					

B. Sentence Completion

Please complete each of the following sentences with one of the terms provided. Then translate the resulting sentence into English.

年轻　　　　轻重　　　　力量　　　　许多　　　　优美　　　　可怕

1. 我朋友的身体很大, 他的_____也很大。

_____

2. 世界上有一些地方人们都认为很_____。

_____

3. 那么小的狗, 真的不_____的!

_____

4. 老人常常需要_____人的力气。

_____

5. 搬家的时候家具的＿＿＿＿＿＿＿很重要。

_____

6. 每个星期你可以看新的电影, 每年有＿＿＿＿＿＿＿的新电影。

_____

C. Short Description

Consider each of the following common animals. Then write a short description about the various needs of each animal. This should include the necessary conditions to raise the animal and provide for all of its needs.

鸡	_____
	_____
	_____
鱼	_____
	_____
	_____
牛	_____
	_____
	_____

第　　**dì**

ordinal number

Radical: 竹 # 145 "bamboo"

Compounds, sentences, and meanings

1. 第 **dì** ordinal number

我 是 第二次 世界 大战 后 出生 的。

Wǒ shì Dì'èrcì Shìjiè Dàzhàn hòu chūshēng de.

I was born after the Second World War.

2. 第一声 **dìyīshēng** first tone

第一声

dìyīshēng

First tone in Mandarin (high-level tone)

3. 第二声 **dì'èrshēng** second tone

第二声

dì'èrshēng

Second tone in Mandarin (high-rising tone)

4. 第三声 **dìsānshēng** third tone

第三声

dìsānshēng

Third tone in Mandarin (low-dipping tone)

5. 第四声 **dìsìshēng** fourth tone

第四声

dìsìshēng

Fourth tone in Mandarin (high-falling tone)

Helpful tips: The ninth stroke ends with a hook.											11 strokes
第	丿	丘	夶	竺	竻	竻	等	笒	笃	第	第

CHARACTER 436

等

děng

level, rank; equal; wait

Radical: ⺮ # 145 “bamboo”

Compounds, sentences, and meanings

1. 高等 **gāoděng** high, advanced

   研究生院 是 高等 教育。

   Yánjiūshēngyuàn shì gāoděng jiàoyù.

   Graduate school is an advanced level of education.

2. 等等 **děngděng** et cetera, and so on

   上课 的 时候 我 带 课本, 笔记本, 钢笔, 等等。

   Shàngkè de shíhou wǒ dài kèběn, bǐjìběn, gāngbǐ, děngděng.

   When I go to class I bring a textbook, notebook, pens, and so on.

3. 等同 **děngtóng** equal; equality, the same

   每 个 人 经济 机会 都 不 等同。

   Měi ge rén jīngjì jīhuì dōu bù děngtóng.

   Every person’s economic opportunity is not the same.

4. 等待 **děngdài** to wait

   小狗 在 房子 门口, 等待 主人 回家。

   Xiǎogǒu zài fángzi ménkǒu, děngdài zhǔrén huíjiā.

   At the door, small dogs wait for the family to come home.

5. 等级 **děngjí** grade, rank

   宝石 等级 有 很 多 种。

   Bǎoshí děngjí yǒu hěn duō zhǒng.

   There are many kinds of grades for gemstones.

Helpful tips: Each horizontal stroke should be evenly spaced. **12 strokes**

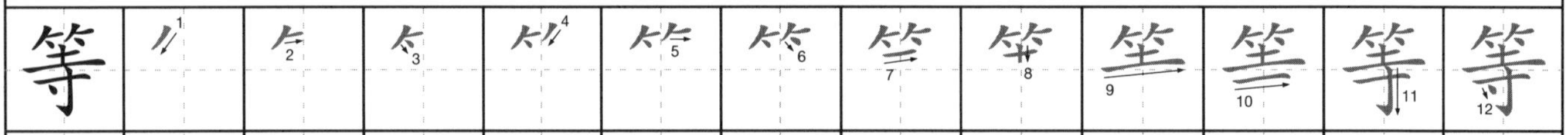

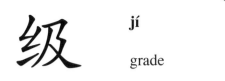

jí

grade

級

Radical: 纟 # 68 "silk"

Compounds, sentences, and meanings

1. 级 **jí** grade

长城 饭店 是 五星级 宾馆。

Chángchéng Fàndiàn shì wǔxīngjí bīnguǎn.

The Great Wall Hotel is a five-star hotel.

2. 级别 **jíbié** rank

她的级别比我 高。

Tāde jíbié bǐ wǒ gāo.

She is my senior.

3. 超级 **chāojí** super grade

这 家 超级 市场 东西 很 全。

Zhè jiā chāojí shìchǎng dōngxi hěn quán.

This supermarket has a wide range of goods.

4. 初级 **chūjí** novice level

这 是 汉语 初级 读本。

Zhè shì Hànyǔ chūjí dúběn.

This is an elementary Chinese reader.

5. 高级 **gāojí** advanced level

这 个 旅馆 真 高级。

Zhè ge lǚguǎn zhēn gāojí.

This hotel is really first class.

Helpful tips: The second stroke of 及 has two bends.　　　　**6 strokes**

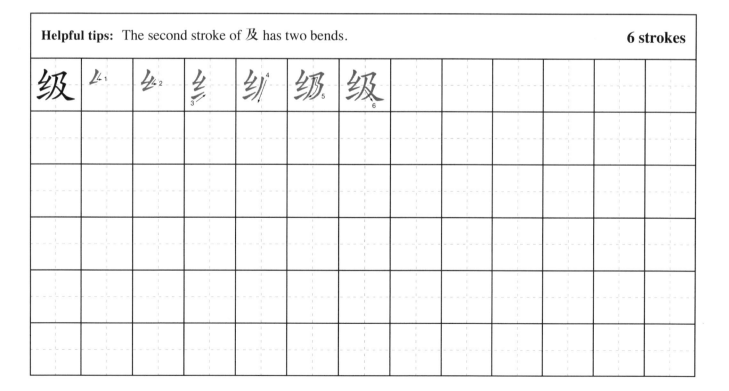

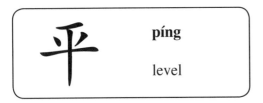

平   **píng**

level

Radical: 一 # 2 "horizontal-stroke"

Compounds, sentences, and meanings

1. 平 **píng** level

   桌面 不平。

   Zhuōmiàn bù píng.

   The table is not level.

2. 平安 **píng'ān** safe

   平安 到达 目的地。

   Píng'ān dàodá mùdìdì.

   Get there safe and sound.

3. 平常 **píngcháng** ordinary

   平常 我 很少 进城。

   Píngcháng wǒ hěnshǎo jìnchéng.

   As a rule, I seldom go to town.

4. 平等 **píngděng** equality

   我们 家里 男 女 平等。

   Wǒmen jiāli nán nǚ píngděng.

   In our family, there is equality between the sexes.

5. 平静 **píngjìng** calm down

   他 很 激动, 心情 久久 不能 平静。

   Tā hěn jīdòng, xīnqíng jiǔjiǔ bùnéng píngjìng.

   He was very excited, and it was a long time before he calmed down.

Helpful tips: The two dots come towards each other at an angle.   **5 strokes**

平	二	二	二	平	平						

cì

position in a series

Radical: 冫 # 7 "ice"

Compounds, sentences, and meanings

1. 次 **cì** [measure word (for number of times)]

   今天 我 来 找过 你 两次。

   Jīntiān wǒ lái zhǎoguo nǐ liǎng cì.

   I looked for you twice today.

2. 次序 **cìxù** order, sequence

   请 按次序 入场。

   Qǐng àn cìxù rùchǎng.

   Please stay in line as you come in.

3. 次要 **cìyào** less important

   把 这 个 问题 推到 次要 地位。

   Bǎ zhè ge wèntí tuīdào cìyào dìwèi.

   Give this problem lower priority.

4. 次数 **cìshù** number of times

   练习 的 次数 越 多, 熟练 的 程度

   Liànxí de cìshù yuè duō, shúliàn de chéngdù

   越 高。

   yuè gāo.

   The more you practice, the better you'll be.

5. 车次 **chēcì** train or bus service

   上下班 的 时候 车次 比较 多。

   Shàngxiàbān de shíhou chēcì bǐjiào duō.

   During peak hours, buses and trains are more frequent.

Helpful tips: The last two strokes taper off. **6 strokes**

次	丶	冫	丷	冹	汃	次					

CHARACTER 440

Traditional Form

极 jí extreme

極

Radical: 木 # 81 "tree"

Compounds, sentences, and meanings

1. 极 **jí** extremely
   我 最近 忙极了。
   Wǒ zuìjìn mángjíle.
   I've been extremely busy lately.

2. 极大 **jídà** enormous
   人类 给 自然 带来极大的 损害。
   Rénlèi gěi zìrán dàilái jídà de sǔnhài.
   Humans have caused great environmental harm.

3. 极端 **jíduān** extreme
   他 是 个 极端 个人主义者。
   Tā shì ge jíduān gèrénzhǔyìzhě.
   He is an out-and-out egoist.

4. 极力 **jílì** do everything possible
   我们 将极力避免 发生 事故。
   Wǒmen jiāng jílì bìmiǎn fāshēng shìgù.
   We'll do our utmost to avoid accidents.

5. 南极 **Nánjí** the South Pole
   中国 也派 探险队 去过 南极。
   Zhōngguó yě pài tànxiǎnduì qùguo Nánjí.
   China also sent an expedition to the South Pole.

Helpful tips: The sixth stroke has two bends.						**7 strokes**

极	一	十	才	木	枞	极	极				

度　**dù**

degree

Radical: 广 # 36 "broad"

Compounds, sentences, and meanings

1. 度 **dù** degree

   这里 夏天 最热是 摄氏三十五度。

   Zhèlǐ xiàtiān zuìrè shì shèshì 35 dù.

   It gets to 35°C in summer here.

2. 度过 **dùguò** pass, spend time in

   他在 农村 度过 童年。

   Tā zài nóngcūn dùguò tóngnián.

   He spent his childhood in the countryside.

3. 风度 **fēngdù** demeanor, bearing

   她的 风度 很 大方。

   Tāde fēngdù hěn dàfāng.

   She has an easy manner.

4. 度假 **dùjià** take a holiday

   下个月我 到 海边 去度假。

   Xià ge yuè wǒ dào hǎibiān qù dùjià.

   I'll be spending my holiday at the beach next month.

5. 湿度 **shīdù** humidity

   广州 夏天 湿度 很 高。

   Guǎngzhōu xiàtiān shīdù hěn gāo.

   The humidity in Guangzhou is very high in summer.

Helpful tips: The last stroke tapers off.								**9 strokes**
度	丶	二	广	广	庐	庐	庐	庐	度

虽 sui

although

雖

Radical: 口 # 50 "mouth" or 虫 # 142 "insect"

Compounds, sentences, and meanings

1. 虽 **suī** although

   问题 虽 小, 但 很 典型。
   Wèntí suī xiǎo, dàn hěn diǎnxíng.
   The problem is trivial, but common.

2. 虽然 **suīrán** although

   路上 虽然 很 辛苦, 但是 他 觉得
   Lùshàng suīrán hěn xīnkǔ, dànshì tā juéde
   很 高兴。
   hěn gāoxìng.
   Although the journey was tiring, he felt very happy.

3. 虽说 **suīshuō** although

   虽说 我 已 认识 他 很 久 了, 但 我
   Suīshuō wǒ yǐ rènshi tā hěn jiǔ le, dàn wǒ
   并 不 了解 他。
   bìng bù liǎojiě tā.
   Though I've known him for a long time, I don't understand him at all.

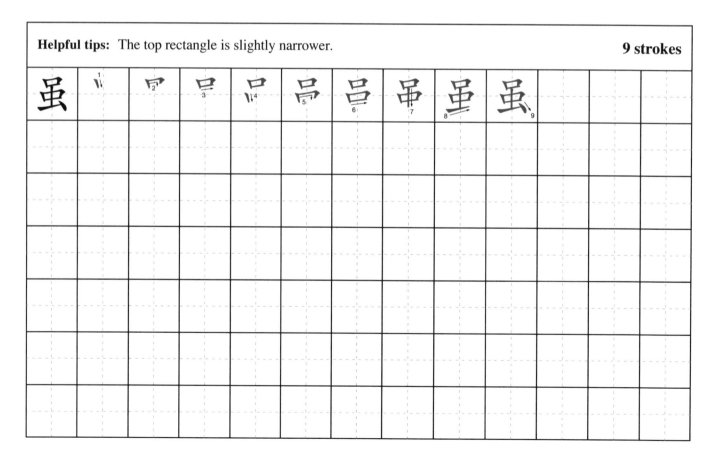

Helpful tips: The top rectangle is slightly narrower.   **9 strokes**

除 chú

except; divide

Radical: 阝 # 27 "left ear-lobe"

Compounds, sentences, and meanings

1. 除了 **chúle** except

除了 我的 朋友，我 只 认识 同班 的
Chúle wǒ de péngyou, wǒ zhǐ rènshi tóngbān de
学生。
xuéshēng.
Except for my friend, I only know students in my same class.

2. 除…以外 **chú…yǐwài** except for

除 旧金山 以外，美国 的 城市
Chú Jiùjīnshān yǐwài, Měiguó de chéngshì
没有 很 大的 唐人街。
méiyǒu hěn dà de tángrénjiē.
Except for San Francisco, American cities don't have very large Chinatowns.

3. 除非 **chúfēi** only if, unless

除非 每个人 改变自己 的 习惯，我们
Chúfēi měi ge rén gǎibiàn zìjǐ de xíguàn, wǒmen
才 能 解决 全球 暖化。
cái néng jiějué quánqiú nuǎnhuà.
Only if everyone changes their own habits, are we then able to solve global warming.

4. 除夕 **chúxī** New Year's Eve

每年 除夕 我 喜欢 办 很 大的 宴会。
Měinián chúxī wǒ xǐhuan bàn hěn dà de yànhuì.
Every New Year's Eve I enjoy throwing a big party.

Helpful tips: The first stroke begins with an angle and continues with a smooth curve.	**9 strokes**

除　阝　阝　阶　除　阴　除　除　除

例
lì

example, case

Radical: 亻 # 19 "person"

Compounds, sentences, and meanings

1. 例子 lìzi example

要 介绍 现代 的 情况，你 需要
Yào jièshào xiàndài de qíngkuàng, nǐ xūyào

给 一个 例子。
gěi yí ge lìzi.

When you want to introduce a modern situation, you need to introduce an example.

2. 例如 lìrú for example

中国 有一些 非常 大的 城市，
Zhōngguó yǒu yīxiē fēicháng dà de chéngshì,

例如北京。
lìrú Běijīng.

Cities in China are very large, for example Beijing.

3. 例外 lìwài exception

这个 事情 跟 大家 都 有 关系，
Zhè ge shìqing gēn dàjiā dōu yǒu guānxi,

没有 例外。
méiyǒu lìwài.

This situation has a connection to everyone without exception.

4. 例句 lìjù example sentence

要 写出 很 好的 例句是 很 难。
Yào xiěchū hěn hǎo de lìjù shì hěn nán.

Writing good example sentences is very difficult.

| **Helpful tips:** Each component is of similar width with the middle section slightly larger. | **8 strokes** |

例	丿	亻	乍	仴	佊	佊	例	例			

品   **pǐn**

product, item

Radical: 口 # 50 "mouth"

Compounds, sentences, and meanings

1. 产品 **chǎnpǐn** product

    每 个 公司 都 有 自己 特色 的 产品。

    Měi ge gōngsī dōu yǒu zìjǐ tèsè de chǎnpǐn.

    Every company has its special products.

2. 品质 **pǐnzhì** moral quality, character

    老师 的 品质 很 高。

    Lǎoshī de pǐnzhì hěn gāo.

    Teachers have high moral character.

3. 品名 **pǐnmíng** name of a product (on labels)

    品名: 青岛 啤酒

    Pǐnmíng: Qīngdǎo píjiǔ

    Product: Qingdao Beer

4. 品牌 **pǐnpái** brand name

    德国 有 很多 很 有名 的 汽车 品牌。

    Déguó yǒu hěnduō hěn yǒumíng de qìchē pǐnpái.

    Germany has many very famous brands of automobiles.

5. 品味 **pǐnwèi** taste

    他 只 要 吃 法国菜, 他的 品味 太 高!

    Tā zhǐ yào chī Fǎguó cài, tā de pǐnwèi tài gāo!

    He only wants to eat French food, his taste is too good!

Helpful tips: Each component is the same size.									9 strokes		
品	⌐¹	口²	口³	口⁴	口⁵	吕⁶	品⁷	品⁸	品⁹		

A. Pronunciation Identification

Please transcribe the following statements utilizing *pinyin*. For additional practice, use these statements to begin a conversation in Chinese.

1. 每天早上第一个人来办公室得开灯。

_____

2. 除了有高级的名牌, 啤酒平常很便宜。

_____

3. 你的汉语水平怎么样?

_____

B. Example Creation

For each of the following general conditions please provide a specific example. Introduce the example effectively with appropriate Chinese grammar structures.

1. 第一个。。。

_____

2. 高度。。。

_____

3. 特别产品。。。

_____

4. 等级。。。

_____

C. Short Story

Write a story on the following topic. Communicate each event in connected order. Make special note of significant and important moments throughout the experience.

请介绍你第一次自己做饭的经历。你要做什么饭，有没有遇到什么问题？

Traditional Form

赢

yíng

win, victory

赢

Radical: 亠 # 6 "top of 六"

Compounds, sentences, and meanings

1. 赢 **yíng** win, be victorious

   我们 都 希望自己喜欢 的 队 赢。

   Wǒmen dōu xīwàng zìjǐ xǐhuan de duì yíng.

   We all want the teams we enjoy to win.

2. 赢利 **yínglì** profit (coll.)

   每 次你卖 东西 你要 赢利。

   Měi cì nǐ mài dōngxi nǐ yào yínglì.

   Every time you sell something you want to profit.

3. 赢得 **yíngde** win, achieve

   人 都 希望 赢得 家人的 赞美。

   Rén dōu xīwàng yíngde jiārén de zànměi.

   All people hope to achieve the respect of their family.

Helpful tips: Each component on the bottom is equal in width.											17 strokes

输　shū
loss, lose

輸

Radical: 车 # 84 "vehicle"

Compounds, sentences, and meanings

1. 输了 **shūle**　lose; a loss

    每 个 球赛 都 有 一个 队 赢，
    Měi ge qiúsài dōu yǒu yí ge duì yíng,
    一个 队 输。
    yī ge duì shū.
    Every competition has a team that wins and a team that loses.

2. 输赢 **shūyíng**　victory or defeat; outcome

    有 人说：比赛 输赢 不 重要，
    Yǒu rénshuō: bǐsài shūyíng bú zhòngyào,
    过程 才 重要。
    guòchéng cái zhòngyào.
    It is said: victory or defeat isn't important; it is the experience that is important.

Helpful tips: The last stroke ends with a left hook.											**13 strokes**
输	一₁	左₂	车₃	车₄	车₅	车₆	车₇	输₈	输₉	输₁₀	输₁₁	输₁₂
输₁₃											

sài

competition, match

賽

Radical: 宀 # 34 "roof"

Compounds, sentences, and meanings

1. 比赛 **bǐsài** competition

   今天，学校 足球队 参加 比赛。

   Jīntiān, xuéxiào zǔqiú duì cānjiā bǐsài.

   Today, the school's soccer team is taking part in a match.

2. 赛跑 **sàipǎo** footrace, running race

   奥运会 的 赛跑 很 有名。

   Àoyùnhuì de sàipǎo hěn yǒumíng.

   The Olympics have famous footraces.

3. 赛过 **sàiguò** surpass

   很 少　中国　大学 赛得 过 北京

   Hěn shǎo Zhōngguó dàxué sài de guò Běijīng

   大学 的 研究。

   dàxué de yánjiū.

   Very few Chinese universities surpass the research at Beijing University.

Helpful tips: Pay attention to appropriate character height with multiple components.　　**14 strokes**

赛	丶	宀	宀	宀	宣	寅	寅	寒	寒	寒	寒	寒
	1	2	3	4	5	6	7	8	9	10	11	12
赛	赛											
13	14											

成   chéng

become

Radical: 戈 # 85 "spear"

Compounds, sentences, and meanings

1. 成 **chéng** become

他们 两个人 成了 好 朋友。
Tāmen liǎng ge rén chéngle hǎo péngyou.
The two of them became good friends.

2. 成绩 **chéngjī** result (of work or study)

他的学习 成绩 不太 好。
Tāde xuéxí chéngjī bútài hǎo.
He's not doing very well in his studies.

3. 成就 **chéngjiù** achievement

她是个很有 成就 的科学家。
Tā shì ge hěn yǒu chéngjiù de kēxuéjiā.
She is an accomplished scientist.

4. 成问题 **chéng wèntí** be a problem

雨再不停， 明天 的比赛就要
Yǔ zài bù tíng, míngtiān de bǐsài jiù yào

成 问题了。
chéng wèntí le.
If the rain doesn't stop, I doubt we can have the competition tomorrow.

5. 完成 **wánchéng** finish

她的 论文 完成 了。
Tāde lùnwén wánchéng le.
She has finished her thesis.

Helpful tips: The third stroke is a horizontal-bend-hook.   **6 strokes**

成	一¹	厂²	厉³	成⁴	成⁵	成⁶				

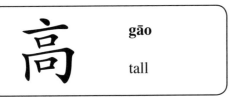

gāo

tall

Radical: 亠 # 6 "top of 六"

Compounds, sentences, and meanings

1. 高 **gāo** high, tall
   他比 小王 高一头。
   Tā bǐ Xiǎowáng gāo yì tóu.
   He is a head taller than Xiaowang.

2. 高矮 **gāo'ǎi** height
   这 两 棵树 高矮 差不多。
   Zhè liǎng kē shù gāo'ǎi chàbuduō.
   These two trees are nearly the same height.

3. 高低 **gāodī** high and low
   每个人的 声音 高低 不同。
   Měi ge rén de shēngyīn gāodī bùtóng.
   Everyone's voice has a different pitch.

4. 高大 **gāodà** tall and big
   那 栋 建筑物 很 高大。
   Nà dòng jiànzhùwù hěn gāodà.
   That building is huge.

5. 高兴 **gāoxìng** happy, pleased
   很 高兴 看见 你。
   Hěn gāoxìng kànjiàn nǐ.
   It's nice to see you.

Helpful tips: The second 口 is slightly larger than the first.									**10 strokes**

兴　xīng/xìng

prosper/interest

Radical: 八 # 17 "eight"

Compounds, sentences, and meanings

1. 兴 xìng mood, desire
   兴　高　采　烈
   Xìng gāo cǎi liè
   In high spirits

2. 兴奋 xīngfèn be excited
   我　兴奋得　睡不着　觉。
   Wǒ xīngfènde shuìbuzháo jiào.
   I'm so excited I can't sleep.

3. 兴趣 xìngqù interest
   我　对下棋很　感　兴趣。
   Wǒ duì xiàqí hěn gǎn xìngqù.
   I'm very interested in chess.

4. 兴头 xìngtóu enthusiasm
   我的　朋友　对体育　活动　兴头
   Wǒde péngyou duì tǐyù huódòng xìngtóu
   很　大。
   hěn dà.
   My friends are very into sports.

5. 高兴 gāoxìng happy
   认识　你很　高兴。
   Rènshi nǐ hěn gāoxìng.
   I'm pleased to meet you.

Helpful tips: The third stroke sweeps down from right to left.										**6 strokes**
兴	丶	丷	丷丿	䒑	兴	兴				

照

zhào

shine

Radical: 灬 # 71 "fire"

Compounds, sentences, and meanings

1. 照 **zhào** light up

   车灯 把大路 照得 通亮。
   Chēdēng bǎ dàlù zhàode tōngliàng.
   The headlights lit up the road.

2. 照相 **zhàoxiàng** take a picture

   我们 星期天 照相 去。
   Wǒmen Xīngqītiān zhàoxiàng qù.
   Let's go and take photographs this Sunday.

3. 照片 **zhàopiàn** photograph

   我 想 加印 照片。
   Wǒ xiǎng jiāyìn zhàopiàn.
   I want to print off copies from a negative.

4. 照旧 **zhàojiù** as before

   演唱会 改期， 入场券 照旧
   Yǎnchànghuì gǎiqī, rùchǎngquàn zhàojiù
   有效。
   yǒuxiào.
   The concert has been postponed, but the tickets remain valid.

5. 照常 **zhàocháng** as usual

   足球 比赛遇雨也 照常 进行。
   Zúqiú bǐsài yù yǔ yě zhàocháng jìnxíng.
   The soccer match will be played as scheduled in the event of rain.

Helpful tips: The two character components above the radical should be evenly balanced.											**13 strokes**
照	⎮⎮¹	⎰²	日³	日⁴	日⁵	昭⁶	昭⁷	昭⁸	照⁹	照¹⁰	照¹¹	照¹²
照¹³											

相

xiàng

looks, appearance

Radical: 木 # 81 "tree"

Compounds, sentences, and meanings

1. 相 **xiàng** appearance

   他 坐 在那儿, 一副 可怜 相。

   Tā zuò zài nàr, yí fù kělián xiàng.

   He sat there with a pitiful appearance.

2. 相貌 **xiàngmào** facial features

   那 小伙子 好 相貌!

   Nà xiǎohuǒzi hǎo xiàngmào!

   That young man is really handsome!

3. 相片 **xiàngpiàn** photograph

   我 喜欢 这 张 相片。

   Wǒ xǐhuan zhè zhāng xiàngpiàn.

   I like this photo.

4. 相声 **xiàngshēng** comic dialogue/cross-talk

   我 觉得 相声 很 有意思。

   Wǒ juéde xiàngshēng hěn yǒu yìsi.

   I enjoy comic dialogue.

5. 长相 **zhǎngxiàng** looks, features

   看 他们 的 长相 好像 是 兄弟。

   Kàn tāmen de zhǎngxiàng hǎoxiàng shì xiōngdì.

   They look like brothers.

Helpful tips: Each of the two character components should be evenly balanced.   **9 strokes**

相	一	十	才	木	杓	相	相	相			

片 **piàn**

part, slice

Radical: 片 # 100 "slice"

Compounds, sentences, and meanings

1. 片面包 **piànmiànbāo** sliced bread

   要 用 片面包 做 三明治。

   Yào yòng piànmiànbāo zuò sānmíngzhì.

   You want to use sliced bread to make a sandwich.

2. 照片 **zhàopiàn** photograph, picture

   看一看 这 张 照片 是我的

   Kàn yí kàn, zhè zhāng zhàopiàn shì wǒ de

   老 朋友。

   lǎo péngyou.

   Take a look, this picture is of my good friend.

3. 肉片 **ròupiàn** sliced meat

   很多 中国 菜用 肉片。

   Hěn duō Zhōngguó cài yòng ròupiàn.

   Many Chinese dishes use sliced meat.

4. 片段 **piànduàn** part, clip

   电影 片段 非常 有意思。

   Diànyǐng piànduàn fēicháng yǒu yìsì.

   The movie clip is really interesting.

Helpful tips: The left downward stroke does not have an exaggerated bend.   **4 strokes**

加

jiā

add, increase

Radical: 力 # 31 "strength"

Compounds, sentences, and meanings

1. 加 **jiā** add

   这 道 菜 的 味道 不太 好, 应该
   Zhè dào cài de wèidào bú tài hǎo, yīnggāi
   加 什么?
   jiā shénme?
   The flavor of this food isn't too good, what should be added?

2. 加入 **jiārù** enter, join

   国家　常常　加入 国际 贸易 组织。
   Guójiā chángcháng jiārù guójì màoyì zǔzhǐ.
   Countries often enter into international trade organizations.

3. 加油 **jiāyóu** Let's go!, fight!

   学校　队 加油 加油!
   Xuéxiào duì jiāyóu jiāyóu!
   Let's go team, fight, fight, fight!

4. 加倍 **jiābèi** multiply

   有　困难 的 时候, 你 得 加倍 努力。
   Yǒu kùnnan de shíhou, nǐ děi jiābèi nǔlì.
   When you have difficulties, you need to multiply your efforts.

5. 加快 **jiākuài** accelerate, increase in speed

   中国　经济 发展　每年　加快。
   Zhōngguó jīngjì fāzhǎn měinián jiākuài.
   Every year, the Chinese economy is growing at a faster rate.

Helpful tips: Each component is equal in size.													5 strokes
加	刁	力	加	加	加								

CHARACTER 456

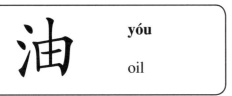

油

yóu

oil

Radical: 氵 # 32 "water"

Compounds, sentences, and meanings

1. 食油 **shíyóu** cooking oil

   做 饭 的 时候, 用 食油 炒饭 吧。

   Zuò fàn de shíhou, yǒng shíyóu chǎofàn ba.

   When cooking, use cooking oil to fry the food.

2. 石油 **shíyóu** petroleum, gasoline

   世界 上 石油 一年 比 一年 贵。

   Shìjiè shàng shíyóu yìnián bǐ yìnián guì.

   Across the world petroleum is getting more expensive year by year.

3. 油腻 **yóunì** oily, greasy

   中国 菜 常常 太 油腻。

   Zhōngguó cài chángcháng tài yóunì.

   Chinese food can often be too greasy.

Helpful tips: The vertical stroke does not cross the final stroke.

8 strokes

A. Pronunciation Practice

Please transcribe the following statements using *pinyin*. Then, in Chinese characters, answer the question provided.

1. 运动的比赛有两个队。

_____

2. 这场比赛每个队有十一个球员。

_____

3. 只有一个球员可以用手拿球。

_____

4. 进了一球给那队一分。

_____

5. 哪一队有最多分就赢了那场比赛。

_____

问题：这些句子介绍什么运动？

_____

B. Sentence Description

Describe for each of the situations below an instance when it would apply. When possible please describe in a connected sentence both the time and the situation.

1. （你很高兴）_____

_____

2. （你的队赢了）_____

_____

3.（你说加油加油！）_____

_____

4.（你要有很多照片）_____

_____

5.（你有成功）_____

_____

C. Short Description

Describe the illustration below. Express the components of the illustration, but also the context for the situation as a whole.

_____

_____

_____

_____

_____

_____

_____

_____

A. Vocabulary Identification

For each of the colors below, sketch a term that you identify with the color. Then provide the characters and *pinyin* for each term you provided.

白色		（汉字）
		(pinyin)
深红色		（汉字）
		(pinyin)
粉黄色		（汉字）
		(pinyin)

黑色		（汉字）
		(pinyin)
绿色		（汉字）
		(pinyin)
深蓝色		（汉字）
		(pinyin)

B. Short Description

Describe the illustration, expressing both the overall context for the figures in the illustration and the relationship between the different people. A strong description will convey accurately the relationship between the location and the people.

_____

_____

_____

_____

_____

_____

C. Place Description

Consider the following topic. Then create a description that demonstrates an understanding of locations, placement, and related activities. A strong description will express the traditional elements of a Suzhou garden, and also will show the cultural elements involved with understanding garden layout and design.

苏州花园是中国最有名的地方之一。除了苏州以外，一个苏州花园需要什么特点？请也介绍中国文化的山水思想跟苏州花园的关系。

_____

_____

_____

_____

_____

_____

D. Reflective Questions

Use these questions to both check the expressiveness of the previous section and to confirm your understanding of the previous topic. For additional practice, say and then respond to these questions aloud.

苏州花园都在什么中国城市？

花园有什么有名的例子？

你有没有去过一个苏州花园？

苏州花园有很长的历史，你会介绍一点吗？

苏州花园都有水，都有一些小楼，对不对？

对你来说，苏州的花园是很大还是很小？

在苏州花园你可以做什么？

对你来说，山水的思想有什么特点？

人们常常认为山水画好象介绍别的世界，你同意吗？

到过苏州花园后，启发你的新思想吗？

254

计 jì count

計

Radical: 讠 # 9 "word"

Compounds, sentences, and meanings

1. 计 **jì** calculate, count

现在 有博士 学位 的人 不计其数。

Xiànzài yǒu bóshì xuéwèi de rén bú jì qí shù.

Nowadays there are countless people with PhD degrees.

2. 计划 **jìhuà** plan

我们 计划 下周 出发。

Wǒmen jìhuà xiàzhōu chūfā.

We plan to leave next week.

3. 计较 **jìjiào** haggle over, fuss about

他不 计较 小事。

Tā bú jìjiào xiǎoshì.

He doesn't fuss about trifles.

4. 计时 **jìshí** reckon by time

这 是一份计时 工作。

Zhè shì yí fèn jìshí gōngzuò.

This work is paid by the time.

5. 计算 **jìsuàn** planning

做事 不能 没个计算。

Zuòshì bùnéng méi ge jìsuàn.

We shouldn't do anything without a plan.

Helpful tips: The second stroke is a horizontal-vertical-lift.				4 strokes
计	丶	讠	讠	计

划 huà delimit

劃

Radical: 刂 # 15 "upright knife" or 戈 # 85 "spear"

Compounds, sentences, and meanings

1. 划 **huà** draw, stroke (of a Chinese character)
   这 个 字 有 八 划。
   Zhè ge zì yǒu bā huà.
   This Chinese character has eight strokes.

2. 划定 **huàdìng** delimit, designate
   在 划定 的 区域 内 游泳。
   Zài huàdìng de qūyù nèi yóuyǒng.
   Swim within the designated areas.

3. 划一不二 **huà yì bú èr** fixed, rigid
   写 文章 没有 划一不二的 公式。
   Xiě wénzhāng méiyǒu huà yì bú èr de gōngshì.
   There are no hard and fast rules for writing essays.

4. 划分 **huàfēn** divide
   中国 划分 为 三 种 行政
   Zhōngguó huàfēn wéi sān zhǒng xíngzhèng
   区域。
   qūyù.
   China is divided into three types of administrative areas.

5. 划时代 **huàshídài** epoch-making
   中国 加入 世贸 具有 划时代
   Zhōngguó jiārù Shìmào jùyǒu huàshídài
   的意义。
   de yìyì.
   China's entry into the WTO was a historic event.

Helpful tips: The last stroke ends with a hook.						**6 strokes**

难　**nán**

difficult

難

Radical: 又　# 24 "again"

Compounds, sentences, and meanings

1. 难 **nán** difficult

   说起来 容易, 做起来难。

   Shuōqǐlai róngyì, zuòqǐlai nán.

   It is easier said than done.

2. 难得 **nándé** rare

   像 他 这样 的 人 很 难得。

   Xiàng tā zhèyàng de rén hěn nándé.

   It's rare to find a person like him.

3. 难说 **nánshuō** it's hard to say

   很 难说 谁 对 谁 不对。

   Hěn nánshuō shéi duì shéi búduì.

   It's hard to say who's right and who's wrong.

4. 难过 **nán'guò** sad

   他 听到 朋友 去世的 消息 非常

   Tā tīngdào péngyou qùshì de xiāoxi fēicháng

   难过。

   nán'guò.

   He was deeply saddened by the death of his friend.

5. 难为 **nánwéi** press, embarrass

   他 不会 唱歌 就别 难为 他了。

   Tā búhuì chànggē jiù bié nánwéi tā le.

   He can't sing, so don't press him to.

Helpful tips: There is equal spacing between the horizontal strokes.　　　　**10 strokes**

难	フ	又	刄	刃	对	对	邓	邓	难	难		

CHARACTER 460

容

róng

contain

Radical: 穴 # 110 "cave"

Compounds, sentences, and meanings

1. 容 **róng** hold, contain

   这 个 礼堂 能 容 五百 人。

   Zhè ge lǐtáng néng róng wǔbǎi rén.

   This room can hold 500 people.

2. 容纳 **róngnà** have a capacity of

   这 个 体育馆 能 容纳 一万 观众。

   Zhè ge tǐyùguǎn néng róngnà yīwàn guānzhòng.

   This stadium has a seating capacity of 10,000.

3. 容忍 **róngrěn** put up with

   你 怎么 能 容忍 他的 脾气?

   Nǐ zěnme néng róngrěn tāde píqi?

   How can you put up with his temper?

4. 容许 **róngxǔ** tolerate, permit

   请 容许 别人 把 话 说完。

   Qǐng róngxǔ biéren bǎ huà shuōwán.

   Please allow others to finish speaking.

5. 笑容 **xiàoróng** smiling face

   他 常常 满面 笑容。

   Tā chángcháng mǎnmiàn xiàoróng.

   He often has a grin on his face.

Helpful tips: Note the difference between 容 and 客.									**10 strokes**
容	⼀	⼆	宀	宀	宀	宀	宀	容	容

易 yì

change; easy

Radical: 日 # 90 "sun"

Compounds, sentences, and meanings

1. 易 yì easy

   冬天 易 患 感冒。

   Dōngtiān yì huàn gǎnmào.

   It is easy to catch a cold in winter.

2. 易经 **Yìjīng** the Book of Changes

   易经 这 本 书 很 难 懂。

   Yìjīng zhè běn shū hěn nán dǒng.

   It is difficult to understand the Book of Changes.

3. 交易 **jiāoyì** transaction

   对不起, 这里 现款 交易。

   Duìbuqǐ, zhèlǐ xiànkuǎn jiāoyì.

   I'm sorry, it's cash transactions here only.

4. 轻易 **qīngyì** easily

   不要 轻易地 下 结论。

   Búyào qīngyìde xià jiélùn.

   Don't jump to conclusions.

5. 容易 **róngyì** easy

   在 美国 生活 不太 容易。

   Zài Měiguó shēnghuó bú tài róngyì.

   Life is not easy in America.

Helpful tips: The bottom section is 勿.								8 strokes

易

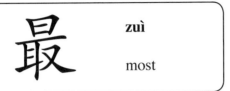

最

zuì

most

Radical: 日 # 91 "speech"

Compounds, sentences, and meanings

1. 最 **zuì** most

   同学 之 中 可算 小王 最
   Tóngxué zhī zhōng kě suàn Xiǎowáng zuì
   为积极。
   wéi jījí.
   Of all our classmates, Xiaowang's the most active.

2. 最多 **zuìduō** at most, maximum

   我 最多 只能 等 半个 小时。
   Wǒ zuìduō zhǐ néng děng bàn ge xiǎoshí.
   I can wait half an hour at the most.

3. 最好 **zuìhǎo** best, first rate

   这 是 最好 的 办法。
   Zhè shì zuìhǎo de bànfǎ.
   This is the best way.

4. 最后 **zuìhòu** last, final

   我 坐 在 最后 一排。
   Wǒ zuò zài zuìhòu yì pái.
   I sat in the last row.

5. 最近 **zuìjìn** recently, of late

   我 最近 很 忙。
   Wǒ zuìjìn hěn máng.
   I've been very busy lately.

Helpful tips: The fifth stroke extends to cover 又.											**12 strokes**

最　｜　冂　日　旦　旱　昂　昂　昂　昂　晨　最　最

fǎ

law, method

Radical: 氵 # 32 "3 drops of water"

Compounds, sentences, and meanings

1. 法 **fǎ** law

   国家 不能 无法。

   Guójiā bùnéng wú fǎ.

   All countries need laws.

2. 法国 **Fǎguó** France

   法国 大革命 对 美国 独立 战争

   Fǎguó Dàgémìng duì Měiguó Dúlì Zhànzhēng

   影响 很 大。

   yǐngxiǎng hěn dà.

   The French Revolution greatly influenced the American War of Independence.

3. 法定人数 **fǎdìng rénshù** quorum

   法定 人数 不足。

   Fǎdìng rénshù bùzú.

   We haven't got a quorum.

4. 法律 **fǎlǜ** law

   法律 面前 人人 平等。

   Fǎlǜ miànqián rénrén píngděng.

   Everyone is equal before the law.

5. 法子 **fǎzi** way, method

   我们 要 想 个法子解决 这 个问题。

   Wǒmen yào xiǎng ge fǎzi jiějué zhè ge wèntí.

   We have to think of a way to solve this problem.

Helpful tips: The second horizontal stroke is longer.　　　　**8 strokes**

法	丶	冫	氵	汀	汁	法	法	法			

rú

similar

Radical: 女 # 65 "female"

Compounds, sentences, and meanings

1. 如 **rú** resemble; as if

   事情 不如 他们 所 想 那么 简单。
   Shìqing bùrú tāmen suǒ xiǎng nàme jiǎndān.
   Things are not as simple as they think.

2. 如此 **rúcǐ** so, like that

   他的脾气 向来 如此。
   Tāde píqi xiànglái rúcǐ.
   His temper has always been like this.

3. 如果 **rúguǒ** if

   你如果 要 来, 请 事先 告诉 我。
   Nǐ rúguǒ yào lái, qǐng shìxiān gàosu wǒ.
   Let me know in advance if you're coming.

4. 如何 **rúhé** how, what

   这个 电影 你觉得如何?
   Zhè ge diànyǐng nǐ juéde rúhé?
   How did you like the film?

5. 如今 **rújīn** nowadays

   如今 很少 有 人 用 毛笔 了。
   Rújīn hěnshǎo yǒu rén yòng máobǐ le.
   Hardly anyone uses writing brushes these days.

Helpful tips: Each of the two character components should be evenly balanced.   **6 strokes**

果

guǒ

fruit, result

Radical: 木 # 81 "tree"

Compounds, sentences, and meanings

1. 果 **guǒ** as expected

果 不 出 所 料。

Guǒ bù chū suǒ liào.

Just as you would expect.

2. 果断 **guǒduàn** decisive, resolute

他 办事 果断。

Tā bànshì guǒduàn.

He works decisively.

3. 果然 **guǒrán** really, as expected

他 说 要 下雪, 果然 就 下雪 了。

Tā shuō yào xiàxuě, guǒrán jiù xiàxuě le.

He said it would snow, and sure enough it did.

4. 苹果 **píngguǒ** apple

我 买 一 斤 苹果。

Wǒ mǎi yì jīn píngguǒ.

I'd like to buy a catty [500 grams] of apples.

5. 后果 **hòuguǒ** consequence

后果 不堪 设想。

Hòuguǒ bùkān shèxiǎng.

The consequences would be too ghastly to contemplate.

Helpful tips: The vertical stroke does not protrude at the top. **8 strokes**

果	丨	冂	日	旦	旦	甲	界	果			

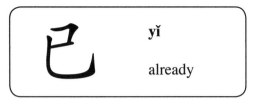

已　yǐ

already

Radical: 已 # 62 "self"

Compounds, sentences, and meanings

1. 已 **yǐ** already

   天 已 黑 了。

   Tiān yǐ hēi le.

   It's already dark.

2. 已经 **yǐjīng** already

   问题 已经 解决 了。

   Wèntí yǐjīng jiějué le.

   The problem has already been solved.

3. 已往 **yǐwǎng** in the past

   已往 的 事 不要 再提 了。

   Yǐwǎng de shì búyào zài tí le.

   Don't mention the past.

4. 而已 **éryǐ** that is all

   我 只 是 个 学生 而已。

   Wǒ zhǐ shì ge xuésheng éryǐ.

   I'm just a student, that is all.

Helpful tips: Note the difference between 已 and 己.										**3 strokes**
已	乛	乛	已							

经

jīng

classics; pass through

經

Radical: 纟 # 68 "silk"

Compounds, sentences, and meanings

1. 经 **jīng** pass through

   他 经 新加坡 回 广州。

   Tā jīng Xīnjiāpō huí Guǎngzhōu.

   He returns to Guangzhou via Singapore.

2. 经常 **jīngcháng** frequently

   他 经常 上 图书馆 去。

   Tā jīngcháng shàng túshūguǎn qù.

   He goes to the library regularly.

3. 经过 **jīngguò** pass

   这 路 车 经过 动物园 吗?

   Zhè lù chē jīngguò dòngwùyuán ma?

   Does this bus go past the zoo?

4. 经理 **jīnglǐ** manager

   她 在 一 家 饭馆 当 经理。

   Tā zài yì jiā fànguǎn dāng jīnglǐ.

   She works as a manager in a restaurant.

5. 经验 **jīngyàn** experience

   他的 经验 很 丰富。

   Tāde jīngyàn hěn fēngfù.

   He's got a lot of experience.

Helpful tips: The final vertical stroke does not go through the upper horizontal stroke.　　　**8 strokes**

经	纟	纟	纟	纫	纴	经	绐	经			

CHARACTER 468

始　shǐ

beginning

Radical: 女 # 65 "female"

Compounds, sentences, and meanings

1. 始 shǐ begin

不 知 始 于 何 时。

Bù zhī shǐ yú héshí.

It's not known exactly when this came into being.

2. 始末 shǐmò beginning and end

事情 的 始末 是 这样 的。

Shìqing de shǐmò shì zhèyàng de.

This is the story from A to Z.

3. 始终 shǐzhōng from start to finish

会议 始终 在 友好 的 气氛 中 进行。

Huìyì shǐzhōng zài yǒuhǎo de qìfēn zhōng jìnxíng.

The talks proceeded in a friendly atmosphere from start to finish.

4. 开始 kāishǐ begin

一 种 新的 工作, 开始 总 会

Yì zhǒng xīnde gōngzuò, kāishǐ zǒng huì

遇到 一些 困难。

yùdào yìxiē kùnnan.

You always run into some difficulties at the beginning of a new job.

5. 原始 yuánshǐ primeval, primitive

这是 原始 森林。

Zhè shì yuánshǐ sēnlín.

This is a primeval forest.

Helpful tips: The first stroke of 台 is a downward-left-bend.　　**8 strokes**

A. Character Practice and Pronunciation

First write the *pinyin* for each of the following characters. Then, in sequence in each of the boxes provided, write each of the character's strokes cumulatively (as shown in the character introductions).

难												
nán												
最												
如												
容												
经												
果												

B. Sentence Completion

Complete the following sentences by completing the "if…then…" statement. Demonstrate your effective use of context to understand the grammar construction. Please also notice that the topic is general and serves as a challenge for effective expression. The dominant question to consider is: "你就做什么？"

1. 如果第一次我试不成功。。。

_____

2. 如果我做得非常容易。。。

_____

3. 如果我不知道要用什么办法做。。。

_____

4. 如果我已经做过。。。

_____

5. 如果我还没开始做。。。

_____

C. Short Description

Create a short description based on the topic below. Attempt to express the initial planning concepts but also discuss the possible results of such planning. The expression of consequences should be done using strong connected statements.

请介绍你计划怎么找到新的，又很有意思的工作。

_____

_____

_____

_____

_____

_____

_____

告　　gào

tell

Radical: 口 # 50 "mouth"

Compounds, sentences, and meanings

1. 告 **gào** tell

   什么 时候 离开, 盼 告。

   Shénme shíhou líkāi, pàn gào.

   Please tell me when you are leaving.

2. 告别 **gàobié** bid farewell to

   我 向 你告别 来了。

   Wǒ xiàng nǐ gàobié lái le.

   I've come to say goodbye.

3. 告假 **gàojià** take leave

   我 身体不 舒服, 明天 告假。

   Wǒ shēntǐ bù shūfu, míngtiān gàojià.

   I don't feel well, I won't come in tomorrow.

4. 告诉 **gàosu** tell

   告诉 他们别 等 了。

   Gàosu tāmen bié děng le.

   Tell them not to wait.

5. 报告 **bàogào** report

   报告 大家一个 好 消息。

   Bàogào dàjiā yí ge hǎo xiāoxi.

   Here's a piece of good news for us all.

Helpful tips: The second horizontal stroke is longer than the first.　　　**7 strokes**

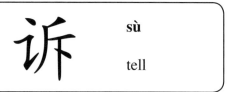

sù

tell

诉

Radical: 讠 # 9 "word"

Compounds, sentences, and meanings

1. 诉 sù tell

   他 常常 向 我 诉苦。

   Tā chángcháng xiàng wǒ sù kǔ.

   He often tells me his troubles.

2. 诉说 sùshuō relate, recount

   她 向 我 诉说 苦衷。

   Tā xiàng wǒ sùshuō kǔzhōng.

   She tells me her troubles.

3. 诉讼 sùsòng litigation

   他 提出 离婚 诉讼。

   Tā tíchū líhūn sùsòng.

   He has started divorce proceedings.

4. 控诉 kòngsù accuse, denounce

   她 控诉 社会 对 她的 歧视。

   Tā kòngsù shèhuì duì tā de qìshì.

   She spoke out against the way society had discriminated against her.

5. 倾诉 qīngsù pour out one's heart

   我 是你的 好 朋友， 有 什么 事可以

   Wǒ shì nǐde hǎo péngyou, yǒu shénme shì kěyǐ

   向 我 倾诉。

   xiàng wǒ qīngsù.

   I'm your good friend, you can pour your heart out to me.

| **Helpful tips:** Don't forget to end 斤 firmly with a dot. | **7 strokes** |

诉

信　xìn

letter; trust

Radical: 亻 # 19 "upright person"

Compounds, sentences, and meanings

1. 信 **xìn** letter

你 到 了 那儿 就 给 我 来 个 信。

Nǐ dàole nàr jiù gěi wǒ lái ge xìn.

Please send me a letter when you arrive.

2. 信不过 **xìnbuguò** distrust

你 是 信不过 我, 所以 不肯 对 我

Nǐ shì xìnbuguò wǒ, suǒyǐ bùkěn duì wǒ

讲　真话。

jiǎng zhēnhuà.

You are not telling me the truth because you don't trust me.

3. 信得过 **xìndeguò** trust

你 要是 信得过 我, 就 交 给 我 办。

Nǐ yàoshi xìndeguò wǒ, jiù jiāo gěi wǒ bàn.

If you trust me, let me do it for you.

4. 信心 **xìnxīn** confidence, faith

我 对 这 药 信心 不大。

Wǒ duì zhè yào xìnxīn bú dà.

I haven't much faith in this medicine.

5. 信用 **xìnyòng** trustworthiness

他 信用 好, 完全 可以 信任。

Tā xìnyòng hǎo, wánquán kěyǐ xìnrèn.

His credit is good. You can trust him.

Helpful tips: The top horizontal stroke is longer than those below.										**9 strokes**	
信	亻	亻	亻	信	信	信	信	信	信		

言　yán

word

Radical: 言 # 154 "whole word"

Compounds, sentences, and meanings

1. 言 **yán** word

你 为什么 一言 不发?

Nǐ wèishénme yì yán bù fā?

Why don't you say something?

2. 言论 **yánlùn** opinion on public affairs

西方 社会 有 言论 自由。

Xīfāng shèhuì yǒu yánlùn zìyóu.

There is freedom of speech in Western societies.

3. 言行 **yánxíng** words and deeds

这 个 人 言行 不一。

Zhè ge rén yánxíng bù yī.

This man's words don't match his deeds.

4. 言谈 **yántán** the way one speaks

言谈 之间 可以 看出 他 很 懂事。

Yántán zhījiān kěyǐ kànchū tā hěn dǒngshì.

It's clear from the way he talks that he is very mature.

5. 言语 **yányǔ** speech

这 个 人 言语 粗鲁。

Zhè ge rén yányǔ cūlǔ.

This man speaks crudely.

Helpful tips: The top horizontal stroke is the longest.　　　　**7 strokes**

言	丶	二	三	言	言	言	言				

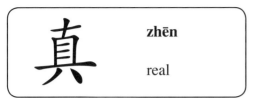

真 **zhēn**

real

Radical: 十 # 11 "ten"

Compounds, sentences, and meanings

1. 真 **zhēn** really

   时间 过得 真 快。

   Shíjiān guòde zhēn kuài.

   How time flies.

2. 真话 **zhēnhuà** truth

   朋友 之间 要 说 真话。

   Péngyou zhījiān yào shuō zhēnhuà.

   Friends should be honest with each other.

3. 真相 **zhēnxiàng** the real situation

   这 就是 事情 的 真相。

   Zhè jiù shì shìqing de zhēnxiàng.

   This is the actual state of affairs.

4. 真心 **zhēnxīn** sincere

   我 知道 你是 真心 对我 好。

   Wǒ zhīdao nǐ shì zhēnxīn duì wǒ hǎo.

   I know your affections for me are genuine.

5. 真正 **zhēnzhèng** genuine

   这是 真正 的吉林 人参。

   Zhè shì zhēnzhèng de Jílín rénshēn.

   This is genuine Jilin ginseng.

Helpful tips: There are three horizontal strokes inside.										**10 strokes**
真	一	十	广	古	直	直	直	直	真	真

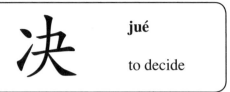

jué

to decide

Radical: 冫 # 7 "ice"

Compounds, sentences, and meanings

1. 决 **jué** definitely

   女儿 对她的 婚事 决 不 让步。

   Nǚ'ér duì tāde hūnshì jué bú ràngbù.

   With regard to her marriage, their daughter won't make any concessions.

2. 决不 **juébù** absolutely not

   在 这 方面 我 决不 退让。

   Zài zhè fāngmiàn wǒ juébù tuìràng.

   I will not give in under any circumstances.

3. 决定 **juédìng** decide

   我 一时 决定不了。

   Wǒ yìshí juédìngbuliǎo.

   I can't make up my mind right now.

4. 决心 **juéxīn** determination

   我 下定 决心 学好 汉字。

   Wǒ xiàdìng juéxīn xuéhǎo Hànzì.

   I'm determined to learn Chinese characters well.

5. 解决 **jiějué** resolve

   这 件 事情 不 容易 解决。

   Zhè jiàn shìqing bù róngyì jiějué.

   This matter is not easily resolved.

Helpful tips: The last stroke firms and then tapers off.											6 strokes
决	丶	冫	冖	冮	决	决					

定　　dìng

calm

Radical: 宀 # 34 "roof"

Compounds, sentences, and meanings

1. 定 **dìng** fix, establish

开会 时间 定 在 后天　上午
Kāihuì shíjiān dìng zài hòutiān shàngwǔ
十点。
shídiǎn.
The meeting is fixed for the day after tomorrow at 10 a.m.

2. 定做 **dìngzuò** have something made to order

我 这 双　跳舞鞋 是 定做 的。
Wǒ zhè shuāng tiàowǔxié shì dìngzuò de.
My dancing shoes were made to order.

3. 定期 **dìngqī** regular

我 定期 检查 身体。
Wǒ dìngqī jiǎnchá shēntǐ.
I have a regular medical checkup.

4. 一定 **yídìng** certainly

七点 以前 我 一定　能　回家。
Qīdiǎn yǐqián wǒ yídìng néng huíjiā.
I'll certainly be home before 7:00.

5. 约定 **yuēdìng** arrange

我们　约定 在　火车站　见面。
Wǒmen yuēdìng zài huǒchēzhàn jiànmiàn.
We've arranged to meet at the station.

Helpful tips: The last stroke curves, then levels off.									**8 strokes**
定	丶	丷	宀	宁	宇	宦	疋	定	

xiàng

resemble

Radical: 亻 # 19 "upright person"

Compounds, sentences, and meanings

1. 像 **xiàng** resemble

   这 孩子 像 他 父亲。

   Zhè háizi xiàng tā fùqin.

   The child takes after his father.

2. 像样 **xiàngyàng** up to the mark, presentable

   她 跳舞 还 挺 像样 的。

   Tā tiàowǔ hái tǐng xiàngyàng de.

   Her dancing is pretty good.

3. 不像话 **bú xiànghuà** unreasonable

   这 种 行为 真 不像话。

   Zhè zhǒng xíngwéi zhēn búxiànghuà.

   Behavior like that is really shocking.

4. 好像 **hǎoxiàng** seem, be like

   这 个 人 我 好像 是 在哪儿 见过。

   Zhè ge rén wǒ hǎoxiàng shì zài nǎr jiànguo.

   I seem to have met this man before.

5. 录像 **lùxiàng** videotape

   这 是 你 跳舞 的 录像。

   Zhè shì nǐ tiàowǔ de lùxiàng.

   This is a videotape of your dancing.

Helpful tips: The ninth stroke curves and ends with a hook.   **13 strokes**

像	ノ	亻	亻	伫	伫	伯	俜	俜	像	像	像	像
像												

清   qīng

clear

Radical: 氵 # 32 "3 drops of water"

Compounds, sentences, and meanings

1. 清 **qīng** clear

   谁 是 谁 非, 我 也 搞不清。

   Shéi shì shéi fēi, wǒ yě gǎobuqīng.

   I can't work out who's right and who's wrong.

2. 清楚 **qīngchu** clear

   她的发音 很 清楚。

   Tāde fāyīn hěn qīngchu.

   Her pronunciation is very clear.

3. 清理 **qīnglǐ** put in order

   请把 房间 清理一下。

   Qǐng bǎ fángjiān qīnglǐ yíxià.

   Please tidy (my) room.

4. 清静 **qīngjìng** quiet

   我们 找 个 清静 的 地方 谈谈。

   Wǒmen zhǎo ge qīngjìng de dìfang tántan.

   Let's find a quiet place to chat.

5. 清闲 **qīngxián** at leisure, idle

   他 过不惯 清闲 的 退休 生活。

   Tā guòbuguàn qīngxián de tuìxiū shēnghuó.

   He can't get used to having nothing to do, now that he's retired.

Helpful tips: Each horizontal stroke is evenly spaced.										**11 strokes**
清	丶	冫	氵	泸	泸	泮	清	清	清	清

楚

chǔ

clear, neat

Radical: 疋 # 130 "rolls of cloth"

Compounds, sentences, and meanings

1. 楚 **Chǔ** one of the Warring States

   楚 才 晋 用。

   Chǔ cái Jìn yòng.

   The talents of Chu used by Jìn.
   (meaning: brain drain)

2. 楚楚可怜 **chǔchǔ kělián** (of young woman)
   delicate and charming

   她 长得 楚楚 可怜 的。

   Tā zhǎngde chǔchǔ kělián de.

   She is delicate and charming.

3. 楚楚 **chǔchǔ** tidy, neat

   她 今天 穿得 衣冠 楚楚 的。

   Tā jīntiān chuānde yīguān chǔchǔ de.

   She is immaculately dressed today.

4. 苦楚 **kǔchǔ** suffering

   艾滋病 给 这 个 国家 带来了 极大的 苦楚。

   Àizībìng gěi zhè ge guójiā dàiláile jídàde kǔchǔ.

   AIDS has brought great misery to this country.

5. 清楚 **qīngchu** clear

   她的 发音 很 清楚。

   Tāde fāyīn hěn qīngchu.

   Her pronunciation is very clear.

Helpful tips: The ninth stroke ends with a hook.												**13 strokes**
楚	二	廿	才	木	杧	杧	杜	林	梺	梺	替	梺
楚												

唱　chàng

sing

Radical: 口 # 50 "mouth"

Compounds, sentences, and meanings

1. 唱 **chàng** sing

   他 唱得 很 难听。

   Tā chàngde hěn nántīng.

   He sings badly.

2. 唱歌 **chànggē** sing

   他 就 喜欢 人 听 他 唱歌。

   Tā jiù xǐhuan rén tīng tā chànggē.

   He likes people to listen when he sings.

3. 唱片 **chàngpiàn** phonograph record

   现在 不 用 唱片 了。

   Xiànzài bú yòng chàngpiàn le.

   Nowadays (people) don't play phonograph records.

4. 歌唱家 **gēchàngjiā** singer, vocalist

   他 是 个 有名 的 歌唱家。

   Tā shì ge yǒumíng de gēchàngjiā.

   He is a famous singer.

5. 合唱团 **héchàngtuán** choir

   我 最近 参加了 一个 合唱团。

   Wǒ zuìjìn cānjiāle yí ge héchàngtuán.

   Recently I joined a choir.

Helpful tips: The bottom 日 component is wider than the one above.										**11 strokes**

唱　口¹　吕²　吕³　吕⁴　吕⁵　唱⁶　唱⁷　唱⁸　唱⁹　唱¹⁰　唱¹¹

歌
gē

song

Radical: 欠 # 104 "owe"

Compounds, sentences, and meanings

1. 歌 **gē** song

   唱 首歌给 我们 听听, 怎么样?
   Chàng shǒu gē gěi wǒmen tīngting, zěnmeyàng?
   How about singing us a song?

2. 歌星 **gēxīng** singer (star)

   宋 祖英是 中国 有名 的 歌星。
   Sòng Zǔyīng shì Zhōngguó yǒumíng de gēxīng.
   Song Zuying is a famous Chinese singer.

3. 歌剧院 **gējùyuàn** opera house

   悉尼歌剧院 世界 有名。
   Xīní Gējùyuàn shìjiè yǒumíng.
   Sydney Opera House is world-famous.

4. 歌迷 **gēmí** fan (of singer)

   他是 宋 祖英 的 忠实 歌迷。
   Tā shì Sòng Zǔyīng de zhōngshí gēmí.
   He is a fan of Song Zuying.

5. 歌声 **gēshēng** sound of singing

   她的 歌声 很 清晰。
   Tāde gēshēng hěn qīngxī.
   Her (singing) voice is very clear.

Helpful tips: The fifth stroke is a vertical stroke.											**14 strokes**

Lesson 44: Review Activities

A. Radical Recognition and Pronunciation

Transcribe each of the following characters using *pinyin*. Each character is also a commonly used radical for Chinese characters; please provide four characters that utilize each of the radicals.

Radical:	言	人	水	木	口	心	食
pinyin:							
汉字：							

B. Sentence Completion

Please complete each of the following sentences with one of the terms provided. Then translate the resulting sentence into English.

真话   清楚   好像   相信   复杂

1. 政治家得说_____, 如果他们没说真相, 国家就受到困难。

_____

2. 现在你穿很奇怪的衣服, 你_____是外星人。

_____

3. 我听不懂你的话, 请说_____一点。

_____

4. 有人的生活很_____，每个人的生活都不一样。

_____

5. 别_____他，上个星期他骗过我！

_____

C. Short Description

Describe the illustration with a short paragraph. Identify and effectively express the multiple possibilities that can be seen within the same illustration. Use effective grammar and expressive techniques to clearly express the multiple possibilities.

_____

_____

_____

_____

_____

_____

_____

刚 gāng

just

刚

Radical: 刂 # 15 "upright knife"

Compounds, sentences, and meanings

1. 刚 **gāng** just

   这 双 鞋 大小 刚 合适。

   Zhè shuāng xié dàxiǎo gāng héshì.

   This pair of shoes is just the right size.

2. 刚才 **gāngcái** just now

   他 刚才 还 说 要 去 呢。

   Tā gāngcái hái shuō yào qù ne.

   He was saying only a moment ago that he wanted to go.

3. 刚刚 **gānggāng** a moment ago

   他 刚刚 走, 你 去 追 吧。

   Tā gānggāng zǒu, nǐ qù zhuī ba.

   He left just a minute ago. Run and try to catch him.

4. 刚好 **gānghǎo** exactly

   你们 来得 刚好。

   Nǐmen láide gānghǎo.

   You came in the nick of time.

5. 刚巧 **gāngqiǎo** by chance

   我 刚巧 在 车站 碰见 她。

   Wǒ gāngqiǎo zài chēzhàn pèngjiàn tā.

   I happened to run into her at the station.

Helpful tips: 冈 does not close at the bottom.											**6 strokes**
刚	刂¹	冂²	刃³	冈⁴	冈⁵	刚⁶					

Traditional Form

随 suí

follow, let

随

Radical: 阝 # 27 "left earlobe"

Compounds, sentences, and meanings

1. 随地 **suídì** without regard, everywhere

   请 勿随地吐痰。

   Qǐng wù suídì tǔtán.

   Please do not spit all over.

2. 随便 **suíbiàn** with no inclination, whatever

   去 什么 饭店 都可以, 我 随便 你。

   Qù shénme fàndiàn dōu kěyǐ, wǒ suíbiàn nǐ.

   What restaurant to go to is all okay, I'll follow your choice.

3. 随时 **suíshí** all the time, always

   好人 随时 关心 别人。

   Hǎorén suíshí guānxīn bié rén.

   No matter when, good people care about others.

4. 随意 **suíyì** as one pleases

   小 孩子可以随意做 喜欢 的 事情。

   Xiǎo háizi kěyǐ suíyì zuò xǐhuan de shìqing.

   Small children can do as they please.

| **Helpful tips:** The final three strokes fit clearly between the previous components. | | | | | | | | | | | **11 strokes** |

随	阝	阝	阝	阝	陏	陏	陏	陏	陏	随	随

新　xīn

new

Radical: 斤 # 101 "ax"

Compounds, sentences, and meanings

1. 新 **xīn** new

这 本 书 是 我 新 买 的。

Zhè běn shū shì wǒ xīn mǎi de.

This is the book I've just bought.

2. 新年 **xīnnián** new year

新年 好!

Xīnnián hǎo!

Happy New Year!

4. 新闻 **xīnwén** news

现在 是 新闻 简报。

Xiànzài shì xīnwén jiǎnbào.

Here are the (news) headlines.

4. 新奇 **xīnqí** strange, novel

他 初 到 北京 时, 处处 觉得 新奇。

Tā chū dào Běijīng shí, chùchù juéde xīnqí.

When he first got to Beijing, everything struck him as new.

5. 新鲜 **xīnxiān** fresh

这 条 鱼 有点 不 新鲜。

Zhè tiáo yú yǒudiǎn bù xīnxiān.

This fish is slightly stale.

Helpful tips: The bottom horizontal stroke of 亲 is shorter.　　　　**13 strokes**

新	丶¹	二²	六³	立⁴	立⁵	立⁶	辛⁷	亲⁸	亲⁹	亲¹⁰	新¹¹	新¹²
新¹³												

旧

jiù

old

舊

Radical: | # 3 "vertical stroke"

Compounds, sentences, and meanings

1. 旧 **jiù** old, used

   你的鞋旧了,买一 双 新的吧。

   Nǐde xié jiù le, mǎi yì shuāng xīnde ba.

   Your shoes are worn. Buy a new pair.

2. 旧货 **jiùhuò** secondhand goods

   我 买 的 是 旧货。

   Wǒ mǎi de shì jiùhuò.

   I bought it secondhand.

3. 旧事 **jiùshì** a past event

   请 不要 重提 旧事 了。

   Qǐng búyào chóngtí jiùshì le.

   Please don't dwell on the past.

4. 陈旧 **chénjiù** outdated

   你也 应该 改改你的 陈旧 思想。

   Nǐ yě yīnggāi gǎigai nǐde chénjiù sīxiǎng.

   You should change your outdated thinking.

5. 破旧 **pòjiù** old and shabby

   那个老头儿 穿着 一 身 破旧的衣服。

   Nà ge lǎotóur chuānzhe yì shēn pòjiù de yīfu.

   That old man is shabbily dressed.

Helpful tips: The vertical stroke takes up one third of the space.　　　**5 strokes**

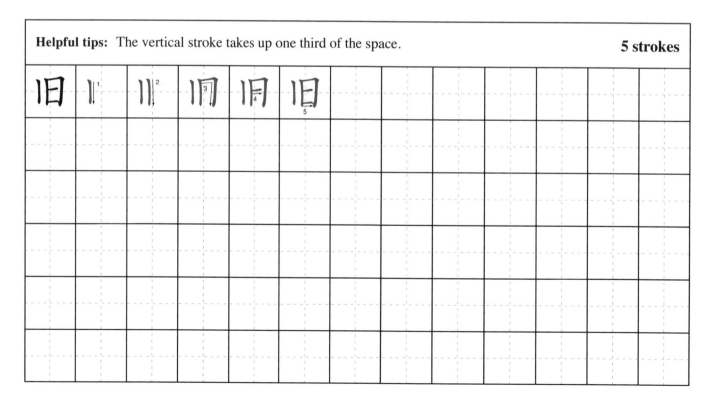

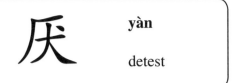

厌　yàn

detest

厭

Radical: 厂　# 12 "building"

Compounds, sentences, and meanings

1. 厌 **yàn**　be fed up with

   这 个　广告　我　看厌 了。

   Zhè ge guānggào wǒ kànyàn le.

   I've seen more than enough of this ad.

2. 厌烦 **yànfán**　be fed up with

   这 首 歌我 听　多少　次也不 觉得

   Zhè shǒu gē wǒ tīng duōshao cì yě bù juéde

   厌烦。

   yànfán.

   I never tire of listening to this song.

3. 厌恶 **yànwù**　detest

   大家 都　厌恶 他。

   Dàjiā dōu yànwù tā.

   Everyone is disgusted with him.

3. 厌倦 **yànjuàn**　be tired of

   整天　坐　办公室，我 早 就

   Zhěngtiān zuò bàngōngshì, wǒ zǎo jiù

   厌倦 了。

   yànjuàn le.

   Long ago, I grew tired of sitting in an office all day.

4. 厌食症 **yànshízhèng**　(esp. in young women)
   anorexia

   她 什么　都 不 吃，恐怕　是 得了

   Tā shénme dōu bù chī, kǒngpà shì déle

   厌食症。

   yànshízhèng.

   She's not eating anything. I'm worried that she has become anorexic.

Helpful tips: Note the difference between 厌 and 庆.											6 strokes
厌	一	厂	厂	厉	厌	厌					

合   hé

join

Radical: 人 # 18 "people"

Compounds, sentences, and meanings

1. 合 **hé** close
   把 书 合上。
   Bǎ shū héshàng.
   Close the book.

2. 合不来 **hébulái** be incompatible
   她 跟 母亲 合不来。
   Tā gēn mǔqin hébulái.
   She doesn't get along with her mother.

3. 合口 **hékǒu** (of a dish) be to one's taste
   你 做 的 菜 很 合口。
   Nǐ zuò de cài hěn hékǒu.
   The food you cook is very much to my taste.

4. 合理 **hélǐ** reasonable
   这 家 饭馆儿 收费 合理。
   Zhè jiā fànguǎnr shōufèi hélǐ.
   Prices at this restaurant are reasonable.

5. 合适 **héshì** suitable, appropriate
   这 个 词 用 在 这里 不 合适。
   Zhè ge cí yòng zài zhèlǐ bù héshì.
   This isn't the right word to use here.

Helpful tips: The line in the middle does not touch the side strokes.   **6 strokes**

合	ノ¹	人²	今³	合⁴	合⁵	合⁶							

适　shì

appropriate

適

Radical: 辶 # 38 "movement"

Compounds, sentences, and meanings

1. 适 **shì** suitable

   这个 电影 不 适于 儿童 观看。

   Zhè ge diànyǐng bú shì yú értóng guānkàn.

   This movie is not suitable for children.

2. 适当 **shìdàng** appropriate

   到 适当 的 时候 我 会 告诉 你。

   Dào shìdàng de shíhou wǒ huì gàosu nǐ.

   I'll tell you in due course.

3. 适合 **shìhé** suit, fit

   他 适合 做 教师。

   Tā shìhé zuò jiàoshī.

   He's well suited to a teaching career.

4. 适宜 **shìyí** suitable

   游泳 对 老年人 也是 适宜 的。

   Yóuyǒng duì lǎoniánrén yě shì shìyí de.

   Swimming is good for old people too.

5. 适中 **shìzhōng** well situated

   这家 饭店 地点 适中。

   Zhè jiā fàndiàn dìdiǎn shìzhōng.

   This hotel is well situated.

Helpful tips: The top stroke of 舌 sweeps from right to left.　　**9 strokes**

适	ノ	二	チ	千	舌	舌	舌	活	适			

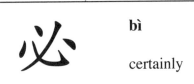

必 **bì**

certainly

Radical: 心 # 76 "heart"

Compounds, sentences, and meanings

1. **必 bì** must

   我 明天 下午 两点半 必到。

   Wǒ míngtiān xiàwǔ liǎngdiǎnbàn bì dào.

   I'll definitely be there at 2:30 tomorrow.

2. **必得 bìděi** have to

   你必得去一趟。

   Nǐ bìděi qù yí tàng.

   You simply must go.

3. **必定 bìdìng** must

   她 必定 知道。

   Tā bìdìng zhīdao.

   She must have known it.

4. **必然 bìrán** inevitable

   他 必然 失败。

   Tā bìrán shībài.

   He will certainly fail.

5. **必要 bìyào** necessary

   我们 没有 必要 再 讨论 了。

   Wǒmen méiyǒu bìyào zài tǎolùn le.

   There's no need for us to discuss this any further.

Helpful tips: Note the difference between 必 and 心.											**5 strokes**
必	丿	心	心	必	必						

dài

represent

Radical: 亻 # 19 "upright person"

Compounds, sentences, and meanings

1. 代 **dài** take the place of

请 代 我 向 您 父母 问候。

Qǐng dài wǒ xiàng nín fùmǔ wènhòu.

Please give my regards to your parents.

2. 代办 **dàibàn** do something for somebody

这 件 事 请 你 代办 吧。

Zhè jiàn shì qǐng nǐ dàibàn ba.

Could you do this for me?

3. 代表 **dàibiǎo** represent

老师 让 她 代表 我们 班 同学

Lǎoshī ràng tā dàibiǎo wǒmen bān tóngxué

讲话。

jiǎnghuà.

The teacher asked her to speak on behalf of the class.

4. 代价 **dàijià** price, cost

我们 不惜 任何 代价 也 要 完成

Wǒmen bùxī rènhé dàijià yě yào wánchéng

任务。

rènwù.

We have to finish the job at any cost.

5. 代替 **dàitì** replace

将来 很多 工作 都 能 用

Jiānglái hěnduō gōngzuò dōu néng yòng

机器人代替。

jīqìrén dàitì.

In the future, robots will replace people in many jobs.

Helpful tips: The second to last stroke is a slanting hook.

5 strokes

代	丿	亻	仁	代	代								

gēng/gèng

change, replace/even, moreover

Radical: 一 # 2 "horizontal stroke"

Compounds, sentences, and meanings

1. 更 **gèng** even, more so

   这 张 画 比别的画 更好, 更
   Zhè zhāng huā bǐ bíede huā gènghǎo, gèng
   有意思。
   yǒu yìsi.
   This painting is extremely good, it's more interesting than other paintings.

2. 更加 **gèngjiā** more so, moreover

   这 个 课 比 上 个 课 更加 难。
   Zhè ge kè bǐ shàng ge kè gèngjiā nán.
   This class is even more difficult than the last one.

3. 更改 **gēnggǎi** change, alter

   现在 我 的 生活 非常 好, 一点 也
   Xiànzài wǒ de shēnghuó fēicháng hǎo, yìdiǎn yě
   不要 更改!
   bú yào gēnggǎi.
   Right now my life is really good, I wouldn't change it even a little bit.

4. 更替 **gēngtì** to replace

   新的 东西 如果 有 毛病, 公司
   Xīn de dōngxì rúguǒ yǒu máobing, gōngsī
   常常 让 你 更替 新的。
   chángcháng ràng nǐ gēngtì xīn de.
   When a new thing breaks, companies often let you replace it for a new one.

Helpful tips: The vertical stroke has a slight bend to the left.											**7 strokes**

Lesson 45: Review Activities

A. *Pinyin* and Pronunciation Practice

Please transcribe the following questions into *pinyin*. For additional practice, say and then respond to these questions aloud.

1. 我要写更好的文章, 你有没有意见?

_____

2. 我随便你, 你要去哪儿? 要做什么?

_____

3. 我们的朋友刚刚来了, 我们一起可以做什么?

_____

B. Adjective Descriptions

Please place one of the provided adjectives with each of the items below. Then sketch a small illustration of the item that depicts the adjective effectively. Finally, write a sentence that describes the item accurately.

新　　　重　　　旧　　　贵　　　便宜

汽车		
楼		_____
书		_____
		_____

毛衣	
照相机	

C. Short Descriptions

For each of the following problems, present a possible method for solution. Attempt to also indicate the severity of the problem and offer some advice as to how quickly and effectively the solution needs to happen.

1. 你想做更好吃的饭。

_____

_____

_____

2. 你刚刚到达一个新的城市。

_____

_____

_____

3. 你必需再上大学的课。

_____

_____

_____

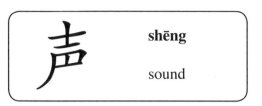

声　shēng

sound

Radical: 士 # 41 "scholar"

Compounds, sentences, and meanings

1. 声 **shēng** sound

   你 听见 脚步 声 了 没有?

   Nǐ tīngjiàn jiǎobù shēng le méiyǒu?

   Did you hear the sound of footsteps?

2. 大声 **dàshēng** loudly

   请 你 说 大声 点儿。

   Qǐng nǐ shuō dàshēng diǎnr.

   Please speak up a little.

3. 小声 **xiǎoshēng** in a low voice

   请 小声 说话。

   Qǐng xiǎoshēng shuōhuà.

   Please speak softly.

4. 声调 **shēngdiào** tones

   学 汉语 一定 要 学好 声调。

   Xué Hànyǔ yídìng yào xuéhǎo shēngdiào.

   In learning Chinese, one must learn the tones properly.

5. 声旁 **shēngpáng** phonetic element of a character

   "请" 的 声旁 是 "青"。

   "Qǐng" de shēngpáng shì "qīng".

   The phonetic element for the character "qǐng" is "qīng."

Helpful tips: The second horizontal stroke of 士 is shorter. **7 strokes**

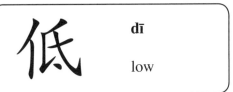

低   **dī**

low

Radical: 亻 # 19 "upright person"

Compounds, sentences, and meanings

1. 低 **dī** low
   飞机飞得 很 低。
   Fēijī fēide hěn dī.
   The plane flew very low.

2. 低沉 **dīchén** (of voice) low and deep
   他的 声音 很 低沉。
   Tāde shēngyīn hěn dīchén.
   He's got a low voice.

3. 低估 **dīgū** underrate
   我低估了她的 英语 水平。
   Wǒ dīgūle tāde Yīngyǔ shuǐpíng.
   I underestimated the standard of her English.

4. 低头 **dītóu** yield, submit
   我 决不 向 困难 低头。
   Wǒ juébù xiàng kùnnan dītóu.
   I will never give in to difficulties.

5. 降低 **jiàngdī** drop, lower
   今天 气温 降低 了。
   Jīntiān qìwēn jiàngdī le.
   The temperature has dropped today.

Helpful tips: Note the final stroke placed at the bottom of the character.   **7 strokes**

低	丿	亻	仁	仹	仾	低	低				

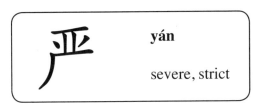

严 yán

severe, strict

Radical: 一 # 2 "horizontal stroke"

Compounds, sentences, and meanings

1. 严肃 yánsù serious, severe

   我 朋友 的 脸面 很 严肃。

   Wǒ péngyou de liǎnmiàn hěn yánsù.

   My friend's face looks very severe.

2. 严重 yánzhòng serious, weighty

   我们 不 希望 生 严重 的病。

   Wǒmen bù xīwàng shēng yánzhòng de bìng.

   We all wish not to get a serious disease.

3. 严酷 yánkù harsh, difficult

   水灾 以后人民的 生活 很

   Shuǐzāi yǐhòu rénmín de shēnghuó hěn

   严酷 的。

   yánkù de.

   After a flood people's lives are very difficult.

Helpful tips: The horizontal strokes are of even length.											7 strokes
严	一	丅	丌	亚	亚	亚	严				

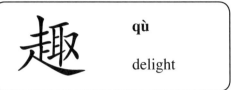

qù

delight

Radical: 走 # 156 "walk"

Compounds, sentences, and meanings

1. 趣 **qù** interest, delight

我 觉得 他 表演得 很 有趣。

Wǒ juéde tā biǎoyǎnde hěn yǒuqù.

I found his performance quite delightful.

2. 趣味 **qùwèi** taste

这 种 电影 迎合 低级 趣味。

Zhè zhǒng diànyǐng yínghé dījí qùwèi.

This type of movie caters to vulgar tastes.

3. 乐趣 **lèqù** interest, delight

我 觉得 跳舞 的 乐趣 无穷。

Wǒ juéde tiàowǔ de lèqù wúqióng.

I think dancing is truly wonderful.

4. 兴趣 **xìngqù** interest

我 对 下棋 很 感 兴趣。

Wǒ duì xiàqí hěn gǎn xìngqù.

I'm very interested in chess.

5. 有趣 **yǒuqù** interesting

这 是 个 有趣 的 游戏。

Zhè shì ge yǒuqù de yóuxì.

This is an interesting game.

Helpful tips: End the last stroke firmly.											**15 strokes**
趣	二¹	土²	土³	丰⁴	丰⁵	走⁶	走⁷	走⁸	赴⁹	赳¹⁰	趋¹¹	趋¹²
趋¹³	趣¹⁴	趣¹⁵									

表

biǎo

show, express

Radical: 一 # 2 "horizontal stroke"

Compounds, sentences, and meanings

1. 表 **biǎo** show, express

   我们 对你的遭遇 深 表 同情。

   Wǒmen duì nǐde zāoyù shēn biǎo tóngqíng.

   We would like to express our deep sympathy for what you went through.

2. 表达 **biǎodá** express

   我 激动 的 心情 难以 用 语言

   Wǒ jīdòng de xīnqíng nán yǐ yòng yǔyán

   来 表达。

   lái biǎodá.

   Words can hardly express my excitement.

3. 表面 **biǎomiàn** surface

   你 不能 只看 事情 的 表面。

   Nǐ bùnéng zhǐ kàn shìqing de biǎomiàn.

   Don't judge a book by its cover.

4. 表情 **biǎoqíng** expression

   他的 面部 没有 表情。

   Tāde miànbù méiyǒu biǎoqíng.

   He doesn't have any expression on his face.

5. 表演 **biǎoyǎn** perform

   他 表演得 很 好。

   Tā biǎoyǎnde hěn hǎo.

   He performed very well.

Helpful tips: The middle horizontal stroke is shorter.								**8 strokes**

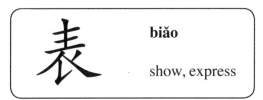

299

放   **fàng**

release, put

Radical: 攵 # 99 "tap" or 方 # 74 "direction"

Compounds, sentences, and meanings

1. 放 **fàng** put

   把 书 放 在 桌子 上。

   Bǎ shū fàng zài zhuōzi shàng.

   Put the book on the table.

2. 放大 **fàngdà** enlarge

   我 想 把 这 几 张　照片 放大。

   Wǒ xiǎng bǎ zhè jǐ zhāng zhàopiàn fàngdà.

   I'd like to enlarge these photographs.

3. 放过 **fàngguò** let off, let slip

   这 是 好 机会, 不要　放过。

   Zhè shì hǎo jīhuì, búyào fàngguò.

   This is a good opportunity. Don't let it slip.

4. 放假 **fàngjià** have a holiday

   你 什么　时候　放假。

   Nî shénme shíhou fàngjià?

   When do you go on holiday?

5. 放心 **fàngxīn** be at ease

   你 放心 吧, 一切 都　安排好了。

   Nǐ fàngxīn ba, yíqiè dōu ānpáihǎole.

   Don't worry, everything has been arranged.

Helpful tips: Note the difference between 攵 and 又.   **8 strokes**

放	丶	二	方	方	方	放	放				

危　**wēi**

danger, risk

Radical: 刀 # 30 "knife"

Compounds, sentences, and meanings

1. 危险 **wēixiǎn** risky, dangerous

   山路　很　危险。

   Shānlu hěn wēixiǎn.

   Mountain roads are very dangerous.

2. 危机 **wēijī** crisis

   有　人说: 危机　就是　时机。

   Yǒu rénshuō: wēijī jiùshì shíjī.

   People say that a crisis is an opportunity.

3. 危害 **wēihài** endanger, put at risk

   抽烟　危害　健康。

   Chōuyān wēihài jiànkāng.

   Smoking endangers one's health.

Helpful tips: The final stroke ends in a hook.　　　　　**6 strokes**

危	⺈¹	⺈²	产³	广⁴	危⁵	危⁶								

险 xiǎn

danger, vicious

險

Radical: 阝 # 27 "left earlobe"

Compounds, sentences, and meanings

1. 保险 **bǎoxiǎn** insurance, safe

   在 美国 开车 需要 有 汽车 保险。

   Zài Měiguó kāi chē xūyào yǒu qìchē bǎoxiǎn.

   In America to drive one must have auto insurance.

2. 避险 **bìxiǎn** hedge fund

   每个 公司 都 有 自己避险 方法。

   Měi ge gōngsi dōu yǒu zìjǐ bìxiǎn fāngfǎ.

   Every company has its own method of avoiding risk.

3. 冒险 **màoxiǎn** adventurous

   年轻人　都 喜欢　冒险。

   Niánqīngrén dōu xǐhuan màoxiǎn.

   Youth all like to seek out adventures.

Helpful tips: The fifth stroke should fit underneath the previous two strokes.											**9 strokes**

险	3 阝	阝	阝	阶	险	险	险	险	险		

普   pǔ

general

Radical: 日 # 90 "sun"

Compounds, sentences, and meanings

1. 普 **pǔ** general

   今天   阳光   普照。

   Jīntiān yángguāng pǔ zhào.

   Today, the sun is shining everywhere.

2. 普通 **pǔtōng** ordinary

   这 件衣服 很 普通。

   Zhè jiàn yīfu hěn pǔtōng.

   This garment is nothing special.

3. 普通话 **Pǔtōnghuà** Mandarin

   他的 普通话 带 南方   腔调。

   Tāde Pǔtōnghuà dài nánfáng qiāngdiào.

   His Mandarin has a southern accent.

4. 普及 **pǔjí** be made popular among

   中国   正普及法律 常识。

   Zhōngguó zhèng pǔjí fálù chángshí.

   China is making basic legal principles widely known.

5. 普洱茶 **Pǔ'ěrchá** Pu'er tea (red tea from Yunnan province)

   普洱茶 能   帮助   消化。

   Pǔ'ěrchá néng bāngzhù xiāohuà.

   Pu'er tea is a digestive aid.

Helpful tips: The vertical strokes do not cross through the second horizontal stroke.   **12 strokes**

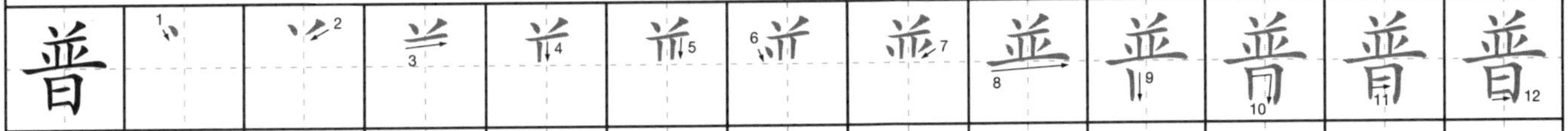

| 普 | ヽ¹ | ˡ�′² | ˭³ | 丷⁴ | 丷⁵ | 并⁶ | 並⁷ | 並⁸ | 普⁹ | 普¹⁰ | 普¹¹ | 普¹² |

tōng

through

Radical: 辶 # 38 "movement"

Compounds, sentences, and meanings

1. 通 **tōng** go to

   这 趟 列车 直通 西安。

   Zhè tàng lièchē zhítōng Xī'ān.

   This train goes straight to Xian.

2. 通常 **tōngcháng** usually

   我 通常 七点 起床。

   Wǒ tōngcháng qīdiǎn qǐchuáng.

   I usually get up at 7:00.

3. 通过 **tōngguò** by means of

   通过 姐姐 介绍，我 认识了她。

   Tōngguò jiějie jièshào, wǒ rènshile tā.

   I got to know her through my older sister.

4. 通知 **tōngzhī** notify

   请 马上 通知他。

   Qǐng mǎshàng tōngzhī tā.

   Please notify him immediately.

5. 交通 **jiāotōng** transport

   北京 的 交通 很 方便。

   Běijīng de jiāotōng hěn fāngbiàn.

   The transport system in Beijing is very convenient.

Helpful tips: The second stroke of 甬 is a dot.										**10 strokes**	
通	丁	马	孑	肖	肖	肖	甬	甬	诵	通		

Lesson 46: Review Activities

A. Character Practice

Please complete the two-character words that are provided, reflecting an understanding of character combinations.

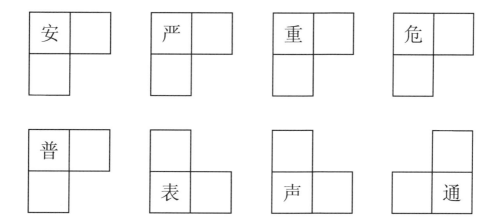

B. Translation Exercise

Please translate this classic poem from the Chinese literary tradition into English. The title is given for the poem, but only limited additional vocabulary is provided. This poem is by the Tang Dynasty poet 王维 (701–761 CE).

鹿柴 lùchái　　　　　　**Deer Park**

空山不见人，　　　　　　_____

但闻人语响。　　　　　　_____

返景入深林，　　　　　　_____

复照青苔上。　　　　　　_____

柴　**chái**　enclosure, park
响　**xiǎng**　noise, sound
苔　**tái**　moss

C. Short Description

Create a short description based on the topic below. Attempt to express both the usual circumstances and what can be considered unusual. A strong description will also include an effective response to the situation.

一般上普通的情况也有危险性。对你来说，在每天生活中，哪些运动是有危险性的？

_____

_____

_____

_____

_____

_____

_____

A. Pronunciation and *Pinyin* Practice

Transcribe the following song using *pinyin*. If possible, listen to a recording of the song and match the singing to the romanization.

中国共和国的国歌歌词：

Lyrics for the People's Republic of China National Anthem:

起来！不愿做奴隶的人们！

_____

把我们的血肉，

_____

筑成我们新的长城！

_____

中华民族到了最危险的时候，

_____

每个人被迫着发出最后的吼声。

_____

起来！起来！起来！

_____

我们万众一心，

_____

冒着敌人的炮火，前进！

_____

冒着敌人的炮火，前进！

_____

前进！前进！进！

_____

B. Short Description

Describe the situation depicted in the illustration. When describing the situation please also comment on why this situation should be considered dangerous and how it might have occurred. A strong description will also express solutions to the situation and possible additional complications.

_____

_____

_____

_____

_____

_____

_____

_____

C. Problem Description

Consider the following topic. Then create a description that demonstrates understanding of topics with complex causes and difficult solutions. Clearly compare the two types of situations being discussed; attempt to use examples, relationships, and precise vocabulary to communicate a complete and structured understanding.

目前问题有两种：一，是一个永久的问题（从古到今人都要解决这样的问题）；二，是一个更新的问题（刚刚发现的情况）。请介绍这个新问题。也请介绍你的意见来解决这个新问题。

_____

_____

_____

_____

_____

_____

_____

D. Reflective Questions

Use these questions to both check the expressiveness of the previous section and to confirm your understanding of the previous topic. For additional practice, say and then respond to these questions aloud.

什么问题是长久问题？请用例子介绍介绍。

什么问题是现代问题？请用例子介绍介绍。

什么情况是人生活中永远的情况？

你想现代的问题跟老百姓有没有关系？

这个情况需要很大的变化解决吗？

在什么时候人开始了解这个情况是一个很大的问题？

如果人类不改变，我们大概会遇到什么结果？

以前的人跟这样的问题有经历吗？

别人同意你的意见吗？

你所介绍的问题是不是世界上最重要的问题？

Alphabetical Index

The number on the right of each column refers to the character number, followed by the compound/sentence number.

A

ài	爱	330.1
àihào	爱好	330.5
àihù	爱护	330.3
àiqíng	爱情	330.2
àixī	爱惜	330.4
ānjìng	安静	395.1
ānquán	安全	395.2
ānxīn	安心	395.4
ānwēi	安危	395.5

B

bǎ	把	311.1
bǎbìng	把柄	311.3
bǎwò	把握	311.4
bǎxì	把戏	311.5
bái	白	405.1
báibái	白白	405.2
báicài	白菜	405.3
báifèi	白费	405.4
báitiān	白天	405.5
bǎiwàn	百万	381.2
bàn	办	350.1
bànfǎ	办法	350.2
bàn gōngshì	办公室	350.3/351.1
bànlǐ	办理	350.4
bànshì	办事	350.5
bāng	帮	266.1
bāng dào máng	帮倒忙	266.5
bāngmáng	帮忙	266.4/268.5
bāngshǒu	帮手	266.3
bāngzhù	帮助	266.2/267.2
bǎngpiào	绑票	390.4

bǎoxiǎn	保险	498.1
bǎoyǎng	保养	425.3
bàogào	报告	469.5
bēi	杯	324.1
bēizi	杯子	324.2
běn	本	252.1
běndì	本地	252.2
běnháng	本行	252.3
běnlái	本来	252.4
běnlǐng	本领	252.5
bǐjiào	比较	344.3
bǐsài	比赛	448.1
bì	必	494.1
bìděi	必得	488.2
bìdìng	必定	488.3
bìrán	必然	488.4
bìyào	必要	488.5
bìxiǎn	避险	498.2
biǎo	表	495.1
biǎodá	表达	495.2
biǎomiàn	表面	495.3
biǎoqíng	表情	495.4
biǎoyǎn	表演	495.5
bié	别	400.1
biéde	别的	400.2
biéren	别人	400.4
biézhì	别致	400.3
bìng	病	286.1
bìngjià	病假	286.2
bìnglì	病历	286.3
bìngqíng	病情	286.4
bìngrén	病人	286.5
búxiànghuà	不像话	476.3
búguò	不过	363.5
bùxǔ	不许	432.4

C

cái	才	281.1
cáihuá	才华	281.3
cáishí	才识	281.4
cài	菜	317.1
càidān	菜单	317.3
càishìchǎng	菜市场	317.2
cè	厕	397.1
cèsuǒ	厕所	397.2
chábēi	茶杯	324.3
chǎnpǐn	产品	445.1
cháng	长	378.1
chángchù	长处	378.2
chángduǎn	长短	379.4
Chángjiāng	长江	378.5
chángyuǎn	长远	361.5
cháng	常	338.1
chángcháng	常常	338.2
chángjiàn	常见	338.3
chángshí	常识	338.4
cháng	场	384.1
chàng	唱	479.1
chànggē	唱歌	479.2
chàngpiàn	唱片	479.3
chāojí	超级	437.3
chē	车	386.1
chēcì	车次	439.5
chēfèi	车费	386.2
chēhuò	车祸	386.5
chénjiù	陈旧	484.4
chéng	成	449.1
chénggōng	成功	341.4
chéngjī	成绩	449.2
chéngjiù	成就	449.3
chéng wèntí	成问题	449.4
chéngchē	乘车	392.1
chéngjī	乘机	392.3
chéngkè	乘客	392.2
chīgòu	吃够	326.2

chóng	重	306.1
chóngfù	重复	306.2
chū	出	367.1
chūchāi	出差	367.2
chūcuò	出错	367.3
chūfā	出发	367.4
chūqu	出去	367.5
chūjí	初级	437.4
chúfēi	除非	443.3
chúle	除了	443.1
chúxī	除夕	443.4
chú...yǐwài	除…以外	443.2
chǔ	楚	478.1
chǔchǔ	楚楚	478.3
chǔchǔ kělián	楚楚可怜	478.2
chuán	船	389.1
chuánpiào	船票	389.2
chuáng	床	314.1
chuángdān	床单	314.3
chuángshang	床上	314.2
chuīniú	吹牛	428.5
cí	词	253.1
cídiǎn	词典	253.2/254.4
cíhuìbiǎo	词汇表	253.5
cì	次	439.1
cìshù	次数	439.4
cìxù	次序	439.2
cìyào	次要	439.3
cóng	从	359.1
cóng ... dào	从…到	359.2
cónglái	从来	359.3
cóngqián	从前	359.4
cóngxiǎo	从小	359.5

D

dàhuà	大话	265.2
dàshēng	大声	491.2
dài	代	489.1
dàibàn	代办	489.2

dàibiǎo	代表	489.3
dàijià	代价	489.4
dàitì	代替	489.5
dài	带	398.1
dàilǐng	带领	398.3
dàitóu	带头	398.4
dàizi	带子	398.2
dān	单	402.1
dānchéng	单程	402.2
dāncí	单词	253.4
dāndān	单单	402.3
dāndú	单独	402.4
dānrénchuáng	单人床	314.4
dānshēn	单身	402.5
dānwèi	单位	323.3
dé (verb)	得	274.1
déyì	得意	274.3
dézuì	得罪	274.4
de (verbal particle)	得	274.2
děi	得	274.5
dēng	灯	313.1
dēngguāng	灯光	313.2
dēnghuǒ guǎnzhì	灯火管制	313.3
dēnglóng	灯笼	313.4
dēngpào	灯泡	313.5
děngdài	等待	436.4
děngděng	等等	436.2
děngjí	等级	436.5
děngtóng	等同	436.3
dī	低	492.1
dīchén	低沉	492.2
dīgū	低估	492.3
dītóu	低头	492.4
dì	第	435.1
dì'èrshēng	第二声	435.3
dìsānshēng	第三声	435.4
dìsìshēng	第四声	435.5
dìyīshēng	第一声	435.2
diǎn	典	254.1
diǎnlǐ	典礼	254.2

diǎnxíng	典型	254.3
diànhuà	电话	265.3
diànnǎo	电脑	260.4
diàoyú	钓鱼	427.2
dìng	定	475.1
dìngqī	定期	475.3
dìngzuò	定做	475.2
dōngjì	冬季	329.5
dǒng	懂	269.1
dǒngde	懂得	269.2
dǒngshì	懂事	269.3
dòng	动	262.1
dòngrén	动人	262.3
dòngshēn	动身	262.2
dòngtīng	动听	262.4
dòngwùyuán	动物园	262.5
dòufu'nǎor	豆腐脑儿	260.5
dú	读	251.1
dúběn	读本	251.3
dúshū	读书	251.2
dúzhě	读者	251.4/279.3
dù	度	441.1
dùguò	度过	441.2
dùjià	度假	441.3
duǎn	短	379.1
duǎnchù	短处	379.5
duǎnqī	短期	379.2
duǎnqiǎn	短浅	379.3

E

è	饿	300.1
èsǐle	饿死了	300.2
éryǐ	而已	466.4

F

fā	发	312.1
fāhuǒ	发火	312.2
fārè	发热	312.3

fāshēng	发生	312.4
fāyán	发言	312.5
fǎ	法	463.1
fǎdìng rénshù	法定人数	463.3
Fǎguó	法国	463.2
fǎlǜ	法律	463.4
fǎzi	法子	463.5
fānchuán	帆船	389.3
fángjiān	房间	352.1/353.5
fángkè	房客	352.3
fángzi	房子	352.2
fángwū	房屋	355.5
fàng	放	496.1
fàngdà	放大	496.2
fàngguò	放过	496.3
fàngjià	放假	496.4
fàngxīn	放心	496.5
fēi	飞	382.1
fēijī	飞机	382.2
fēijīchǎng	飞机场	382.5
fēikuài	飞快	382.3
fēisù	飞速	382.4
fēi	非	337.1
fēi … bù	非…不	337.2
fēicháng	非常	337.3
fēidàn	非但	337.4
fēifǎ	非法	337.5
féi	肥	294.1
féidà	肥大	294.2
féipàng	肥胖	294.3
féishòu	肥瘦	294.4
féiwò	肥沃	294.5
fěnbǐ	粉笔	411.4
fěnhóng	粉红	411.2
fěnsuì	粉碎	411.3
fēngdù	风度	441.4
fùjìn	附近	362.5
fùzá	复杂	255.4

G

gāi	该	297.1
gāidāng	该当	297.4
gāisǐ	该死	297.2
gǎi	改	345.1
gǎibiàn	改变	345.2
gǎidiào	改掉	345.3
gǎigé	改革	345.4
gǎizhèng	改正	345.5
gānbēi	干杯	324.4
gǎn	感	298.1
gǎnjué	感觉	292.5/298.2
gǎnmào	感冒	298.3
gǎnqíng	感情	298.4
gǎnxiè	感谢	298.5
gāng	刚	481.1
gāngcái	刚才	281.2/481.2
gānggāng	刚刚	481.3
gānghǎo	刚好	481.4
gāngqiǎo	刚巧	481.5
gāo	高	450.1
gāo'ǎi	高矮	450.2
gāodà	高大	450.4
gāoděng	高等	436.1
gāodī	高低	450.3
gāogēnxié	高跟鞋	273.5
gāojí	高级	437.5
gāoxìng	高兴	450.5/451.5
gào	告	469.1
gàobié	告别	469.2
gàojià	告假	469.3
gàosu	告诉	469.4
gē	歌	480.1
gēchàngjiā	歌唱家	479.4
gējùyuàn	歌剧院	480.3
gēmí	歌迷	480.4
gēshēng	歌声	480.5
gēxīng	歌星	480.2
gèwèi	个位	323.5

gěi	给	331.1
gěile	给了	331.2
gēn	跟	273.1
gēn ... yíyàng	跟…一样	273.2
gēnshàng	跟上	273.3
gēnzhe	跟着	273.4
gēngǎi	更改	490.3
gēngtì	更替	490.4
gèng	更	490.1
gèngjiā	更加	490.2
gōng'ānjú	公安局	394.5
gōnggòng	公共	327.4
gōnggòngqìchē	公共汽车	386.4
gōngjī	公鸡	426.4
gōng	功	341.1
gōngkè	功课	341.2
gōngnéng	功能	341.3
gōngjǐ	供给	331.3
gòng	共	327.1
gònghéguó	共和国	327.5
gòngtóng	共同	327.2
gòudà	够大	326.4
gòugé	够格	326.5
gòule	够了	326.1
gǔdiǎn	古典	254.5
gǔwán	古玩	334.5
guāndēng	关灯	310.3
guānlián	关联	310.2
guānmén	关门	310.5
guānxi	关系	310.1
guānxīn	关心	310.4
guānyú	关于	310.6
guàn	惯	307.1
guànhuài	惯坏	307.2
guànlì	惯例	307.3
guǎngchǎng	广场	384.2
guǒ	果	465.1
guǒrán	果然	377.3/465.3
guǒduàn	果断	465.2
guò	过	363.1

guòmǐn	过敏	363.2
guòqù	过去	363.3
guòshí	过时	363.4

H

hǎi	海	419.1
hǎibá	海拔	419.4
hǎibian	海边	419.2
hǎiwài	海外	419.3
hǎohuà	好话	265.4
hǎomèng	好梦	305.2
hǎoxiàng	好像	476.4
hé	合	486.1
hébulái	合不来	486.2
héchàngtuán	合唱团	479.5
hékǒu	合口	486.3
hélǐ	合理	486.4
héshì	合适	486.5
hé	河	420.1
Héběi	河北	420.4
héliú	河流	420.2
héyú	河鱼	420.3
hēi	黑	406.1
hēi'àn	黑暗	406.2
hēibái	黑白	406.3
hēibǎn	黑板	406.4
hēirén	黑人	406.5
hóng	红	408.1
hóngbāo	红包	408.2
hónglùdēng	红绿灯	408.3
hóngshǔ	红薯	408.4
hóngyǎn	红眼	408.5
hòuguǒ	后果	465.5
hūrán	忽然	377.5
huálì	华丽	422.2
huà	划	458.1
huà yì bú èr	划一不二	458.3
huàdìng	划定	458.2
huàfēn	划分	458.4

jiàngdī	降低	492.5	jiǔliàng	酒量	318.4
jiāotōng	交通	500.5	jiǔròu péngyou	酒肉朋友	318.2
jiāoyì	交易	461.3	jiù	旧	484.1
jiāo	教	272.1	jiùhuò	旧货	484.2
jiāoshū	教书	272.2	jiùshì	旧事	484.3
jiàoshī	教师	272.3	jú	局	394.1
jiàotáng	教堂	272.4	júbù	局部	394.2
jiàoyù	教育	272.5	júshì	局势	394.4
jiào	觉	292.1	jùchǎng	剧场	384.4
jiào	较	344.1	jué	决	474.1
jiàoliàng	较量	344.5	juébù	决不	474.2
jiàowéi	较为	344.4	juédìng	决定	474.3
jié	节	328.1	juéxīn	决心	474.4
jiéjiàrì	节假日	328.4	juéde	觉得	292.4
jiémù	节目	328.2			
jiéshí	节食	328.3	**K**		
jiějué	解决	474.5			
jiè	界	372.1	kāi	开	391.1
jièxiàn	界限	372.4	kāichē	开车	391.2
jīn	近	362.1	kāifàng	开放	391.3
jīnbiàn	近便	362.4	kāikǒu	开口	391.4
jīnlái	近来	362.2	kāishǐ	开始	391.5/468.4
jīnshì	近视	362.3	kàndǒng	看懂	269.4
jìn	进	369.1	kèchuán	客船	389.5
jìnbù	进步	369.4	kèfáng	客房	352.4
jìnchūkǒu	进出口	369.5	kètáng	课堂	354.3
jìnlai	进来	369.2	kōng	空	415.1
jìnrù	进入	368.2	kōngqì	空气	415.2
jìnxíng	进行	369.3	kōngtiáo	空调	415.4
jīng	经	467.1	kòngxián	空闲	415.5
jīngcháng	经常	467.2	kòngr	空儿	415.3
jīngguò	经过	467.3	kǒngpà	恐怕	431.5
jīnglǐ	经理	467.4	kòngsù	控诉	470.4
jīngyàn	经验	467.5	kǔchǔ	苦楚	478.4
jìng	境	414.1	kuàilè	快乐	336.2
jìngdì	境地	414.2	kùnjìng	困境	414.5
jìngkuàng	境况	414.3			
jìngyù	境遇	414.4	**L**		
jiǔ	酒	318.1			
jiǔhòu	酒后	318.3	lán	蓝	409.1

lánbǎoshí	蓝宝石	409.2
lánjīng	蓝鲸	409.3
lánlǐng	蓝领	409.4
lánsè	蓝色	409.5
lè	乐	336.1
lèguān	乐观	336.3
lèqù	乐趣	494.3
léizhui	累赘	301.2
lèi	累	301.1
lěngyǐn	冷饮	319.5
lí	离	360.1
líbié	离别	360.4
líhūn	离婚	360.2
líkāi	离开	360.3
lítí	离题	360.5
lǐ	礼	332.1
lǐbài	礼拜	332.2
lǐbàisān	礼拜三	332.3
lǐjié	礼节	332.4
lǐmào	礼貌	332.5
lǐwù	礼物	333.5
lǐ	理	304.1
lǐfà	理发	304.2/312.6
lǐjiě	理解	304.3
lǐxiǎng	理想	304.4
lǐyóu	理由	304.5
lì	力	430.1
lìliang	力量	430.2/434.5
lìqi	力气	430.3
lìqiú	力求	430.4
lìzhēng	力争	430.5
lì	利	343.1
lìhai	利害	343.2
lìluo	利落	343.3
lìxī	利息	258.3
lìyì	利益	343.4
lìyòng	利用	343.5
lìjù	例句	444.4
lìrú	例如	444.2
lìwài	例外	444.3

lìzi	例子	444.1
liánlěi	连累	301.5
liáng	量	434.1
liàngcí	量词	434.2
liànglì	量力	434.3
liú	流	421.1
liúchuán	流传	421.2
liúdòng	流动	421.3
liúlì	流利	421.4
liúxíng	流行	421.5
lóu	楼	349.1
lóushang	楼上	349.3
lóutái	楼台	349.5
lùxiàng	录像	476.5
lǚ	旅	373.1
lǚchéng	旅程	373.2
lǚguǎn	旅馆	373.3
lǚtú	旅途	373.4
lǚxíng	旅行	373.5
lǜ	绿	410.1
lǜchá	绿茶	410.2
lǜdēng	绿灯	410.3
lǜdòuyá	绿豆芽	410.4
lǜhuà	绿化	410.5

M

mǎnzú	满足	293.4
máng	忙	268.1
mánglù	忙碌	268.4
mángrén	忙人	268.3
mángzhe	忙着	268.2
màoxiǎn	冒险	498.3
měilì	美丽	422.1
měiwèi	美味	325.4
mén	门	396.1
ménkǒu	门口	396.2
ménlù	门路	396.4
ménpái	门牌	396.3
ménwàihàn	门外汉	396.5

mèngjiàn	梦见	305.4
mèngxiǎng	梦想	305.3
mǐ	米	321.1
mǐfàn	米饭	321.2
mǐfěn	米粉	321.3/411.1
mǐjiǔ	米酒	321.4
miàn	面	358.1
miànji	面积	358.4
miànmào	面貌	358.2
miànshú	面熟	358.3
miànzi	面子	358.5
mín	民	401.1
mín'gē	民歌	401.3
mínzhǔ	民主	401.4
mínzú	民族	401.5

N

ná	拿	309.1
nábuqǐlái	拿不起来	309.3
nádìng zhǔyi	拿定主意	309.4
náshǒu	拿手	309.5
ná zhǔyi	拿主意	309.2
Nánjí	南极	440.5
nán	难	459.1
nándé	难得	459.2
nán'guò	难过	459.4
nánshuō	难说	459.3
nánwéi	难为	459.5
nǎo	脑	260.1
nǎojīn	脑筋	260.2
nǎozhī	脑汁	260.3
nǐ zìjǐ	你自己	340.4
niánqīng	年轻	492.4
niàn	念	259.1
niàn kèwén	念课文	259.4
niànshū	念书	259.2
niàntóu	念头	259.3
niú	牛	428.1
niújìn	牛劲	428.2

niúpíqi	牛脾气	428.4
niúròu	牛肉	320.2
niúyóu	牛油	428.3
nǚcè	女厕	397.3

P

pà	怕	431.1
pàlěng	怕冷	431.3
pàshì	怕事	431.2
pàxiū	怕羞	431.4
pángguānzhě	旁观者	279.5
píjiǔ	啤酒	318.5
piànduàn	片段	454.4
piànmiànbāo	片面包	454.1
piào	票	390.1
piàofáng	票房	390.2
piàojià	票价	390.3
pǐnmíng	品名	445.3
pǐnpái	品牌	445.4
pǐnwèi	品味	445.5
pǐnzhì	品质	445.2
píng	平	438.1
píng'ān	平安	395.3/438.2
píngcháng	平常	338.5/438.3
píngděng	平等	438.4
píngjìng	平静	438.5
píngguǒ	苹果	465.4
pòjiù	破旧	484.5
pǔ	普	499.1
pǔ'ěrchá	普洱茶	499.5
pǔjí	普及	499.4
pǔtōng	普通	499.2
Pǔtōnghuà	普通话	499.3

Q

qì	汽	385.1
qìchē	汽车	385.4
qìchuán	汽船	385.5

shēncái	身材	284.4	shìnèi	室内	351.4
shēn'gāo	身高	284.5	shìwài	室外	351.3
shēnshang	身上	284.3	shì	适	487.1
shēntǐ	身体	284.2/285.2	shìdàng	适当	487.2
shēnchén	深沉	412.1	shìhé	适合	487.3
shēnlánse	深蓝色	412.4	shìyí	适宜	487.4
shēnshēn	深深	412.2	shìzhōng	适中	487.5
shēnshuǐ	深水	412.3	shǒu	手	288.1
shēnsì	深思	412.5	shǒuqì	手气	288.3
shēngcí	生词	253.3	shǒuxù	手续	288.5
shēnghuó	生活	261.5	shǒuyì	手艺	288.4
shēng	声	491.1	shǒuzhǐ	手纸	288.2
shēngdiào	声调	491.4	shòubuliǎo	受不了	342.1
shēngpáng	声旁	491.5	shòugòu	受够	326.3
shēngyīn	声音	335.4	shòushāng	受伤	342.2
shīdù	湿度	441.5	shòuyì	受益	342.3
shíyóu	石油	456.2	shòuzāi	受灾	342.4
shíjiān	时间	353.3	shòu	瘦	295.1
shí	食	357.1	shòuroù	瘦肉	295.5
shíliáng	食粮	357.3	shòuruò	瘦弱	295.2
shípǐn	食品	357.2	shòuxiǎo	瘦小	295.4
shítáng	食堂	354.1	shū	舒	316.1
shíwù	食物	333.4/357.4	shūchàng	舒畅	316.2
shíyán	食言	357.5	shūfu	舒服	316.3
shíyóu	食油	456.1	shūsàn	舒散	316.4
shǐ	始	468.1	shūshì	舒适	316.5
shǐmò	始末	468.2	shūcài	蔬菜	317.4
shǐzhōng	始终	468.3	shūle	输了	447.1
shì	世	371.1	shūyíng	输赢	447.2
shìgù	世故	371.2	shù	树	423.1
shìjì	世纪	371.3	shùlì	树立	423.2
shìjiè	世界	371.4	shùlín	树林	423.3
Shìjièbēi	世界杯	324.5	shùyīn	树阴	423.4
shìshàng	世上	371.5	shùzhī	树枝	423.5
shìchǎng	市场	384.5	shuāngrénchuáng	双人床	314.5
shì	事	356.1	shuǐ	水	418.1
shìgù	事故	356.3	shuǐguǒ	水果	418.2
shìhòu	事后	356.4	shuǐlóngtóu	水龙头	418.3
shìqing	事情	356.2	shuǐpíng	水平	418.4
shìxiān	事先	356.5	shuì	睡	291.1

shuìjiào	睡觉	291.2
shuì lǎnjiào	睡懒觉	292.2
shuìmián	睡眠	291.4
shuì wǔjiào	睡午觉	292.3
shuìyī	睡衣	291.5
sī	思	303.1
sīkǎo	思考	303.4
sīlù	思路	303.2
sīsuǒ	思索	303.5
sīxiǎng	思想	303.3
sǐ	死	302.1
sǐbǎn	死板	302.2
sǐjì	死记	302.4
sǐxīn	死心	302.3
...sǐle	…死了	302.5
sù	诉	470.1
sùshuō	诉说	470.2
sùsòng	诉讼	470.3
suī	虽	442.1
suīrán	虽然	442.2
suīshuō	虽说	442.3
suíbiàn	随便	482.2
suídì	随地	482.1
suíshí	随时	482.3
suíyì	随意	482.1

T

tā zìjǐ	他自己	340.5
tán	谈	264.1
tánhuà	谈话	264.2
tánpàn	谈判	264.3
tántiān	谈天	264.4
tántù	谈吐	264.5
tángtáng	堂堂	354.4
tè	特	399.1
tèbié	特别	400.5
tècháng	特长	399.2
tèdiǎn	特点	399.3
tèsè	特色	399.4

tèyǒu	特有	399.5
tǐ	体	285.1
tǐlì	体力	285.4
tǐtiē	体贴	285.5
tǐwēn	体温	285.3
tīngdǒng	听懂	269.5
tīnghuà	听话	265.5
tōng	通	500.1
tōngcháng	通常	500.2
tōngguò	通过	500.3
tōngzhī	通知	500.4
tóngzhì	同志	256.3
tòng	痛	289.1
tòngkū	痛哭	289.2
tòngkǔ	痛苦	289.3
tòngkuài	痛快	289.4
tòngxīn	痛心	289.5
tóu	头	287.1
tóuděng	头等	287.2
tóufa	头发	287.3
tóunǎo	头脑	287.4
tóutòng	头痛	287.5
tóupiào	投票	390.5

W

wàijiè	外界	372.3
wánchéng	完成	449.5
wán	玩	334.1
wánjù	玩具	334.2
wánxiào	玩笑	334.3
wányìr	玩意儿	334.4
wàn	万	381.1
wànshì	万事	381.4
wànyī	万一	381.5
wǎng	往	364.1
wǎngcháng	往常	364.3
wǎngfǎn	往返	364.4
wǎnglái	往来	364.5
wǎngwǎng	往往	364.2

wàngjì	忘记	347.5
wēihài	危害	497.3
wēijī	危机	497.2
wēixiǎn	危险	497.1
wéi	为	277.1
wéinán	为难	277.2
wéiqī	为期	277.3
wèile	为了	277.4
wèishénme	为什么	277.5
wèi	位	323.1
wèiyú	位于	323.4
wèi	味	325.1
wèidao	味道	325.2
wèijīng	味精	325.3
wǒ zìjǐ	我自己	340.3
wū	屋	355.1
wūdǐng	屋顶	355.2
wūlǐ	屋里	355.3
wūzi	屋子	355.4
wǔ fēnzhī yī	五分之一	275.4
wǔyán-liùsè	五颜六色	403.5
wǔshuì	午睡	291.3
wù	物	333.1
wùjià	物价	333.2
wùpǐn	物品	333.3

X

xī	息	258.1
xíguàn	习惯	307.4
xǐshǒu	洗手	308.1
xǐshuā	洗刷	304.5
xǐxuě	洗雪	308.4
xǐyī	洗衣	308.2
xǐzǎo	洗澡	308.3
xiān	先	376.1
xiānhòu	先后	376.2
xiānqián	先前	376.3
xiānsheng	先生	376.4
xiāntóu	先头	376.5

xiāngjiào	相较	344.2
xiàng	向	365.1
xiàngdǎo	向导	365.2
xiànglái	向来	365.3
xiànglì	向例	365.4
xiàngwǎng	向往	365.5
xiàng	相	453.1
xiàngmào	相貌	453.2
xiàngpiàn	相片	453.3
xiàngshēng	相声	453.4
xiàng	像	476.1
xiàngyàng	像样	476.2
xiǎoshēng	小声	491.3
xiǎoxīn	小心	290.5
xiàoróng	笑容	460.5
xiēxi	歇息	258.5
xīn	心	290.1
xīnlǐ	心理	290.2
xīnqíng	心情	290.3
xīnténg	心疼	290.4
xīn	新	483.1
xīnnián	新年	483.2
xīnqí	新奇	483.4
xīnwén	新闻	483.3
xīnwénjiè	新闻界	372.5
xīnxiān	新鲜	483.5
xìn	信	471.1
xìnbuguò	信不过	471.2
xìndeguò	信得过	471.3
xìnxīn	信心	471.4
xìnyòng	信用	471.5
xìnxī	信息	258.2
xīngfèn	兴奋	451.2
xìng	兴	451.1
xìngqù	兴趣	451.3/494.4
xìngtóu	兴头	451.4
xìngyùn	幸运	263.3
xiū	休	257.1
xiūjià	休假	257.2
xiūxi	休息	257.4

xiūxishì	休息室	351.2
xiūyǎng	休养	257.3
xiūyè	休业	257.5
xiūyǎng	修养	425.4
xǔ	许	432.1
xǔduō	许多	432.2
xǔjiǔ	许久	432.3

Y

yán	言	472.1
yánlùn	言论	472.2
yántán	言谈	472.4
yánxíng	言行	472.3
yányǔ	言语	472.5
yánkù	严酷	493.3
yánsù	严肃	493.1
yánzhòng	严重	493.2
yán	颜	403.1
yánliào	颜料	403.3
yánmiàn	颜面	403.2
yánsè	颜色	403.4
yǎnjiè	眼界	372.2
yàn	厌	485.1
yànfán	厌烦	485.2
yànjuàn	厌倦	485.4
yànshízhèng	厌食症	485.5
yànwù	厌恶	485.3
yǎng	养	425.1
yǎngshén	养神	425.2
yāoqiú	要求	271.5
yào	药	315.1
yàocái	药材	315.2
yàodiàn	药店	315.4
yàofāng	药方	315.3
yàoshuǐ	药水	315.5
yěxǔ	也许	432.5
yèjiān	夜间	353.2
yībǎi mǐ	一百米	321.5
yīlóu	一楼	349.2

yídìng	一定	475.4
yígòng	一共	327.2
yì bǎ dāozi	一把刀子	311.2
yì qiānwàn	一千万	381.3
yìzhí	一直	370.2
yǐ	已	466.1
yǐjīng	已经	466.2
yǐwǎng	已往	466.3
yì	易	461.1
Yìjīng	易经	461.2
yīn	因	276.1
yīncǐ	因此	276.2
yīnxún	因循	276.3
yīnwèi	因为	276.4
yīn	音	335.1
yīnxiǎng	音响	335.2
yīnyuè	音乐	335.3/336.5
yǐn	饮	319.1
yǐnliào	饮料	319.2
yǐnshí	饮食	319.3
yǐnyòngshuǐ	饮用水	319.4
yīng	应	296.1
yīngdāng	应当	296.4
yīnggāi	应该	296.2/297.5
yìngchóu	应酬	296.3
yìngfu	应付	296.5
yíngyǎng	营养	425.5
yíng	赢	446.1
yíngde	赢得	446.3
yínglì	赢利	446.2
yònggōng	用功	341.5
yōu	优	433.1
yōudài	优待	433.3
yōudiǎn	优点	433.4
yōuměi	优美	433.5
yōuxiān	优先	433.2
yóu	邮	393.1
yóubāo	邮包	393.2
yóudìyuán	邮递员	393.3
yóujì	邮寄	393.4

yóujú	邮局	394.3
yóupiào	邮票	393.5
yóu	游	374.1
yóulǎn	游览	374.5
yóurén	游人	374.4
yóuxì	游戏	374.3
yóuyǒng	游泳	374.2
yóunì	油腻	456.3
yǒuqù	有趣	494.5
yòu	又	282.1/2/4
yòu ... yòu	又…又	282.3
yú	于	283.1/2
yújīn	于今	283.3
yúshì	于是	283.4
yú	鱼	427.1
yúgān	鱼竿	427.3
yúlóng hùnzá	鱼龙混杂	427.4
yúmù hùnzhū	鱼目混珠	427.5
yù	预	348.1
yùbào	预报	348.2
yùbèi	预备	348.3
yùdìng	预订	348.4
yùyuē	预约	348.5
yuánshǐ	原始	468.5
yuányīn	原因	276.5
yuǎn	远	361.1
yuǎnchù	远处	361.2
yuǎndà	远大	361.4
yuǎnjìn	远近	361.3
yuēdìng	约定	475.5
yuèdú	阅读	251.5
yuèqì	乐器	336.4
yún	云	424.1/2
yúncai	云彩	424.4
yúncéng	云层	424.3
yùn	运	263.1
yùndòng	运动	263.4
yùnqi	运气	263.2
yùnyòng	运用	263.5

Z

záhuò	杂货	255.1
záluàn	杂乱	255.2
zázhì	杂志	255.3
zàoyīn	噪音	335.5
zhàn	站	388.1
zhànlì	站立	388.3
zhànwěn	站稳	388.4
zhànzhù	站住	388.5
zhǎngbèi	长辈	378.4
zhǎngdà	长大	378.3
zhǎngxiàng	长相	453.5
zháojí	着急	280.2
zháoliáng	着凉	280.3
zhǎo	找	270.1
zhǎobukāi	找不开	270.5
zhǎo duìxiàng	找对象	270.4
zhǎo máfan	找麻烦	270.3
zhǎoqián	找钱	270.2
zhào	照	452.1
zhàocháng	照常	452.5
zhàojiù	照旧	452.4
zhàopiàn	照片	452.3/454.2
zhàoxiàng	照相	452.2
zhě	者	279.1
zhe	着	280.1
zhēn	真	473.1
zhēnhuà	真话	473.2
zhēnxiàng	真相	473.3
zhēnxīn	真心	473.4
zhēnzhèng	真正	473.5
zhèng	正	346.1
zhèngcháng	正常	346.2
zhènghǎo	正好	346.3
zhèngquè	正确	346.4
zhèngzài	正在	346.5
zhī	之	275.1
zhīhòu	之后	275.2
zhīqián	之前	275.3

zhījǐ	知己	340.2
zhí	直	370.1
zhídào	直到	370.3
zhíjiē	直接	370.4
zhílái-zhíqù	直来直去	370.5
zhìqi	志气	256.2
zhìyuàn	志愿	256.1
zhōngjiān	中间	353.4
Zhōngqiūjié	中秋节	328.5
zhòngdiǎn	重点	306.3
zhòngshì	重视	306.4
zhòngyào	重要	306.5
zhù	助	267.1
zhùshǒu	助手	267.3
zhùxìng	助兴	267.4
zhùxuéjīn	助学金	267.5
zhuóxiǎng	着想	280.4
zhuózhòng	着重	280.5
zì	自	339.1
zìcóng	自从	339.2
zìjǐ	自己	339.3

zìjǐ	自给	331.4
zìxíngchē	自行车	339.4
zìyóu	自由	339.5
zúgòu	足够	293.2
zúqiú	足球	293.1
zúyǐ	足以	293.3
zuì	最	462.1
zuìduō	最多	462.2
zuìhǎo	最好	462.3
zuìhòu	最后	462.4
zuìjìn	最近	462.5
zuòxī	作息	258.4
zuòzhě	作者	279.2
zuò	坐	322.1
zuòbān	坐班	322.5
zuòbuxià	坐不下	322.4
zuòcè	坐厕	397.4
zuò huǒchē	坐火车	322.2
zuòwèi	坐位	322.3/323.2
zuòcài	做菜	317.5
zuòmèng	做梦	305.1

Radical Index

The number on the right of each column refers to the character number.

1 stroke

[、] #1

头	tóu	287
为	wéi/wèi	277
之	zhī	275

[一] #2

表	biǎo	495
才	cái	281
更	gēng/gěng	490
开	kāi	391
丽	lì	422
面	miàn	358
平	píng	438
求	qiú	271
世	shì	371
事	shì	356
万	wàn	381
严	yán	493
于	yú	283
正	zhèng	346

[丨] #3

非	fēi	337
旧	jiù	384

[丿] #4

长	cháng/zhǎng	378
乘	chéng	392
重	chóng/zhòng	306
乐	lè/yuè	336
千	qiān	380
向	xiàng	365

[乙] (一 乛 乚) #5

飞	fēi	382
民	mín	401

2 strokes

[亠] #6

高	gāo	450
离	lí	360
赢	yíng	446

[冫] #7

次	cì	439
决	jué	474

[讠] #9

词	cí	253
读	dú	251
该	gāi	297
话	huà	265
计	jì	457
记	jì	347
诉	sù	470
谈	tán	264
许	xǔ	432

[二] #10

云	yún	424

[十] #11

真	zhēn	473
直	zhí	370

[厂] #12

厕	cè	397
厌	yàn	485

[刂] #15

别	bié	400
刚	gāng	481
划	huà	458
利	lì	343

[冂] #16

肉	ròu	320

[八] (丷) #17

单	dān	402
典	diǎn	254
共	gòng	327
关	guān	310
兴	xīng/xìng	451

[人] (入) #18

从	cóng	359
合	hé	486
拿	ná	309
入	rù	368
舒	shū	316

[亻] #19

代	dài	489
低	dī	492
假	jiǎ/jià	375
例	lì	444
体	tǐ	285
位	wèi	323
像	xiàng	476
信	xìn	471
休	xiū	257
优	yōu	433

[儿] #21

先	xiān	376

[彳] #54		
得	dé/de/děi	274
往	wǎng	364

[夕] #56		
够	gòu	326
梦	mèng	305

[饣] #59		
饿	è	300
饮	yǐn	319

[尸] #61		
局	jú	394
屋	wū	355

[己]（巳）#62		
己	jǐ	340
已	yǐ	466

[女] #65		
如	rú	464
始	shǐ	468

[纟] #68		
给	gěi/jǐ	331
红	hóng	408
级	jí	437
经	jīng	467
绿	lǜ	410

4 strokes

[灬] #71		
然	rán	377
照	zhào	452

[方] #74		
放	fàng	496
旅	lǚ	373

[火] #75		
灯	dēng	313
火	huǒ	387

[心] #76		
必	bì	488
感	gǎn	298
念	niàn	259
思	sī	303
息	xī	258
心	xīn	290
志	zhì	256

[户] #77		
房	fáng	352

[礻] #78		
礼	lǐ	332

[王] #79		
环	huán	413
理	lǐ	304
玩	wán	334

[木] #81		
杯	bēi	324
本	běn	252
果	guǒ	465
机	jī	383
极	jí	440
楼	lóu	349
树	shù	423
相	xiàng	453
杂	zá	255

[歹] #83		
死	sǐ	302

[车] #84		
车	chē	386
较	jiào	344

轻	qīng	429
输	shū	447

[戈] #85		
成	chéng	449
划	huà	458
或	huò	278

[止] #88		
正	zhèng	346

[日] #90		
量	liáng/liàng	434
普	pǔ	499
晴	qíng	416
易	yì	461

[曰] #91		
者	zhě	279
最	zuì	462

[见] #93		
觉	jiào/jué	292

[牛]（牛）#95		
牛	niú	428
特	tè	399
物	wù	333

[手] #96		
拿	ná	309
手	shǒu	288

[攵] #99		
放	fàng	496
改	gǎi	345
教	jiāo/jiào	272

[片] #100		
片	piàn	454

Answer Key to Activities

Lesson 24: Review Activities

A. *Pinyin* and Character Practice

Part 1

看书	读课本	休息	念文章	打球
kànshū	dúkèběn	xiūxī	niànwénzhāng	dǎqiú

Part 2

杂志	词典	课堂	电话	老师
zázhì	cídiǎn	kètáng	diànhuà	lǎoshī

B. Day Description

1. (日报) 我的父亲有一天没看日报。
2. (杂志) 有一天我看过四本杂志。
3. (词典) 有一天我借了老师的词典。
4. (电脑) 总有一天我会有自己的电脑。
5. (休息) 有一天我休息得太久了！

C. Short Description

(Open answer) Comprehension Questions

- 你可以在图书馆里的什么地方读书？
- 你用电脑做什么？
- 图书馆的服务员站在哪里？
- 这个图书馆有什么特别的书？
- 这么大的图书馆有没有用？

Lesson 25: Review Activities

A. *Pinyin* and Pronunciation Practice

1. Tā Hànyǔ shuō de hěn qīngchu, nǐmen dōu tīng de dǒng ma?

2. Zhè zhāng huà hěn yǒu yìsi, nǐ zěnme kàn de dǒng?

3. Jièshào wán le, nǐ dǒng le ma?

B. Sentence Completion

1. 我的朋友<u>喜欢</u>踢足球。
   <u>My friend enjoys playing soccer.</u>

2. 我的母亲常常告诉我<u>别</u>做危险的运动。
   <u>My mother often tells me not to do dangerous things.</u>

3. 医生说每天人都<u>需要</u>锻炼锻炼。
   <u>Doctors say that every day, people need to exercise.</u>

4. 离开家以前你<u>应该查</u>有家的钥匙。
   <u>Before leaving your home you should check that you have house keys.</u>

5. 去别的国家你<u>得</u>有护照。
   <u>To go to other countries you must have a passport.</u>

C. Conversation Practice

(Open answer)

1. 现在你在哪儿? 你在做什么?
2. 昨天你做了什么?
3. 请问, 我们有没有汉语功课?
4. 对你来说, 学生应该天天练习说汉语吗?
5. 我们可以一起做这个活动? 还是你太忙?
6. 明天你想做什么? 我们可以见个面吗?
7. 如果可以的话, 你给我打个电话, 好吧?

Lesson 26: Review Activities

A. Character and Pronunciation Practice

	If	Must	Thus	But	Or	With
汉字	如果	得	于是	可是	或者	跟
(pinyin)	rúguǒ	děi	yúshì	kěshì	huòzhě	gēn

B. Sentence Creation

(Open answer)

1. 昨天晚上很晚我才来朋友的家。
2. 你跟男朋友要看新的电影。
3. 明天, 我们两个人去花园或者动物园。
4. 太累了, 不能吃饭。于是上床睡大觉。
5. 我得写很长的文章因为这篇文章是英文课的功课。

C. Connected Discourse

(Open answer; here are some possible responses)

1.（得买一辆新汽车）

因为　今天我得买一辆新汽车, 因为我的旧汽车有毛病。

所以　所以我去一家汽车经销商。我认识那里的老板。

于是　于是我找到了一辆很好, 很便宜的汽车。

2.（要去亚洲旅游）

因为　以前我只想去欧洲旅游。可是今年的夏天我要去亚洲旅游, 因为我的家人想去。

或者　我的父母说, 我们可能去中国或者日本。我们也知道要旅行两个国家得花很长的时间,
　　　　走很长的路。

于是　于是我们都得准备离家很长时间去旅游。

Lesson 27: Review Activities

A. Vocabulary and Pronunciation

头	tóu	心	xīn
身体	shēntǐ	头发	tóufa
胸	xiōng	手	shǒu
口	kǒu	足/脚	zú/jiǎo

B. Answering Questions

(Open answer; here are some possible responses)

1. 因为我生病的时候我不能吃饭, 于是我变了很瘦。

2. 因为每年冬天有许多节日, 吃了许多的东西。

3. 什么时候?我记不起来去年生了病。

4. 因为我的邻居昨晚开了很热闹的派对, 所以我睡不好觉。

5. 因为这里太冷, 我们关一下空调好不好?

C. Short Description

(Open answer) Comprehension Questions

- 你的朋友应不应该去医院, 为什么?
- 你的朋友听得懂还是听不懂医生的话?
- 你的朋友要不要休息, 为什么?
- 你觉得她的病什么时候会好起来?

Section 6 Review (Lessons 24–27)

A. Vocabulary Review and Identification

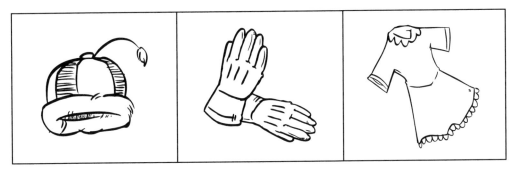

身体：　　　　头　　　　　　　　　手　　　　　　　　上身

衣服：　　　帽子　　　　　　　手套　　　　　　　衬衫

身体：　　　　头　　　　　　　足/脚　　　　　　　眼睛

衣服：　　　围巾　　　　　鞋子 / 靴子　　　　　眼镜

B. Sentence Creation

(Open answer; here are some possible responses.)

（老师）　课堂需要老师因为老师教课。

（课本）　课堂也需要有课本因为学生们从课本学习新知识。

（黑板）　课堂得有黑板因为老师在那黑板上写重点。

（电脑）　现代化的课堂也需要电脑因为学生常常上网络找新知识。

（学生）　最后课堂需要学生。如果没有学生的话，那就不上课了。

C. Lifestyle Description

(Open answer)

D. Reflective Questions

(Open answer)

Lesson 28: Review Activities

A. Vocabulary Identification

饿死了　　　　　　　很累　　　　　　做好梦　　　　　想一想

B. Sentence Creation

(Open answer)

C. Short Descriptions

(Open answer) Comprehension Questions

1.（你很累）休息以后你觉得怎么样？
2.（你饿死了）很饿的时候你应该多吃一些吗？
3.（你非常高兴）每次你感到非常高兴你会要做哪一件事？
4.（你生病了）什么办法最有效利地让你好起来？

Lesson 29: Review Activities

A. Pronunciation and *Pinyin* Practice

1. Nǐ yǒu shénme tiāntiān de xíguàn?

2. Wǎnshàng jǐdiǎn zhōng nǐ chángcháng guān dēng?

3. Nǐ bǎ wǒ de kèběn fàng zài nǎlǐ?

B. Sentence Completion

1. 每天早上很多人 洗 澡。
   Every morning many people take showers.

2. 对不起，我 把 你的帽子放在你的房间里。
   Excuse me, I put your hat in your room.

3. 对你来说，学生应该 带 什么文具上课？
   From your perspective, what supplies should students bring to class?

4. 我的朋友常常很累，他不喜欢很早 上 床。
   My friend is often really tired; he doesn't like to go to bed early.

5. 我不喜欢别人 拿 我的东西。
   I don't like other people touching my belongings.

C. Short Description

(Open answer) Comprehension Questions

- 什么时候你开始准备去睡觉？
- 几点钟你才上床？
- 上床以前还是起床以后你洗澡？
- 对你来说，你需要穿特色衣服去睡觉吗？
- 你的床子怎么样？床上有什么东西？

Lesson 30: Review Activities

A. Pronunciation and *Pinyin* Practice

菜：	$	
鱼香肉丝	.... 8.50	八块五毛钱
红烧牛肉	.... 12.00	十二块钱
家常豆腐	.... 9.50	九块半/九块五毛钱
饭：		
白饭（碗）	.... 1.50	一块五毛钱一碗
饮：		
水（瓶）	.... 2.00	两块一瓶
茶（壶）	.... 5.75	五块七毛五分钱一壶
咖啡（杯）	... 2.30	两块三毛一杯

B. Sentence Creation

(Open answer)

C. Short Description

(Open answer) Comprehension Questions

- 你跟几个朋友一起去饭店？
- 你常常请客，还是很少次请客？
- 美国跟中国请客的习俗不一样，你会用哪一种？
- 你请客的时候你能花多少钱？
- 四个人要吃饭，你们要叫几道菜？

Lesson 31: Review Activities

A. Character Practice

	动
礼	物

	音
快	乐

	春
国	节

B. Sentence Completion

(Open answer)

C. Short Description

(Open answer) Comprehension Questions

- 那个小孩子几岁?
- 你要花多少钱买礼物?
- 对你来说, 小孩子喜欢什么样的东西?
- 什么时候最适合给孩子礼物?
- 你曾经给过这样的礼物吗?

Lesson 32: Review Activities

A. Pronunciation and *Pinyin* Practice

自己	zì jǐ	受利	shòu lì	改变	gǎi biàn
自动	zì dòng	受伤	shòu shāng	改好	gǎi hǎo
自行	zì xíng	受益	shòu yì	改正	gǎi zhèng

B. Sentence Response

(Open answer)

C. Focused Description

(Open answer) Comprehension Questions

- 这个地方是哪里?
- 画里是什么时候, 白天还是夜晚?
- 你喜不喜欢这种的风景吗?
- 形容一下画中的天空。
- 你看过同一样的风景吗?

Section 7 Review (Lessons 28–32)

A. Character Practice

感觉	习惯	节日	礼物	菜
高兴	洗澡	春节	一本书	肉
很累	看日报	生日	钱	鱼
幸福	吃早饭	圣诞节	红包	豆腐
舒服	打电话	国节	小动物	面

B. Short Description

(Open answer)

饿死了

你可以改变吃饭的时间。

很累

你可以晚上早一点睡觉。

记不住

你可以开始做一点笔记。

生病

如果你常常生病，
就应该改变卫生的习惯。

要喝水

随时带着一瓶水，
那么要喝水就有水喝。

给别人很好的礼物

这样的情况不要改变。

C. Holiday Description

(Open answer)

D. Reflective Questions

(Open answer)

Lesson 33: Review Activities

A. Vocabulary and Pronunciation

(Open answer)

饭店　　　fàndiàn

办公室　　bàngōngshì　　　　　　　美容室　měiróngshì

学校　　　xuéxiào

商店　　　shāngdiàn　　　　　　　书店　　shūdiàn

门庭　　　méntīng

B. Short Description

(Open answer; here are some possible responses.)

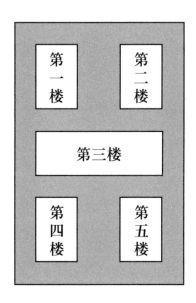

1. 第一楼有图书馆和小咖啡馆。

2. 第二楼是一间学校。

3. 第三楼有体育馆, 小卖部, 和衣服商店。

4. 第四楼有很多办公室。

5. 第五楼是一个很大百货公司。

C. Location Description

(Open answer) Comprehension Questions

- 这种房间需要桌子和椅子吗?
- 这种房间需不需要电脑?
- 房间里有电视比较好吗?

- 如果房间没有床子, 有问题吗?
- 你可以在这种房间工作吗?

Lesson 34: Review Activities

A. Vocabulary Identification

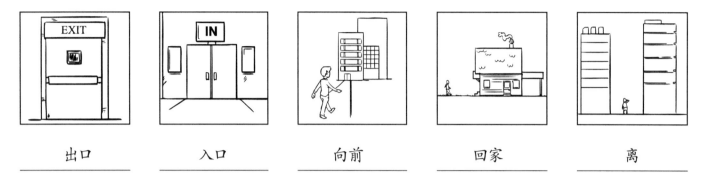

出口　　　　入口　　　　向前　　　　回家　　　　离

B. Sentence Completion

1. 请 <u>进</u>。请坐, 你要不要喝茶?
   <u>Please come in. Take a seat, would you like some tea?</u>

2. 饭店在那里, <u>向</u> 右拐吧。
   <u>The restaurant is over there, take a right turn.</u>

3. 我想家人, 我 <u>离</u> 他们太远啊!
   <u>I miss my family, I'm too far apart from them!</u>

4. 你不可能 <u>从</u> 这里走路到城市中心。
   <u>You can't walk from here to the center of the city.</u>

5. 如果一个人不知道路线, 他会常常说 "一 <u>直</u> 走五分钟。"
   <u>If one doesn't know how to get there, he often says: "Straight ahead five minutes."</u>

C. Route Description

(Open answer) Comprehension Questions

* 从学校你向哪里去?
* 公园在你的右边, 什么地方在你的左边?
* 你的家在什么建筑物的旁边?
* 大饭店在你的左边, 你要向左还是右拐回家?
* 你要穿过广场走路回家吗?

Lesson 35: Review Activities

A. Vocabulary Identification

1. 中国	5. 日本
2. 英国	6. 越南
3. 法国	7. 印度
4. 西班牙	8. 意大利

B. Sentence Completion and Translation

1. <u>千</u>言万语也不能形容一幅好的画。
   <u>Thousands of words cannot clearly describe a good painting.</u>

2. 天天做的事，<u>一</u>来二去地也就变成习惯了。
   <u>By doing the same thing every day, over time it becomes a habit.</u>

3. 好老师<u>百</u>问不烦。
   <u>Good teachers answer many questions without being irritated.</u>

4. 一个有道德的人<u>万</u>夫莫当。
   <u>One virtuous person is mightier than thousands.</u>

5. 水灾之后地区<u>十</u>室九空。
   <u>After a flood the area is depopulated.</u>

C. Route Description
(Open answer) Comprehension Questions

- 你要去欧洲，亚洲，还是美洲？
- 对你来说，有趣城市是不是那国家的首都？
- 你想去参观很多博物馆还是参加很多俱乐部？
- 你要旅游的国家，你会那国的语言吗？
- 回家后你要不要再去那个地方？

Lesson 36: Review Activities

A. Vocabulary Identification and Pronunciation

汉字/拼音	画	汉字/拼音	画	汉字/拼音	画
汽车 qìchē		飞机 fēijī		火车 huǒchē	
船 chuán		自行车 zìxíngchē			

B. Answer Selection

	开	乘	要票		开	乘	要票
汽车	X			马车	X		
出租汽车		X		地铁		X	X
飞机		X	X	自行车	X		
火车		X	X	公共汽车		X	X

C. Location Comparison

(Open answer) Comprehension Questions

- 如果你来早一点你可以做什么?
- 如果你很饿, 你可以找到饭店吗?
- 如果你得买新手表, 你有钱买新的吗?
- 如果你有很多行李, 你会有什么办法处理?
- 你喜欢在哪儿接客人?

Lesson 37: Review Activities

A. Pronunciation and *Pinyin* Practice

1. Duìbuqǐ, cèsuǒ zài nǎr?
2. Qǐng wèn, nǐ de chéngshì yǒu méiyǒu gōng'ān mén?
3. Nǐ zài yóujú kěyǐ mǎi shénme dōngxi?

B. Sentence Creation

(Open answer; here are some possible responses.)

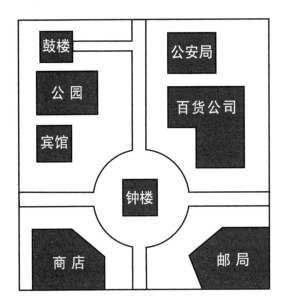

1. 邮局
   邮局在百货公司的对边。
2. 宾馆
   宾馆在大街口的旁边。
3. 钟楼
   钟楼在城市中心。
4. 公园
   公园在鼓楼的左边。
5. 公安局
   公安局在鼓楼的对边。

C. Short Description

(Open answer) Comprehension Questions

（手机）
- 这个手机比较大吗？
- 你可以用手机听音乐吗？
- 你有没有同一样的手机？

（电视）
- 这台电视很大吗？
- 节目在这台电视上看得非常清楚吗？
- 你有没有同一样的电视？

Section 8 Review (Lessons 33–37)

A. Vocabulary Identification

中国	来：飞机
北京	内：地铁

英国	来：船
伦敦	内：走路

美国	来：汽车
纽约	内：地铁

中国	来：飞机	德国	来：火车	美国	来：飞机
上海	内：出租汽车	巴林	内：自行车	洛杉矶	内：汽车

B. Short Description

(Open answer)

C. Travel Description

(Open answer)

D. Reflective Questions

(Open answer)

Lesson 38: Review Activities

A. Vocabulary Identification

中国人民共和国

（东西）	苹果	香蕉	国旗	天空	夜晚
（颜色）	红色	黄色	红色	蓝色	黑色

B. Short Description

(Open answer)

C. Example Description

(Open answer) Comprehension Questions

- 你的三个东西是什么？
- 你的三个东西好不好看？
- 为什么你喜欢这些东西？

- 你喜欢这些东西还是你喜欢东西的颜色？
- 对你来说，这个颜色有什么意思？

Lesson 39: Review Activities

A. Vocabulary Identification and Pronunciation

山 shān	河 hé	云 yún
水 shuǐ	石 shí	天空 tiānkōng
树 shù	雪 xuě	环境 huánjìng

B. Sentence Creation

(Open answer)

C. Short Description

(Open answer) Comprehension Questions

- 自然环境的地方有什么很美丽？
- 城市也有什么地方很漂亮？
- 你在自然环境的地方喜欢做什么？

- 你在城市喜欢做什么？
- 你喜欢做什么运动？

Lesson 40: Review Activities

A. Vocabulary Identification

	(1 kg)	(10 g)	(100 lbs)	(500 lbs)	(1000 kg)
东西：	一条鱼	一支笔	一个很瘦的人	几块木头	一头牛
重量：	一公斤	十克	一百斤	五百斤	一千公斤

B. Sentence Completion

1. 我朋友的身体很大，他的 <u>力量</u> 也很大。
   <u>My friend is really big, he is also very strong.</u>

2. 世界上有一些地方人们都认为很 <u>优美</u>。
   <u>Across the world there are a few places that everyone thinks are magnificent.</u>

3. 那么小的狗，真的不 <u>可怕</u> 的！
   <u>This is a small dog, it really isn't scary.</u>

4. 老人常常需要 <u>年轻</u> 人的力气。
   <u>Elderly people often need to depend on the strength of young people.</u>

5. 搬家的时候家具的 <u>轻重</u> 很重要。
   <u>When moving house, the weight of furniture is very important.</u>

6. 每个星期你可以看新的电影，每年有 <u>许多</u> 的新电影。
   <u>Every week you can see a new movie, every year has a multitude of new movies.</u>

C. Short Description

(Open answer) Comprehension Questions

(鸡)	(鱼)	(牛)
<u>鸡住在什么样的地方？</u>	<u>鱼住在什么样的地方？</u>	<u>牛住在什么样的地方？</u>
<u>鸡吃什么东西？</u>	<u>鱼吃什么东西？</u>	<u>牛吃什么东西？</u>
<u>鸡给人什么？</u>	<u>鱼给人什么？</u>	<u>牛给人什么？</u>

Lesson 41: Review Activities

A. Pronunciation Identification

1. <u>Měitiān zǎoshàng dìyī ge rén lái bàngōngshì děi kāi dēng.</u>
2. <u>Chúle yǒu gāojì de míngpái, píjiǔ píngcháng hěn piányi.</u>
3. <u>Nǐ de Hànyǔ shuǐpíng zěnme yàng?</u>

B. Example Creation

(Open answer)

C. Short Story

(Open answer) Comprehension Questions

- 你第一次要做饭你是多大?
- 你想要做什么饭?
- 你怎么准备做那餐饭?

- 你先做什么?
- 你做的饭好不好吃?

Lesson 42: Review Activities

A. Pronunciation Practice

1. <u>Yùndòng de bǐsài yǒu liǎng ge duì.</u>
2. <u>Zhè chǎng bǐsài, měi ge duì yǒu shíyī ge qiúyuán.</u>
3. <u>Zhǐ yǒu yí ge qiúyuán kěyǐ yòngshǒu ná qiú.</u>
4. <u>Jīnle yī qiú gěi nǎ duì yī fēn.</u>
5. <u>Nǎ yí duì yǒu zuì duō fēn jiù yīngle nà chǎng bǐsài.</u>

问题:这些句子介绍什么运动? <u>这些句子介绍足球。</u>

B. Sentence Description

(Open answer)

C. Short Description

(Open answer) Comprehension Questions

- 这些人都在哪里?
- 他们都参加一样的队吗?
- 你喜欢参加这种的比赛吗?

- 照片是比赛以前还是以后的?
- 这个队也需要什么样的比赛?

Section 9 Review (Lessons 38–42)

A. Vocabulary Identification

(Open answer)

B. Short Description

(Open answer)

C. Place Description

(Open answer)

(Open answer)

Lesson 43: Review Activities

A. Character Practice and Pronunciation

难	(See Character 459)	容	(See Character 460)
nán		róng	
最	(See Character 462)	经	(See Character 467)
zuì		jīng	
如	(See Character 464)	果	(See Character 465)
rú		guǒ	

B. Sentence Completion

(Open answer; here are some possible responses.)

1. 如果第一次我试不成功。。。我就需要多练习练习。
2. 如果我做得非常容易。。。我就决定再做。
3. 如果我不知道要用什么办法做。。。我就问很多人他们的办法。
4. 如果我已经做过。。。我就会觉得每次比较容易。
5. 如果我还没开始做。。。我就得马上开始。

C. Short Description

(Open answer) Comprehension Questions

• 现在你做什么工作？
• 你自己有什么目的？
• 要找新工作你先要准备什么东西？
• 你认识别人现在做一样的工作吗？
• 你怎么找到别人也做很好的工作？

Lesson 44: Review Activities

A. Radical Recognition and Pronunciation

(Example characters are open answer; some possible responses are noted.)

Radical:	讠	亻	氵	木	口	心	饣
pinyin:	yán	rén	shuǐ	mù	kǒu	xīn	shí
汉字：	说	你	河	楼	喝	想	饭
	话	体	汤	机	品	志	饿
	词	做	海	林	听	思	饱
	记	信	流	树	吗	怎	饮

B. Sentence Completion

1. 政治家得说 <u>真话</u> ，如果他们没说真相, 国家就受到困难。
   <u>Politicians need to speak truthfully; if they speak falsely the country endures difficulties.</u>

2. 现在你穿很奇怪的衣服, 你 <u>好像</u> 是外星人。
   <u>You are wearing some strange clothing today, it is like you are from outer space.</u>

3. 我听不懂你的话, 请说 <u>清楚</u> 一点。
   <u>I don't understand what you said, please speak a little more clearly.</u>

4. 有人的生活很 <u>复杂</u> , 每个人的生活都不一样。
   <u>People's lives are really complicated, everyone's is different.</u>

5. 别 <u>相信</u> 他, 上个星期他骗过我！
   <u>Don't believe him, last week he cheated me!</u>

C. Short Description

(Open answer) Comprehension Questions

- 这张画是两个人还是一个花瓶？
- 你能看两个事情都在一张画吗？
- 你用什么办法才可以看到这两个事情吗？
- 你有别的例子吗？
- 能看到这种画可以让我了解人民的情况吗？

Lesson 45: Review Activities

A. *Pinyin* and Pronunciation Practice

1. <u>Wǒ yào xiě gènghǎo de wénzhāng, nǐ yǒu méi yǒu yìjiàn?</u>
2. <u>Wǒ suíbiàn nǐ, nǐ yào qù nǎr? Yào zuò shénme?</u>
3. <u>Wǒmen de péngyou gānggāng láile, wǒmen yìqǐ kěyǐ zuò shénme?</u>

B. Adjective Descriptions

(Open answer; here are some possible responses.)

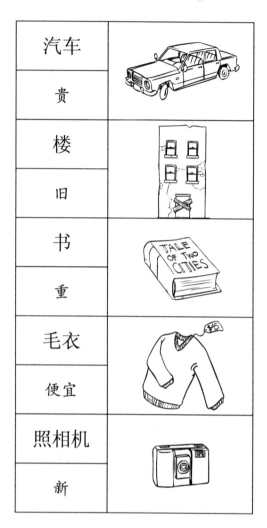

汽车 贵		我经理的汽车很贵。
楼 旧		这栋楼太旧了！
书 重		我最喜欢的书很重。
毛衣 便宜		这件毛衣非常便宜。
照相机 新		要买新照相机是很容易。

C. Short Descriptions

(Open answer)

Lesson 46: Review Activities

A. Character Practice

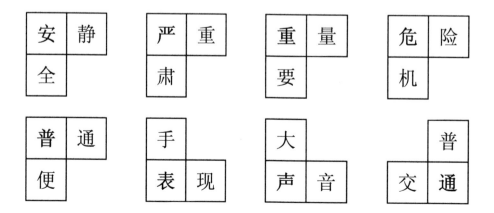

安	静
全	

严	重
肃	

重	量
要	

危	险
机	

普	通
便	

手	
表	现

大	
声	音

	普
交	通

B. Translation Exercise

鹿柴　　　**Deer Park**

空山不见人，	Seeing no one on the empty mountain,
但闻人语响。	Yet hearing the echoes of voices.
返景入深林，	Sun returns into the deep woods,
复照青苔上。	Lighting again the dark moss.

C. Short Description

(Open answer) Comprehension Questions

- 先要问，你做什么工作？
- 对你来说，开车很危险吗？
- 哪一些普通运动也很危险？
- 有人在家里常常受伤，家里哪个情况很危险？
- 城市比农村的地方不一样，你住在哪儿？
- 你面对什么样的问题？

Section 10 Review (Lessons 43–46)

A. Pronunciation and *Pinyin* Practice

中国共和国的国歌歌词：　　**Lyrics for the People's Republic of China National Anthem:**

起来！不愿做奴隶的人们！	Qǐlai! Bú yuàn zuò núlì de rénmen!
把我们的血肉，	Bǎ wǒmen de xuè ròu,
筑成我们新的长城！	zhú chéng wǒmen xīn de chángchéng!
中华民族到了最危险的时候，	Zhōnghuá mínzú dào liǎo zuì wēixiǎn de shíhou,
每个人被迫着发出最后的吼声。	Měi ge rén bèi pòzhe fāchū zuì hòu de hǒushēng.
起来！起来！起来！	Qǐlai! Qǐlai! Qǐlai!
我们万众一心，	Wǒmen wàn zhòng yìxīn,
冒着敌人的炮火，前进！	Màozhe dírén de pàohuǒ, qiánjìn!
冒着敌人的炮火，前进！	Màozhe dírén de pàohuǒ, qiánjìn!
前进！前进！进！	Qiánjìn! Qiánjìn! Jìn!

B. Short Description

(Open answer) Comprehension Questions

- 这个人在哪里？你喜欢这样的地方吗？
- 这个人应不应该看上边？
- 这个人得做什么？
- 石头下来以后，这个人还有问题吗？
- 对你来说，这个人的情况很危险吗？

C. Problem Description

(Open answer)

D. Reflective Questions

(Open answer)